Acts of Faith,
Acts of Love

Acts of Faith, Acts of Love

Gay Catholic Autobiographies as Sacred Texts

Dugan McGinley

continuum
NEW YORK • LONDON

2004

The Continuum International Publishing Group Inc
15 East 26th Street, New York, NY 10017

The Continuum International Publishing Group Ltd
The Tower Building, 11 York Road, London SE1 7NX

Printed in the United States of America

Library of Congress Cataloging-in-Publication Data

McGinley, Dugan.
  Acts of faith, acts of love : gay Catholic autobiographies as sacred texts / Dugan McGinley.
    p. cm.
  Includes bibliographical references and index.
  ISBN 0-8264-1545-8 (hardcover : alk. paper)
  1. Catholic gays – United States – Biography – History and criticism. 2. Gay men – United States – Biography – History and criticism. 3. Autobiography – Religious aspects – Catholic Church. 4. Homosexuality – Religious aspects – Catholic Church. I. Title.
BX4669.M248 2004
282'.73'086642 – dc22

                                                            2003027592

We are handed an identity
before having a say in the matter,
and we spend our lives running from it,
pretending we have left it behind,
or grappling with it as Jacob wrestled
with his angel.

—Fenton Johnson, *Keeping Faith*

Contents

Acknowledgments

A s with any project of this scale, it cannot be accomplished alone. I want to thank everyone who has helped me in the process of making this book a reality. Lucy Bregman, Rebecca Alpert, Leonard Swidler, Regina Bannan, Katie Cannon, and Laura Levitt were all enormously helpful with guidance, feedback, suggestions, and support over the years, especially in helping me to shape this project. Many others made contributions either directly or indirectly, whether they realize it or not. These include Bob Miailovich, David Floss, Dick Young, Bruce Cory (who all gave me suggestions when I put the word out that I was looking for autobiographies), Nancy Krody (one of the first to put herself on the line to declare the reality of being gay and Christian), Ron Karstetter, Frank DeBernardo and New Ways Ministry, Paul Halsall (whose web page bibliography is an incredible resource for gay Catholics), Sally Bourrie, Kathy Coffey, Jim Mallon, Bill Leahy, Paul Michalenko, Kent Epperson, Maria Fama, and Marian Ronan. A special thanks to Frank Oveis at Continuum for believing in this project and for his input.

I owe a lot to my friends in Dignity, especially Dignity Denver, where I learned how faithful Catholics can maintain an intentional community in the face of the church's opposition, and where I first got my feet wet in the world of church reform activism. I also owe a lot to my friends in the National Association of Pastoral Musicians, where I remain connected to the church at large and find the energy to sustain my ministry as a Roman Catholic liturgist and musician. I thank anyone else along the way who made suggestions and shared with me their relevant insights and perspectives.

In terms of financial support, I was given a boost early on from Eileen Mackin. The Temple University Department of Religion also assisted along the way with scholarships and teaching assistantships. I am also greatly indebted to the Jonathan Lax Scholarship for Gay Men, administered by Philadelphia's Bread and Roses Community Fund, for giving me significant support for two years. I am so grateful to have met Mr. Lax before his untimely death in January 1996.

I also need to thank some of my spiritual mentors who have been my guides at various points along the way: Mary Ann Surges, John Dold,

Deborah Voss, Chris Nyholm, and Dale Coski, each of whom is a manifestation of God's presence in this world. Betsy Kelso gave me much needed personal support and guidance years before I undertook this particular project, planting seeds in me to eventually pursue this work. The St. Vincent de Paul Gay and Lesbian Spirituality Group has provided support and friendship throughout the many years I have lived in Philadelphia. Each time I am with this fine group of faithful individuals, I know my work is important. It is for the sake of holy people like them that I undertook this project. I also write in memory of those I have known who have died of complications from AIDS: Thom, Greg, Richard, John, Scott, Tim, Urban, Sonny, Bill, Merrill, Marty, Kevin, Sam, Lou, Ron, and Gary. Their lives cut short on earth, they now exist and offer guidance in the communion of saints.

Most importantly, thanks to my life partner Scott Roulier. In the over three years I worked on this project from start to finish, a number of things occurred, any of which might have completely derailed any hope of progress: our house was burglarized and my computer and disks were stolen; Scott's father died suddenly, just a few years after the death of his mother; we endured a strenuous process to acquire a lovely old house which had stood vacant for a time and needed lots of loving care; my own father suffered a heart attack and underwent subsequent medical treatment, which compromised his mental and physical health to the point that he passed away after an eight-month struggle; the events of September 11, 2001, took an emotional toll, especially for a New York lover like me; and I was diagnosed with and underwent surgery and treatment for testicular cancer. In the face of such overwhelming life events, my dear partner Scott stood with me through it all, performing countless "acts of love." Never have I met a more generous and forgiving person, who truly knows the meaning of unconditional love. He is a constant reminder and embodied representation of God's love and action in my life. I so appreciate Scott's unwavering faith in my abilities and in the value of this work. I could not have written this book without him and I can confidently say I would never have completed it without his support. I hope whatever fruit this project yields will not only serve to "repay" him but also stand as a testament to the procreativity of our union.

Preface

This book explores gay Catholic identity as narrated in autobiographical texts. It builds upon and has been shaped by a body of scholarship related to gay Catholic studies that has emerged over the past several decades to analyze and respond to church teaching on homosexuality and to paint a more complex picture of gay and lesbian reality in the church. John McNeill was one of the first to challenge the Catholic Church's negative assessment of homosexuality. His 1976 book, *The Church and the Homosexual*, set the foundation for much of the liberatory work that would follow.[1] Subsequent scholars have approached this issue through historical studies to see how the tradition has dealt with sexuality at various points in time. Some have analyzed Roman Catholic teachings on homosexuality through the discipline of moral theology.[2] Others have tried to bring lesbian and gay experience to bear directly on the ethical and theological assumptions underlying official church positions on homosexuality. My work fits most closely in this latter category of scholarship.

Scholars across a broad spectrum of religious traditions and other Christian denominations have been doing similar work and adding to our general knowledge of religion and sexuality.[3] Biblical scholars have also taken up the very important task of critically analyzing scripture to determine what it has to say about homosexuality as we understand it today.[4] All of this has taken place within the context of the rise of feminist consciousness in academia, and a number of feminist scholars have made significant contributions to and been influenced by the study of religion and sexuality.[5] Though this book is neither historical, nor a work of biblical analysis, nor explicitly feminist, I owe a great deal to the theoretical and methodological foundations and insights such scholarship has provided.

The autobiographies examined here are in themselves part of the body of literature on being gay and Catholic that has emerged over the past three-plus decades since Vatican II and the Stonewall riots. The concern in this type of literature is to share a life story (or particular aspects thereof) and not necessarily to deal with church teaching in any systematic way. Indeed, the motivations for a person to engage in writing something autobiographical vary from one to another and this is true even among the

1

authors whose works I will discuss. Certainly, many of these writers are
motivated by a perceived need on their part to respond to the conflicted
atmosphere within the church and/or society on sexual issues, to insert
their own personal stories into the debate. Others simply want to share
their personal struggles or discuss important pieces of their spiritual journeys as a way of giving witness to some larger meaning in their lives. Still
others are only marginally concerned, if at all, about the role of religion
in their current lives and may or may not even self-identify as Catholic at
the time of writing their story. Their reasons for writing are probably not
spiritual in any meaningful sense of the word. But all of them have been
marked in some way by Catholicism and all of them are gay (or at least not
heterosexual). These writings have gone largely untapped as a source for
critical analysis and as a starting point for overcoming the problems with
official church teaching on homosexuality I discuss herein. I use them in
this book as the basis for a literary, textual analysis springing from theories
of autobiography.[6]

Limits and Terminology

My study is limited in the following ways, which are summed up in the
phrase "gay Catholic men." First, I only examine autobiographies written by *men*. Although there is a large body of autobiographical writing
by Catholic lesbians, men and women confront different issues in both
society and the church, and their life stories need to be analyzed sep-
arately. A pervasive tendency in much of the relevant scholarship (and
indeed in church teaching itself) is the conflation of gay male and lesbian
experiences. The problem is well articulated by Adrienne Rich:

> Lesbians have historically been deprived of a political existence
> through "inclusion" as female versions of male homosexuality. To
> equate lesbian existence with male homosexuality because each is
> stigmatized is to erase female reality once again. . . . I perceive the
> lesbian experience as being, like motherhood, a profoundly *female*
> experience, with particular oppressions, meanings, and potentiali-
> ties we cannot comprehend as long as we simply bracket it with
> other sexually stigmatized existences.[7]

My intention is not to further marginalize women, as they have been so
frequently in Catholicism, but to take gender differences seriously and
set limits that will do justice to my analysis and women's experience.
This enables me to better address gender issues related specifically to men
and masculinities. Ultimately, my hope is that the same liberatory princi-
ples of my analysis can be applied similarly to lesbian women's life texts,

given that homophobia, antigay bias, and hate crimes do affect all gay, lesbian, bisexual, and transgendered people (though perhaps not in equivalent ways). My conclusions and the impact of my work on church teaching should be beneficial for men and women alike given the conflation of gay men and lesbians in official documents.

Second, I only examine autobiographies written by *gay* men who are self-identified as such. For my purposes, this also includes anyone who identifies himself as bisexual, which is the case in only one of the texts in my survey. It is important to say a few words about the terminology associated with sexual identity because some of these terms have become contentious in both political and academic circles. The debate has to do with how same-sex desire is theorized in relation to the idea of "sexual identity." In his groundbreaking *History of Sexuality*, Michel Foucault charts the nineteenth-century evolution (or devolution, as it might be interpreted) of "sodomy" as a category strictly of forbidden acts to "homosexuality" as a category of persons: "The nineteenth-century homosexual became a personage, a past, a case history, and a childhood. . . . The sodomite had been a temporary aberration; the homosexual was now a species."[8] This could be considered the birth or "invention" of homosexuality as an identity.[9] The use of the term "gay" in place of or as an equivalent to "homosexual" was a strategic move, first deployed in the 1960s, by gay liberationists who viewed it as a counter to the sexual hierarchy that classed heterosexuality as normal and homosexuality as deviant. "Gay" is now widely accepted in popular usage as describing a person with exclusively same-sex desires.[10] It tends to carry a more publicly affirming expediency and linkage to the gay rights movement than the more clinical sounding "homosexual," though both can be politically deployed in different contexts.[11]

The use of "gay" or "homosexual" as identity categories is not entirely unproblematic, however, because as identities the terms become much more restrictive. Consider, for instance, a man who is sexually attracted to women and even maintains a relationship with a woman, but who also engages in occasional sexual encounters with men. He is not likely to identify as "gay" because the popular understanding of that term does not accurately describe his feelings or experience. The category of "bisexual" has been deployed to counter and deconstruct the either/or binary created by the usage of terms like "gay" and "straight" or even the more clinical sounding "homosexual" and "heterosexual"; but some theorists argue "bisexuality" integrates rather than disrupts the binary sexual economy and reifies a third identity category that is still too restrictive and reliant on traditional constructions of gender. Where, for example, does sex-as-recreation or transvestism fit into this model? Much of this hinges on how one understands the concept of sexual identity in the first place. Is it fixed, natural, and innate — often called the *essentialist* position — or is it fluid and dependent on social conditioning and available cultural models — the *constructionist* position?[12]

Critical theorists offer the term "queer" as a way out of this conundrum. "Queer" is an outgrowth of the constructionist position, founded on twentieth-century theories which have destabilized "identity" as a self-evident or natural category. While some might see "queer theory" as the latest institutional transformation of "gay and lesbian studies," those who advocate using the term "queer" see it as something much more complicated and hard to define. "Broadly speaking, queer describes those gestures or analytical models which dramatise incoherencies in the allegedly stable relations between chromosomal sex, gender and sexual desire."[13] The whole purpose of deploying this term is to resist definitions and boundaries that reinscribe the limitations it seeks to overcome. Its usage is also a resistance to what many perceive as a normalizing tendency in the gay rights movement today. Many advances in gay rights realized in the past few decades are seen as signs "not of progress but of how lesbians and gays have been assimilated into mainstream culture and values."[14] In this way, queer advocates would argue, those with marginalized identities are complicit with the identification regimes they hope to counter. By lumping all "non-normative" sexualities and desires under the umbrella of "queer," without drawing boundaries around what that term describes, queer theorists seek to revolutionize the way we think about sexual categories and identities.

But the use of "queer" is still contested by many to whom the label may be applied. The openendedness of the term effectively erases real differences between and among those who are grouped under the umbrella, and potentially effaces injustices and discrimination experienced by some queers but not all. "Queer" also neutralizes the political efficacy of "gay" and "lesbian" as gendered identity categories. This is a serious consideration in the realm of Christian theology, where gays and lesbians have been working hard to assert their equal placement at the "table."[15] While "queerness" works very well to disrupt the givenness of heterosexuality, the content of gay identity needs to be recognized on a par with religious identity before we can destabilize it. Additionally, many gay men and lesbians feel uncomfortable using a term for themselves that has been and often still is used derogatorily toward them by those who want to denigrate them.[16] By far, the terms "gay" and "lesbian" and even "bisexual" are still more widely used than "queer" in terms of self-identification.[17] With few exceptions, the writers of the autobiographies I examine use "gay" to describe themselves. Some use "queer" in addition to "gay," but in most cases they use both in terms of sexual *identity*, which strict queer theorists would resist.

A simple and helpful way of thinking about sexuality is in three component parts: orientation (feelings/desires), behavior, and identification.[18] I am most concerned with questions of identity and self-identification, so I will use the term "gay" most of the time because of its popular usage as an identity category. I do not think "gay" yet represents a category of assimilation, so I think it still accomplishes the goal of challenging the heteronormative status quo. I will use "queer" or "bisexual" when it is more appropriate and if the autobiographer himself uses that term; I will also use "homosexual" as appropriate, especially to separate church teaching that denies gay identity or when referring to "clinical" descriptions of same-sex desire or activity. Despite the nuances of these terms, it must be remembered that in popular usage among gay men these terms are roughly equivalent. Which term is deployed when is largely a matter of context, but "gay" remains the popular term at this point in time.

My limitation of using only gay men's life texts by definition excludes the stories of "ex-gay" men. In spite of my personal misgivings about the "ex-gay" movement, it is not my intention to simply dismiss their experiences. I do think "ex-gays" have something to say about the fluidity of sexual identity and their life texts are worth studying in another project. Indeed, one might theorize "ex-gays" are still "queer" by virtue of their nonfixed sexuality; but most "ex-gays" identify themselves that way in conformity with heterosexual norms. In that respect, they desire "straight" rather than "queer" identity, and an analysis of their autobiographies could be most helpful in revealing how their life stories have been usurped by religious right rhetoric. It is important to note that a "bisexual" man's life story might look sexually similar to "ex-gay" stories if he is not currently engaging in any same-sex behavior. Again, the crucial difference is in self-identification. "Ex-gays" define themselves outside of my methodological paradigm by flatly rejecting gay or even homosexual identity. I do, however, include autobiographies of gay men who (try to) live celibate lives in accord with current Catholic teaching. Living in chastity is not the same as trying to "become heterosexual," and the stories of gay celibates are equally important in my analysis.[19]

My third limitation is using only autobiographies written by gay *Catholic* men. By this, I mean men who were born into or converted to Roman Catholicism. I exclude those who grew up in or write from a Protestant tradition that could broadly be called catholic, like the Episcopal Church. The uniqueness of dealing with Roman authority separates the Roman Catholic tradition from other sacramental churches. I include autobiographers whose commitment to Catholicism ranges from intense and devout to marginal or nonexistent. I operate from the assumption that Catholicism is a culture that is formative beyond whatever faith commitments inhere in the individual.[20] A few of these writers might object that they are no longer Catholic and would not necessarily want to be included in a study like this, but I believe their stories are essential in addressing the problems with church teaching I will discuss.[21] After all, many gay Catholics leave the church precisely because church teaching on homosexuality does not make sense in their lives. Their life stories are important for the life of the church, embodied both in the hierarchical leadership *and* the people in or out of the pews who call themselves Catholic. As Vatican II defined it, the church is the entire people of God.

My study is further limited by time and place. In terms of time, I only examine autobiographies written by gay Catholic men since 1969. This situates my analysis firmly within the contemporary church and contemporary gay culture, post-Vatican II and post-Stonewall. Life stories written before that would reflect a radically different cultural and religious paradigm. As Ken Plummer notes, "Whilst men and women have been coming out for over a hundred years, it is only since 1970 that the stories have gone very public."[22] In terms of place, I only examine autobiographies written by gay Catholic men living in the United States, or whose stories take place or are influential primarily in an American context. The American Catholic Church has its own dynamics that are different in some ways from the global church, and the U.S. bishops have made their own statements on homosexuality and have dealt with Vatican statements in a particular way. Also, American gay culture has its own history and has developed its own dynamics.

Locating MySelf

In recognition of the supposition that all scholarship is engaged in some degree of advocacy work, and in line with the current trend of scholars being forthright about their own social location, I feel compelled to reveal something about my own life circumstances in relation to this project. In a book concerned with life stories, it would seem somewhat disingenuous not to disclose the pertinent details of my own story. My life text (if I had written one) would fit within the parameters I outlined above. I am a gay American Catholic man. I was born during Vatican II — to a quintessentially Catholic family: six kids, regular churchgoers, Catholic grade schools — so I am essentially what is now called a post-Conciliar Catholic, though I am not quite part of "Generation X." When I was very young, I remember the altar rail separating the priest from the people being removed at my church. Around the same time, when I was in grade school in the 1970s, our parish formed its first folk music group. I was envious of my teenage sisters who were old enough to join, and I quickly followed suit once I was in high school. From my earliest memories of going to church, I have always loved church music. It has nurtured my soul and has proven to be my primary point of connection with the Catholic tradition, almost "singing" it into my bones. The sweeping changes in American Catholicism have been represented in my life by the changes in church music styles that have happened simultaneously with my own coming of age. Throughout my adult life I have continued this deep connection by working as a music director and liturgist at a variety of Catholic parishes. I dearly love the Roman Catholic liturgy and have found in its depths the inspiration and power to work for social justice in the world.

My education was profoundly influenced by the Sisters of Loretto, arguably the most radical congregation of American nuns. Not only did they staff my grade school — though by the time I reached eighth grade, only one remained on the faculty — but they also founded the college I attended. At first, I resisted their progressive and challenging vision of being Catholic. I was comfortable at my church and enjoyed making music there. But I was also something of a late bloomer and as I slowly explored my sexual self, I began to experience my own cognitive dissonance in the church. The values I learned in my Catholic education about praying with an open mind, listening to my inner voice, and searching for answers that make sense spiritually and intellectually propelled me to push for reconciliation between who the church said I should be and who I knew myself to be. "Leaving" the church, or rather letting the church abandon me, never really occurred to me. I found affirmative spaces in the Catholic community through Dignity and progressive parishes, so I remain a deeply committed Catholic; yet I know for myself if I were to stop going to Mass, I would still have Catholicism "singing" in my bones. The critical work I am now doing is the culmination of my quest to have my life experience taken seriously by my church, as I have taken the church seriously throughout my life. May it bear good fruit for all gay Catholics.

Introduction

Whispers from the Housetop

Then, one Sunday during mass, my mind adrift in the sea of colorful light filtering down from the stained glass window above as I recited the Apostles' Creed, I made the inconceivable and irrevocable connection, felt the blazing brand of recognition — as if I had finally been given the gift of life, been filled almost unbearably by what I could only identify as the Holy Spirit: *I was the degenerate homosexual whom I imagined my Church so despised.* I felt I had been chosen and, in the same excruciating moment, obliterated. Suddenly, everything made perfect sense to me, and yet was all the more terribly incomprehensible. — Rafael Campo, *The Desire to Heal*

Gay and Catholic. The very idea of being both at once seems almost absurd. The popular conception of traditional religions like Roman Catholicism seems to preclude any hope of claiming both descriptions for oneself. Indeed, the phrase "gay Catholic" strikes many as an oxymoron; a painful, if not impossible, convergence of identities; a combination both morally untenable and theologically problematic. Yet behind such theoretical assumptions, gay Catholics do exist: persons who occupy the space where these two identities collide; people who feel both "chosen" and "obliterated"; people for whom everything becomes "all the more terribly incomprehensible," just as everything begins to make "perfect sense." Yes, gay Catholics do exist and are increasingly visible at the beginning of the twenty-first century, especially in the American context. This unavoidable reality represents an ethical and pastoral dilemma for Roman Catholicism as it embarks on its journey into the next Christian millennium.

Of all the issues polarizing American society at this point in time, homosexuality is one of the most divisive. One might think the events of September 11, 2001, would have made this issue seem less important to Americans. After watching the harrowing images of people falling to their deaths from the burning World Trade Center buildings, one might think newspaper coverage of a same-sex union with a photograph of two men kissing would not be a big deal. One might hope that images of love and commitment would be welcome in a world filled with terrorism and uncertainty. But as time passes, objections to such images are still raised,[1] and we find ourselves in the same old debates over the moral status of gay relationships. If anything, 9/11 reemphasized how unresolved this issue is: within days, a few conservative religious leaders construed the attacks as God's punishment for allowing gay rights and abortions. (They quickly retracted these statements in the face of public pressure, saying they had been misinterpreted.) Later, longtime gay partners of those who died in the attacks had to take legal action to receive the same benefits automatically accorded to legally married others who may have known their spouses only a short time.

The fact that these kinds of debates and legal challenges are going on could be read as a sign of progress. Forty years ago, questions about gay rights were hardly on the radar screens of most Americans. While gay and lesbian subcultures and movements existed and even thrived through-out the twentieth century, the 1960s and the 1969 "Stonewall Riots" in particular pushed the gay movement to a new level of visibility that has grown exponentially ever since.[2] And is it ever visible today! The open-ing years of the twenty-first century have seen the societal discourse on homosexuality taken to a level that seemed unimaginable even one decade earlier. Gay characters in some form or another find their way into some of the most popular television shows and movies, and gay roles have be-come less risky for actors. When Ellen DeGeneres came out both on her television show and in her personal life in 1997, it caused enough of a stir to make the cover of *Time* magazine. Her show quickly faltered as a result of the fallout. Today, the audience cheers as Jay Leno gets a makeover by the fab-five gay-team boys of *Queer Eye for the Straight Guy* on *The To-night Show*. Of course, gay representation in mainstream programming is, like so much in popular entertainment culture, rarely multidimensional. It is built upon and fuels a host of stereotypes and is usually drained of any meaningful sexual content. But this partial invisibility is a form of visibility nonetheless, and it has made gay people seem no more screwy than other television characters.

None of this means gay people are now firmly accepted in American society, however. Gay visibility in the fantasy world of television is one thing; the reality in the world of law and ethics is another. According to a recent Washington Post/Kaiser Family Foundation/Harvard University poll, 72 percent of respondents feel "gay sex" is "unacceptable," yet 87 percent say homosexuals should have equal rights and opportunities in the workplace.[3] This reveals a striking tension between people's moral evaluation of homosexuality, on the one hand, and their respect for in-dividual rights and equal treatment, on the other. Unfortunately, many people feel pressed to choose one over the other. When the question is phrased differently to ask about the acceptability of homosexuality as an alternative "lifestyle" rather than focusing on "gay sex," people are more evenly divided in their moral evaluation: 54 percent say it is acceptable, while 43 percent say it is not.[4] Alan Wolfe's research suggests Americans are largely tolerant of difference, but the vehement expressions of opinions on homosexuality indicate it is the ultimate test of this tolerance: "The line separating gay America from straight America is a line that an unusually large number of middle-class Americans are unwilling to cross."[5] According to Wolfe, Americans remain deeply divided with regard to homosexuality: "The question of homosexuality reveals two genuinely different moral camps in America, which disagree profoundly about the fundamental nature of what they are contesting."[6]

Today's legislative propositions and judicial pronouncements on a variety of gay civil rights issues represent the public manifestations of people grappling with the moral status of gay and lesbian relationships. On June 26, 2003, in one of the most symbolically meaningful victories for advocates of gay rights, the United States Supreme Court found a Texas anti-sodomy law unconstitutional, thus overturning all such laws in the thirteen states that still had them. Writing for the 6–3 majority, Justice Anthony Kennedy states, "Adults may choose to enter relationships in the confines of their homes and their own private lives and still retain their dignity as free persons. . . . The state cannot demean their existence or control their destiny."[7] The significance of this ruling was lost on no one, and it caused those opposed to gay rights to draw more dramatic battle lines. The Reverend Louis P. Sheldon, of the Traditional Values Coalition, immediately called for an impeachment movement against the justices who had sided with the majority opinion, suggesting they had "ushered in a new form of government in the United States."[8] Matt Foreman, of the National Gay and Lesbian Task Force, was both hopeful and cautious: "This is both the most promising and the most frightening moment in this movement's history. There's nothing to compare it to."[9]

Foreman's trepidation stems from his recognition that the situation will become far more divisive and volatile as gay rights issues continue to come to the fore. This is especially true with regard to gay marriage, an issue all sides seem to interpret as the ultimate step in the normalization of same-sex relationships. Vermont already recognizes same-sex unions without calling them marriages and, as I complete the writing of this manuscript, the Massachusetts Supreme Court is poised to issue a ruling on gay marriages. Only a handful of countries have actually legalized gay marriage, but the fact that the Canadian provinces of Ontario and British Columbia have done so has turned up the heat on this issue in the United States. Those opposed to same-sex marriage have proposed the dramatic step of amending the U.S. Constitution to limit marriage to a union between a man and a woman. Thirty-seven states already have "Defense of Marriage" laws so that they do not have to recognize same-sex unions or marriages from other states. By a strange warp of logic, they believe that if more people want to be married and have access to it, this will somehow harm the institution of marriage. Peter La Barbera, of the Culture and Family Institute, takes it a step further: he says gay marriage "is a signal of moral breakdown" in society.[10]

Needless to say, many of these attitudes are driven by religion, and religious people are, in turn, caught up in this societal conflict. Religious bodies have been rocked and torn apart by issues related to homosexuality — most visibly within Christian churches.[11] Debates swirl throughout Christian communities regarding the appropriate theological and pastoral responses to same-sex orientations and relationships. The most recent and visible example is in the Episcopal Church, where the openly gay and partnered Rev. V. Gene Robinson was recently elected and approved as bishop of New Hampshire. As a result of this action, some bishops in the Anglican communion are threatening a schism, and the archbishop of Canterbury has called an emergency meeting to address the issue. The Episcopal convention also acknowledged that the blessing of same-sex unions has occurred in the ordinary life of the church, which drew equally heavy criticism from some quarters. Here again, the issue of gay marriage has touched off a firestorm, pushing people to "take sides" against each other within their own church community. A Washington Post poll taken after the Supreme Court decision invalidating anti-sodomy laws showed nearly three out of four regular churchgoers opposing the Episcopal convention's decisions, while less frequent churchgoers remain nearly evenly divided.[12] In the words of Alan Wolfe, "Americans are saying, 'We're willing to move pretty far on this issue, we're much more tolerant than we used to be, but don't mix it up with religion and God.'"[13]

But debates over homosexuality are unavoidably about religion and God, especially when the question deals with something sacramental like marriage — a fitting topic through which to introduce the particular context of Roman Catholicism. In light of all the recent advances toward full, legal recognition of same-sex relationships, Catholic hierarchical leaders have launched an aggressive campaign against this movement. In April 2003, the Vatican issued a lexicon designed to clarify church doctrine and define terminology church leaders find problematic or misused in modern political agendas. Besides making the blanket assertion that homosexuality is "without any social value," the document also characterizes legislative bodies that grant legal recognition to same-sex relationships as being filled with "deeply disordered minds."[14] Later, the bishops of Massachusetts, concerned their Supreme Court might decide the state constitution allows same-sex marriage, urged Catholics in the state to lobby for an amendment that would restrict marriage to heterosexual unions.

Most recently, the Vatican issued one of its most emphatic statements on the subject to date: "Considerations Regarding Proposals to Give Legal Recognition to Unions Between Homosexual Persons." Though the document says nothing new in terms of church teaching, it is notable for its sweeping statements and defensive, reactionary posturing. It is a challenge not only to Catholic politicians, but a call for all Catholics "to refuse to cooperate with measures that suggest an analogy between same-sex unions and traditional marriage between a man and a woman."[15] According to the document, "Not even in a remote analogous sense do homosexual unions fulfill the purpose for which marriage and family deserve specific categorical recognition."[16] Although most people, even those opposed to any kind of legal recognition, would acknowledge something at least remotely analogous about gay unions and legally valid marriages, the Vatican absolutely denies it. Seemingly blind to the historical malleability of the reasons and purpose for marriage, the document also assumes there is unanimous agreement as to why (and whether) marriage and family deserve special categorical recognition.[17] Riding the wave of such debatable assertions, and despite the diversity of opinion among other Christians and Catholics, the Vatican insists that denying the recognition of same-sex relationships is not opposed to justice: "On the contrary, justice requires it."[18]

The full reality of Catholic teaching on homosexuality is far less clear cut. Within the Catholic Church, concerned Catholics negotiate a delicate position between Vatican condemnations of homosexual behavior and church teachings affirming the inherent dignity of all human persons. Over the past four decades, the church has left a legacy of teachings on homosexuality that represents developments in understanding and sends decidedly mixed messages to the Catholic faithful. Beginning with the Second Vatican Council, 1962–65, the Roman Catholic Church deliberately turned itself toward engaging with the modern world. Pope John XXIII was explicit in his call for the *aggiornamento* (It., updating) of the Catholic Church and the necessity of the church to constantly renew and reform itself (*ecclesia semper reformanda*). Though primarily pastoral in nature, the Council affirmed the idea that doctrine could develop.[19] This was especially true with the 1965 promulgation of the "Declaration on Religious Freedom" (*Dignitatis Humanae*), which built upon human rights ideals set forth in John XXIII's 1962 encyclical *Pacem in Terris* and radically reversed earlier condemnations of religious liberty. The Council also affirmed the primacy of one's well-formed conscience in moral decision making and religious matters.[20] The confluence of these factors with the heightened visibility of the lesbian and gay movement provided fertile ground for an array of Catholic responses to homosexuality.[21]

Official Catholic teaching since Vatican II has consistently maintained that sexuality in general is properly expressed only within the confines of a sacramentally valid marriage.[22] Even then, sexual acts are circumscribed by the requirement that they must always be both "unitive" and "procreative."[23] Regarding homosexuality in particular, the church has attempted to integrate Vatican II teachings on the innate dignity of all human beings and the mandate to learn from and dialogue with the modern world by marking a difference between homosexual orientation and homosexual acts. This was first emphasized in the 1975 "Declaration on Certain Questions Concerning Sexual Ethics" (*Persona Humana*) by the Congregation for the Doctrine of the Faith (CDF). The separation between acts and orientation has allowed the church to "respect" homosexual people and at the same time "deplore" homosexual behavior. As Andrew Sullivan describes it, church teaching is now directed in two simultaneous and opposite directions: "A deeper respect for and understanding of homosexual persons, and a sterner rejection of almost anything those persons might do."[24] This has been stressed to various degrees and to various ends in all subsequent Vatican statements on the subject. The CDF's 1986 "Letter to the Bishops of the Catholic Church on the Pastoral Care of Homosexual Persons" exploited this difference not only to condemn homosexual acts but also to describe homosexual orientation as an "objective disorder."[25] The split between behavior and orientation is echoed in the 1995 *Catechism of the Catholic Church*, in which Catholics are reminded "homosexual acts are gravely disordered," but homosexual men and women "must be accepted with respect, compassion and sensitivity."[26]

The Bifurcation Problem

Robert Westerfelhaus discusses the Roman Catholic Church's teachings on homosexuality since the Second Vatican Council in terms of a shift in rhetorical stance. Prior to Vatican II, the church condemned both act (homosexual behavior) and actor (homosexual person). That rhetorical stance has been replaced by two distinctly different rhetorics: a moral rhetoric (to condemn the act) and a pastoral rhetoric (to uphold the person). Westerfelhaus argues that this has resulted in an uneasy bifurcation of the institutional church's position regarding homosexuality.[27] Within the frame of this teaching, the church creates a category of persons who — unlike heterosexual persons, whose nonmarital sexual acts are similarly forbidden, and unlike those who have actively chosen to abstain from sex — are required to be celibate simply because of who they are. The peculiar notion of the church that it is okay to be a homosexual as long as you do not act like one reflects an attempt by the church to balance its two rhetorics. The moral and pastoral rhetorics tenuously balance each other like a see-saw waiting to tilt, if it hasn't careened already. The problem is that by simultaneously trying to elevate both rhetorics, "the Church effectively elevates neither."[28]

The Catholic bishops of the United States have upheld the distinction defined by the two rhetorics, but even they do not seem convinced of its efficacy. In 1981, the United States Catholic Conference stated, "The person who is ostracized in his/her own Church community because of a homosexual orientation finds little comfort that the Church distinguishes between homosexual orientation and homosexual activity."[29] Even more tellingly, in a document distributed ten years later designed to reinforce the distinction "between being homosexual and doing homosexual actions," the bishops note that this distinction is "not always clear and convincing."[30] They want to maintain the church's bifurcated position, even as they admit the underlying reasoning for it may not be completely persuasive.

On a practical level, this bifurcation carries some problematic implications. Primarily, it causes the church to assert itself in inconsistent and troubling ways. For example, the *Catechism* argues with respect to gay and lesbian people, "Every sign of unjust discrimination in their regard should be avoided."[31] Yet in 1992, at a time when several American states and cities were considering legislation concerning the civil rights of gays and lesbians, the CDF issued a statement specifically to assert, "There are areas in which it is not unjust discrimination to take sexual orientation into account, for example, in the placement of children for adoption or foster care, in employment of teachers or athletic coaches, and in military recruitment."[32] In their most recent statement on gay rights legislation, the Vatican argues that allowing children to be adopted by persons living in same-sex unions "would actually mean doing violence to these children."[33] Apparently, the moral rhetoric is now so important to church leaders that they would rather ignore the evidence of thousands of children already being raised by gay and lesbian parents.[34] Surely these children deserve the same protections of family and marriage — an important pastoral concern — as children of heterosexual unions, who we know are not immune to violence simply because they have two opposite-sex parents. Similarly, the church's response to AIDS has been implicated in this problem. Although the pastoral rhetoric might support the use of condoms in order to protect the human person, the moral rhetoric absolutely could not.[35]

The tensions in church teaching have been even more evident since the release of the U.S. Bishops' most recent document concerning homosexuality: "Always Our Children: A Pastoral Message to Parents of Homosexual Children and Suggestions for Pastoral Ministers."[36] The original statement clearly emphasizes the pastoral rhetoric in its insistence that parents of lesbian and gay children should do everything possible to show love to their children. The reasoning is that every child is a gift from God and a homosexual orientation by itself cannot be considered sinful because it is not freely chosen. Here, the American bishops acknowledge the contemporary psychological argument that regardless of what factors "cause" homosexuality, most people who describe themselves as homosexual experience their orientation as a given.[37] Overall, the message in their statement is quite positive and accepting, though nowhere does it negate the moral rhetoric of the church. In fact, in response to those who favor the moral over the pastoral stance, the document was eventually revised and reissued in July of 1998. In the revision, a footnote was added to the above passage concerning the neutrality of the orientation: "This inclination, which is objectively disordered, constitutes for most a trial."[38] While most Catholic lesbians and gays still view the document in a mostly positive light, they find the distinction between orientation and activity confusing and problematic. In the words of Robert Miailovich, then-President of Dignity USA (the nation's largest organization of lesbian, gay, bisexual, and transgendered Catholics), in a statement released the same day as the bishops' letter, "This is a distinction that makes little sense to us and will be a stumbling block in the way of any effective pastoral program seeking to encompass the letter's recommendations."[39]

As recently as December 2000, an American bishop found himself in a delicate situation as a result of the mixed messages in church teaching. Baltimore Bishop William Newman commendably presided at an Advent liturgy for gay/lesbian people, their families, and friends. In the Spirit of "Always Our Children" and the jubilee year launched by Pope John Paul II for the millennium, Bishop Newman used his homily to seek reconciliation between the church and gays and lesbians:

> In this spirit today I lead the Church Community in seeking the forgiveness of our loving God for the sins individually and collectively the Church has committed against the gay and lesbian community. We all are children of God made in God's image and should enjoy the dignity of being a human person.[40]

Needless to say, this action by a bishop was greeted with cheers by lesbian and gay Catholics and celebrated in progressive Catholic publications. After a favorable editorial in the *National Catholic Reporter*, however, the director of communications of the archdiocese of Baltimore issued a clarification in his own letter to the editor. In his letter, he reiterates the moral rhetoric by noting the church "does proscribe intimate acts of sexuality that are reserved in God's plan for a man and a woman in union with one another through marriage." He further notes that the absence of the moral rhetoric in the bishop's homily "does not signal a withdrawal from the truth, but recognition that in an ongoing ministry of outreach, it does not have to be underscored on every occasion."[41] Lesbian and gay Catholics then expressed frustration with the clarification through their own statements and letters. Indeed, one wonders why this clarification was necessary if it is not necessary to underscore the moral rhetoric on every occasion. The clarification from Bishop Newman's office, obviously sent with his authorization, effectively undermined the effort at reconciliation he was putting forth in the first place. Any pastoral ministers in the church will inevitably find themselves between a rock and a hard place attempting to straddle the bifurcated church teaching on homosexuality.

From Bifurcation to Fragmentation: Division in the Church Community

This bifurcation problem negatively impacts those in the church who seek to minister to lesbian and gay Catholics. At the heart of the concept of ministry is the ideal of service. The Roman Catholic Church has a hierarchy of "ministers," both lay and ordained, whose "vocation" or "job" it is to serve the faithful, even as all Catholics are called to be "ministers" to each other and to the world. The goal is for everyone in the church to be served by and through various ministries. Some ministries are based on various church functions and offices (e.g., liturgy, music, education), while others are focused on particular groups of people with special needs (e.g., poor, homeless, youth, elderly). All such ministries are usually called "pastoral ministries" because they are concerned with the spiritual formation and well-being of human persons.

Reflecting the visibility of lesbian and gay people in modern society, there have arisen new ministries designed to reach this group in particular. The nature of these ministries varies according to the ministers' biases and political views about homosexuality and what they perceive is needed. Officially sanctioned ministries, such as Courage,[42] view homosexuality as a problem to be overcome, and they seek to effect a change in the person. They avoid using terms like gay and lesbian because they represent identity categories. Some dioceses maintain various outreach programs for gays and lesbians, grouped under the umbrella National Association of Catholic Diocesan Lesbian and Gay Ministries (NACDLGM). Most of these are designed to keep gay and lesbian Catholics connected to the church by offering opportunities for spiritual enrichment, without challenging church teaching. At the opposite end of the spectrum from Courage, ministries such as Dignity view homosexuality as a reality to which the church must adapt. Founded in 1969, Dignity thrives without official recognition from the church and operates independent of church support. The organization has chapters across the United States offering liturgies and community for gay, lesbian, bisexual, and transgendered Catholics. Dignity publicly dissents from the church's official moral condemnation of homosexual relationships and offers commitment ceremonies to bless same-sex unions.[43]

In 1977, Sister Jeannine Gramick, SSND, and Father Robert Nugent, SDS, cofounded New Ways Ministry in response to a void they perceived in the church's official response to gay and lesbian Catholics. They were also motivated by a sympathetic statement made by the American bishops in 1976.[44] From the outset, they envisioned themselves as bridge-builders between the church, which they "officially" represent as consecrated religious, and lesbian and gay Catholics, with whom they had already developed a pastoral relationship.[45] Their goal was to listen to gay people, communicate their concerns and needs to the church, and thereby begin to bring about reconciliation between the two groups. Their mode of ministry has been primarily educational presentations, seminars, and retreats, in which they discuss church teaching, scripture, and tradition and give participants the chance to voice their concerns. Gramick and Nugent's work has always reflected a recognition that real pastoral ministry must first and foremost demonstrate a true respect for persons as they are in the context of who they believe themselves to be. In that regard, their presentations have always underscored the church's pastoral rhetoric without overemphasizing the doctrinal condemnation of homosexual acts. They have always been clear about the content of the moral rhetoric, but they interpret it as one evolving piece of a multifaceted set of teachings in which the pastoral rhetoric deserves more attention.

In 1984, they were ordered by the Holy See through their community superiors to cease their association with New Ways Ministry and not to "engage in any apostolate or participate in any program or write on any subject concerning homosexuality unless [he/she] makes clear that homosexual acts are intrinsically and objectively wrong."[46] They stopped functioning formally under the auspices of New Ways but continued their ministry as extensions of their work in their own religious congregations. They believed they had adequately addressed the Vatican's concerns; but in 1988, an investigation was launched by the Vatican's Congregation for Religious and Secular Institutes to evaluate the orthodoxy of Gramick and Nugent's ministry. Thus began a long ordeal which would eventually culminate in July 1999, with an order from the Congregation for the Doctrine of the Faith, for Nugent and Gramick to terminate all of their ministry to gays and lesbians. A year later, circumstances had escalated to the point where they were even ordered not to speak about their ministry, the investigation, or anything having to do with lesbian and gay issues.

How did such an ugly situation come to pass for two relatively moderate ministers of the church? Anyone who attended their presentations or read any of their publications would be hard-pressed to characterize Nugent and Gramick as radicals. They even faced some degree of criticism from activist gay Catholics for not insisting on changes in the church's moral rhetoric. I contend the heart of the problem was and is the bifurcated church teaching on homosexuality. The chasm between the moral and pastoral rhetorics cannot reasonably be bridged in a way that makes sense in the lives of those toward whom the teaching is geared or for those who try to carry out a pastoral ministry for their sake. In the appendix, I offer my appraisal of the investigation of Nugent and Gramick by dissecting some of the statements made in the documents related to the case. While myriad problems emerge related to the way the Vatican conducts its business, especially in terms of what constitutes due process, my analysis demonstrates how the underlying dilemma lies in the impossibility of realistically applying church teaching on homosexuality as it currently stands.[47]

As one might expect, the investigation and silencing of Nugent and Gramick caused a considerable uproar in the community, with concerned Catholics caught in the middle and taking sides against each other, mirroring the polarization in American society on the issue of homosexuality in general. Immediately after the initial Vatican notification against Nugent and Gramick, Dignity released a statement denouncing the action. Charles Cox, Executive Director at the time, was quoted as saying, "The CDF's continued use of 'intrinsic evil' to describe homosexual acts, and implicitly homosexual persons, is a chilling reminder of the Church's on-going attempt to marginalize and stigmatize pastoral care for gay men, lesbians, bisexuals, and transgendered persons."[48]

In quick succession, the Gramick and Nugent case became a cause célèbre among Catholic organizations who used it to accentuate their differences with regard to negotiating authority in the church. Reformist Catholic associations like Call to Action circulated petitions asking Catholics to object to the order of silence, while conservative organizations like the Catholic League used it as an opportunity to reiterate the moral rhetoric against homosexual relationships and to urge fidelity to the Vatican. Nugent and Gramick were given awards and were featured speakers at a variety of local and national progressive conferences and retreats,[49] and letters to the editor flooded Catholic publications that covered the story. Responses ranged from outrage and anger toward the Vatican, to demands that Nugent and Gramick follow their religious vows and obey the Vatican orders to the letter.

The case of Nugent and Gramick did not create new tensions; it only exacerbated divisions already in place. The bifurcated teachings have struck a raw nerve among American Catholics, who are more and more likely to be personally acquainted with a gay or lesbian person. The discrepancy between what the church teaches about homosexuals and what some Catholics feel about the lesbian and gay people they know creates a sense of cognitive dissonance.[50] Other Catholics cling to the moral rhetoric as a shield against a creeping secularism that threatens to undermine religious values. Not surprisingly, even the American bishops are divided. While most of them struggle valiantly to walk the narrow line "between Roman authority and American pastoral practice" (see appendix), some are more extreme. I will briefly highlight two of these, arguably the most extremely conservative and the most radically liberal bishops: Fabian Bruskewitz, of Lincoln, Nebraska, and Thomas Gumbleton, of Detroit. When the Nebraska chapter of Call to Action invited Jeannine Gramick to speak at one of their gatherings, Bishop Bruskewitz wrote the following in his diocesan newspaper:

> In a failed attempt to infect decent people with their ideological pathologies, the anti-Catholic sect Call to Action has recently reached into a theological sewer and brought to Nebraska Sister Jeannine Gramick, SSND, an apostle of sexual perversion.[51]

At the other end of the spectrum, Bishop Gumbleton has stated, in reference to church teaching on homosexuality:

> If you tell someone that at the very core of your being you're disordered and you've got a strong inclination [toward sin], what does that do to you? It's cruel to say to anybody. There's no basis to say it to anybody.[52]

While both bishops' statements might be considered inflammatory, they represent a palpable rift in the Catholic community on the issue of homosexuality.

The polarization was starkly visible a few years ago at the fifth annual conference of the National Association of Catholic Diocesan Lesbian and Gay Ministries, held in Rochester, New York, with the full support of Bishop Matthew Clark. A wide variety of speakers talked of hope, love, justice, and reconciliation between the church and its lesbian and gay members. Though none of the speakers at this officially sanctioned event directly challenged the magisterial position on the moral status of homosexual acts,[53] the overall theme of the conference was acceptance and advocacy of lesbian and gay participation in the church. Outside, however, the picture was very different. Protesters made their objections clear by carrying a variety of signs: "Practicing Catholics cannot practice homosexuality"; "Bishop Clark: Love the Homosexual with the Truth";

"Homosexual Persons Are Called to Chastity." The scene was a micro-cosm of the American Catholic Church's "tense and increasingly public struggle over homosexuality."[54]

Less than two months earlier, the Rochester diocese had been the center of yet another controversy related at least partially to the issue of homo-sexuality. This time Bishop Clark appeared to be on the other side of the rift. In late August 1998, Bishop Clark removed Fr. Jim Callan from his position as pastor of Corpus Christi Parish because Callan regularly al-lowed a woman to co-preside at Eucharist and also because he had blessed same-sex unions.[55] The Corpus Christi community had attracted a large number of gays and lesbians since Fr. Callan first came to the parish in 1976, and it had become well known as a place where Catholic lesbians and gays could openly participate and share their gifts. The new pastor was charged with the task of "cleaning up" the parish, bringing it in line with "traditional" norms. Unfortunately, the situation became both divi-sive and explosive, with parishioners voting to protest the removal of their pastor and to continue their inclusive ministries. In December 1998, six parish staff members were fired for "refusal to cooperate with the new pastor."[56] In the meantime, Fr. Callan, originally reassigned to a rural par-ish, was suspended from administering sacraments or celebrating Mass at any parish until he agreed to "abide by Church regulations."[57] The rift in the Corpus Christi community ultimately resulted in a schism and the excommunication of dissident members.[58] Supporters of Fr. Callan have formed a breakaway church and are now functioning independently with their own paid staff, under the name Spiritus Christi. They still claim au-thentic membership in the Catholic community and have ordained two women of their community as priests.[59]

The above examples depict fragmentation on a large and visible scale, but tensions surrounding church teaching on homosexuality can be ob-served at the most localized levels, affecting individuals and families. A case in point involves Anne and Ed Reynolds, parishioners of St. Aedan Parish in Pearl River, New York, since its founding in 1966. The Reynold-ses wrote a letter to their local newspapers in support of Nugent and Gramick in August 1999. Their son Andrew (then twenty-eight years old) is gay and the Reynoldses had attended four retreats led by Nugent and Gramick. In their letter, they voiced their distress over the church's moral rhetoric which labeled their son "objectively disordered": "As par-ents of a gay man, we cannot fully assent to the Church's teaching on homosexuality. To do so would be to deny our son and violate our con-sciences."[60] After the parish pastor received complaints about the letter, he called the Reynoldses into his office and pressured them into resign-ing as eucharistic ministers, a liturgical ministry they had exercised since 1977. They agreed to resign, but were quite shaken by the confrontation and now encounter only tacit support and even disapproval from their fellow parishioners. Anne and Ed Reynolds represent the most mainstream of American Catholics. They both attended Catholic schools through college, and all eight of their children attended Catholic elementary and high schools; yet church teaching created a moral dilemma for them. "We're not political people, We're both just tired of secrecy and shame. . . . [We] agree with the bishops on so many things. We're really very conservative,"[61] states Ms. Reynolds. She maintains church teaching on homosexuality does not reflect her family's reality, and words like "evil" and "disordered" justify violence against gays and lesbians: "The bishops don't mean to do that, but I don't live in an ivory tower. I live with real people in a real house and I can see how harmful that wording is."[62]

Ms. Reynolds is concerned about the ramifications of church teaching when it seeps into the public square. If church teaching reflects societal prejudices, then it can easily be used to justify and reinforce those prejudices, perpetuating rifts not only in the church but also in society at large. This is an especially important concern when Catholics hold positions of public office and base decisions on their religious beliefs. Recently, in an interview held before the Supreme Court's ruling against anti-sodomy laws, conservative Catholic Senator Rick Santorum, R-PA, compared homosexuality to bigamy, polygamy, incest, and adultery, as he expressed his hope that the Court would not overturn the Texas law. He feared that allowing consensual gay sex based on a right to privacy would then open the legal door to a host of other sexual behaviors like those he listed. His remarks touched off the expected storm of objectors and supporters throughout the country and made starkly visible the ruptures in American Catholicism over issues related to homosexuality.[63] When he spoke less than a month later at the St. Joseph's University Commencement (a Catholic institution), several students and faculty walked out to protest his remarks, marking further dissension in the Catholic community.

In the same interview, Santorum made remarks echoing the bifurcated church teaching: "I have no problem with homosexuality — I have a problem with homosexual acts, as I would with acts of other [sic] . . . acts outside of traditional heterosexual relationships."[64] Though it is not entirely clear, it seems Santorum was trying to draw the same difference church teaching does between gay persons and their behavior. This makes his analogy to other sexual behaviors all the more puzzling. Would he ever say something like, "I have no problem with incest, just incestuous acts"? I doubt it. The confusing separation between homosexual behavior and homosexual orientation, between gay act and gay actor, obscures his real message. Clearly, Santorum does have a problem with homosexuality —

both the acts and the people who do them — otherwise why draw the analogy to other sexual behaviors that do not fit the same mold?

Whose Reality? The Subjectivity Problem

Gay people reject any comparison between homosexuality and any of the sexual behaviors Santorum mentioned because they know being gay involves more than same-sex acts. On this much, Santorum would agree, as his clumsy statements reveal. This is also the reason for the church's distinction between sexual orientation and behavior, and the assumption underlying the bifurcated rhetoric. But the problem is that being gay does in some way involve same-sex acts. Being gay and doing gay are connected. Any clean separation of these aspects does not make sense in the reality of gay existence. From a gay perspective, the bifurcation masks a different reality: the church has a problem with gay persons. Let's say, however, the church sincerely does want to respect gay persons as the pastoral rhetoric states. Why is it not enough for them to say it? What will it take for gay people to believe it and take the pastoral rhetoric seriously?

It is one thing for a public official to say he has no problem with gay people and then denounce the actions that inform gay identity in the first place; but when a church representative says it, it directly implicates church teaching and produces a sort of theological dissonance. Here is where Nugent and Gramick were caught in the middle. The Nugent and Gramick case not only highlights the fragmentation of the Catholic community around this issue but also raises important questions about ministry and the role of ministers. In one of their written responses during the investigation, Gramick and Nugent draw an analogy to other ministries in the church to justify their method:

> Those who minister today to the divorced and remarried are not expected to constantly proclaim the immorality of divorce and remarriage. Hospital chaplains are not expected to constantly proclaim the immorality of neglecting and endangering one's health. Those in prison ministry are not expected to constantly proclaim the immorality of criminal acts. Military chaplains are not expected to constantly proclaim the immorality of war. The expectations of those in lesbian and gay ministry should be similar.[65]

At first glance, this comparison offers an insight into the way Gramick and Nugent view their ministry. For them, pastoral ministry is to some extent always already separate from any moral evaluation of those for whom the ministry exists. In that respect, it would seem their ministry and the others they mention actually rely on some degree of bifurcation. They would assert all people deserve pastoral care regardless of the choices they have made in their lives. In broader Christian circles, especially Evangelical strands, this idea is represented by the phrase, "Love the sinner, hate the sin."

But I do not think the above analogy is helpful in relation to the church's teaching on homosexuality. First, if the church's moral teachings were under fire in relation to any of the above groups, I think church officials would indeed expect pastoral ministers to reiterate the moral doctrines. Second, the church does not recognize soldiers, criminals, hospital patients, and divorced and remarried people in the same way it does homosexuals. Soldiers and divorced and remarried people are not said to have an innate orientation related to these life choices. Criminals and hospital patients may indeed have some inborn inclination or trait which led them to their current situation, but they are then accorded the label of "sick." This is a designation which has been roundly rejected by most lesbian and gay Catholics for themselves. When someone is "sick," their subjective culpability is mitigated and pastoral care becomes an act of charity. Most lesbian and gay Catholics do not want "charity" in place of authentic respect, and they want to take full responsibility for their subjective moral choices.[66]

Nugent and Gramick attempted to build the bridge between the moral and pastoral rhetorics by capitalizing on this distinction between objective immorality and subjective culpability, even as they tried to take seriously the lived experience of gays and lesbians. But this negation of subjective responsibility compounds the bifurcation problem by further separating gay and lesbian persons from their actions. In effect, the gay voice is silenced because gay subjectivity is still lacking. In my usage of these terms, *experience* and *subjectivity* are closely linked to each other and ideally function together, but they are not exactly the same thing. *Experience* is the act and result of participation in one's life as a person with same-sex desires. It informs a self-knowledge that is particular and individual, which is what makes it problematic as a criterion for any moral theology claiming to be "objective." *Subjectivity* is the act and result of being the narrator and interpreter of one's own experience.[67] Experience is communicated through subjectivity. Experience cannot be the only criterion for determining church teaching on sexuality, but it must be one of the criteria.[68] Otherwise, sexual ethics remains entirely theoretical. In fact, gay and lesbian Catholics are increasingly demanding that their experience be taken into account in church teaching.[69] Indeed, their experience should be given priority with regard to moral teachings that directly affect them and about which they are the most knowledgeable. This experience must be ascertained from their own voices, from the kind of subjectivity that is an integral aspect of autobiography.

This focuses attention on the other key problem, integrally related to the bifurcation problem, in official church teaching on homosexuality: the apparent absence of gay subjectivity in the documents. Consistently, "homosexuals" are presented as objects of study, abstractions almost, about whom the teaching is written. As Gramick and Nugent note in reference to the CDF's 1986 "Halloween" Letter, it "obviously did not begin from the experience of being lesbian or gay."[70] It is as if no gay or lesbian people exist either in the group of men who constructed the documents[71] or in the group of people to whom the documents are addressed. Though some of the church documents are addressed only to bishops, most of them are designed to address the church at large, the entire community of believers. The implicit assumption then is that gay and lesbian people are legitimate only outside the Catholic community, or within the community only as disembodied orientations denied realization. Unfortunately (or fortunately, depending on one's rhetorical stance), this does not correspond with the reality of the church community regardless of what the official moral stance would like to dictate.

A sort of hidden gay subjectivity could be said to exist in the documents because some of the writers themselves may be homosexual, but they would not necessarily claim a gay identity, and they certainly would not do so in any remotely public way. They do not write openly from a "sexual subject" position because their own sexuality is displaced and superseded by obligatory celibacy. Of course, the issue of homosexuality within the hierarchy is much more complicated than that. There is certainly homosexual activity going on at all levels of church leadership, the "secrecy" of which is maintained and enhanced by church doctrine on homosexuality. Mark Jordan's recent book, *The Silence of Sodom*, deals with the way Catholic clerical culture simultaneously suppresses and encourages, condemns and elicits, persecutes and instructs homoeroticism. The tension between acceptance and condemnation that plays out in gay Catholic lives and ministries as a result of the bifurcated church teaching actually mirrors an institutional schizophrenia. Indeed, Catholic clerical culture has long offered a relatively safe haven for homosexuals, and the similarities and parallels between that culture and modern gay culture are striking. The power structure provides an arrangement through which same-sex desire can be exercised in secret, without the risks of self-identification, and the official teachings in turn support that structure and its subjective silence.[72]

Jordan's goal is to demystify the Catholic clerical culture which makes church teaching on homosexuality unlikely to change. My goal is to fill in the reality gap in church teaching by introducing gay subjectivity into the equation. Fr. Robert Nugent has suggested gays and lesbians have a *responsibility* to articulate their experiences for the broader community:

"You are the experts in this area ... and you cannot be silent — for your own good or for the comfort of others."[73] Even the Catholic Theological Society is having discussions about the gap between church teaching and gay experience. At a recent meeting of the Society, Augustinian Fr. Daniel Doyle said Catholic theology "had reached an 'impasse' in its approach to homosexuality, ... a point where the natural law tradition 'can no longer carry us,' given the insights gleaned from 'the positive experiences of same-sex relationships.' "[74] My analysis of gay Catholic autobiographies — products of gay subjectivity — will carry our theological understanding forward. These first-person narratives represent people who self-identify as gay, for whom sexuality is a defining piece of personal identity, and for whom "objective" teachings on human sexuality are irrelevant by definition. As I have already discussed, the breach in church teaching between the moral and pastoral rhetoric is a void of gay experience, not reflective of reality. Attending to what these autobiographies have to say about gay identity and Catholic identity will help fill in this gap.[75] By doing so, the church community, as Nugent and Gramick state, "will have a more complete understanding of the complex reality of homosexuality as it affects the lives of people in our Church and will be able to respond in a realistic, sensitive and compassionate manner."[76]

For too long, gay Catholic lives have been shrouded in the secrecy advanced by official church teaching. For many gay Catholics, the "closet" remains a powerful metaphor for the secrecy and shame which cause many of us to keep our sexual identity hidden. At times, the decision to stay "in the closet" is carefully calculated and deliberate. At other times, the closet is forced upon us from outside. Yet it is in this context that gay Catholics must reconcile their sexual and spiritual lives. Gay Catholic autobiographical acts reveal the delicate interplay between sexuality, spirituality, and the many other components of identity which make a person unique. These acts of self-disclosure — of confession — stand as revelations of God's intervention and action in gay Catholic lives. I offer a gay interpretation of Matthew 10:27, on open and fearless confession, from which I imagine the framework for understanding these autobiographies as sacred texts. In Jesus's instructions to his apostles, he admonishes them not to be afraid of those who do not welcome them or who would persecute them: disciples of Jesus are not afraid to speak the truth hidden away in their hearts. What gay Catholics learn about themselves and God "in the closet" is revealed in the life narratives they construct and share with the world:

> What I say to you in the dark, tell in the daylight;
> what you hear in whispers, proclaim from the housetops.[77]

When a gay Catholic takes the risk of narrating his gay identity, transforming what was once a secret and publishing it for public dissemination, his autobiographical act becomes a "whisper from the housetop." These autobiographies provide a glimpse of the lives on which the church's twin rhetorics on homosexuality converge and collide, thus creating a space to synthesize and transcend the bifurcation in church teaching and the polarization now being felt over this issue in the Catholic community. Life stories are central to the mythology that creates and legitimates both sexual and religious identities: "All dogma and proof, i.e., formulations and facts of religious belief, are founded deep in autobiography."[78] Spiritual autobiographies have, in fact, played a significant role in shaping the Catholic tradition. Beginning with Saint Augustine's *Confessions*, often considered the founding moment in the Western tradition of an inward autobiographical subject, such writings reflect upon the experience of divine intention in human lives. Gay Catholic autobiographies function similarly and so should be considered sacred texts for the entire Catholic community, voices which must be heard and analyzed in order to paint a more complete picture of what it means to be Catholic.

Overview

In the next chapter, I will survey the many autobiographical works that form the data pool of this study. There are a surprising number of published works out there when one sets his mind to finding them. I bring them together and describe the various styles of autobiographics represented, in addition to briefly introducing the various authors. I also survey some of the most pertinent theoretical concerns associated with this genre of literature, highlighting the peculiarities of using autobiography as a source of analysis.

In the following chapters, I will dwell in the narrative world of these gay Catholic autobiographers in order to become enmeshed in reality as they conceive it. My goal is not to reify any one particular portrait of gay Catholic identity but rather to show its multiplicity and complexity. I will expose trends, patterns, constructions, perceptions, and divergences, and theorize these in terms of identity questions. I am looking for the ways these autobiographies open up the identities of "gay" and "Catholic" and then complicate simplistic conceptions of these categories. In chapter 2, I will focus on the "gay" side of the identity equation. How do these writers experience being gay and how is gay identity performed in these narratives? Is the separation between doing gay and being gay as viable as the bifurcated church teaching would have us believe? What role do gender constructions and masculine expectations play in their lives? In chapter 3, I will focus more on the "Catholic" side of the identity equation, but with an understanding that these religious and sexual identities are deeply entangled. How is gay Catholic identity performed in these narratives? How does Catholicity function both as a "passed on" culture and as a "taught" system of beliefs, and how do both of these dimensions influence the Catholic world view? How and why has problematic church teaching caused some gays to "leave" the church and others to remain?

In chapter 4, I will examine the ethical struggles and decisions of these gay Catholics as a way of bridging the theoretical division between homosexual persons and behaviors that is the foundation for the bifurcated church teaching. When gay people are in relationships with others, be it friends or family or lovers, the concept of "homosexual acts" becomes nebulous. How are the moral and pastoral rhetorics played upon and by gay Catholics as moral agents themselves? How does the integration of sexuality as an identity piece of one's personhood complicate the separation between being and doing? How are these autobiographies moral performances and how is gay Catholic moral agency and conscience reflected in their life texts? My analysis cannot offer the final answers to these questions, nor can it single-handedly "solve" the problems in church teaching, but it is a necessary next step toward the transformation of church teaching. I hope to distill from these autobiographies an intellectual analysis that is useful for and speaks to gay Catholics and the church community at large.

In chapter 5, I will reiterate the need to overcome and adapt problematic church teaching on homosexuality in light of all that has been revealed in this study. I will propose a way forward that relies on the sacramental dimension of life writing. In the encounter between the Catholic reader and these autobiographies, the church has the opportunity to reflect on its own failures. These autobiographers call attention to the ways the church's official teachings and institutionalized attitudes diminish the opportunity for gay Catholics to fully realize their human potential. When gay Catholic autobiographies reveal such failures in human relationships, it is a starting point for reconciliation between the church and its gay members.

Chapter 1

Surveying Autobiographical Acts

We forget the memories that hinder our continuing on; we cherish and embellish those that give us hope. From our stories we each compose our private opera, for playing and replaying to ourselves and others. This is memory's triumph — it filters and shapes the past into a package suitable for remembering. And this is memory's tragedy: All that shaping and filtering is finally so much stage play, for history exacts its dues independent of what memory wants.

— Fenton Johnson, *Geography of the Heart*

W hen I first embarked on this project and told people I was using autobiographies written by gay Catholics as my primary sources, people would invariably ask, "How many are there?" Their thinly disguised incredulity that there would be an adequate number to propel a project like this initially caused me some anxiety. I knew I had seen several, and I knew the literary world had witnessed an explosion of autobiographical writing in the last few decades. Publishers are only too happy to benefit from our contemporary, tell-all culture, which encourages people to devour the most intimate details of other people's lives. What motivates some people to tell their stories varies according to the type of story being told: ethnic "minorities" in America, for example, may wish to tell their stories in order to preserve their cultural heritage or as a way of resisting the hegemonic norms of "white" America; people facing situations of death and dying may tell their stories to bear witness to a life that has passed on, to report their encounters with the medical system, or to relate their experience of grief;[1] prominent celebrities may tell their stories to attest to their struggle for fame or simply to further their own popularity. But where do gay Catholics fit into this scheme of life storytelling at the cusp of the twentieth and twenty-first centuries, and have they published a sufficient number of autobiographies to justify a study such as mine?

As I set out to find the texts to analyze for this project, I decided to open up the definition of autobiography beyond book-length life stories. After all, the word broken into its roots means *self-life-writing*, and my aim was to find instances of self-life-writing by gay Catholics. With that in mind, I decided any such occurrences — whether they are in the form of essays, articles, chapters, or embedded in novels — would be eligible for consideration. For this reason, it is helpful to think of these writings as autobiographical *acts*, not necessarily complete life stories, but moments of lives enacted textually. An autobiographical act is an animated and dynamic gesture — to act is to do — a wonderfully proactive method of exploring the self. And in line with autobiography theory, it is also an "act": a performance of conscious identity construction. Happily, I was able to find an ample number of gay Catholic autobiographies, though there are surely many more to be both found and written. I will begin this chapter with an overview of these texts in order to understand the rich framework of data upon which this analysis is built. The reasons each author has for telling his story inform the style and scope of his autobiographical act. Although their particular motivations are numerous and varied, and not always entirely clear, some general patterns and types emerge when they are studied together. These categories and styles inevitably overlap, but they also provide a way into the world of these sources.

Surveying the Literature

Given my specific location as a scholar of religion, it makes a certain sense to begin by discussing the works that are explicitly *spiritual* autobiographies. While this is a slippery term, especially in contemporary American culture, which labels almost any personal exploration as a "spiritual" project, I am using it here to identify the texts in which the writer is negotiating his spiritual identity in light of his Catholic background. Although spirituality and religion are not synonymous terms,[2] each of these lives begin from a Catholic understanding of ultimate reality, so the two concepts are unavoidably linked for them. Some remain deeply engaged with the tradition, some have found ways of refashioning their relationship with the church, and others have virtually abandoned it in favor of more eclectic understandings of religion. In any case, the spiritual struggle forms the core of each of these works. Not surprisingly, the majority of these autobiographical acts are found in anthologies devoted to this kind of struggle. Foremost among these for my purposes is Raymond Holtz's *Listen to the Stories*, because every one of the contributors to his volume comes from a Catholic perspective. Twenty-two gay Catholic men present their journeys through Catholicism to articulate their current perception of themselves in relation to the church. Each was asked to reflect on three broad questions and their reflections were then converted to text. Because many of the contributors belong to Dignity — the organization for gay, lesbian, bisexual, and transgendered Catholics — their stories tend to reflect an insistence that gay identity should not be an impediment to membership in the Catholic community.[3]

Another substantive anthology, Brian Bouldrey's *Wrestling with the Angel*, features autobiographical essays on faith and religion in gay lives, eight of whom are Catholic: James Morrison, Andrew Holleran, Kevin Killian, Peter Krask, David Plante, Philip Gambone, Fenton Johnson, and Bouldrey himself. Unlike the Holtz anthology, all of the contributors to this volume are professional writers who not only know how to craft compelling stories but also understand the literary issues at stake in the construction of autobiography.[4] Two Catholic contributors to Catherine Lake's *ReCreations: Religion and Spirituality in the Lives of Queer People* are also gifted writers, one widely published (Daniel Curzon) and the other a graduate student in physics (Brian Utter). Their essays are brief, but focused specifically on spiritual concerns.[5] Andrew Sullivan, who was at one time the editor of the *New Republic*, published an essay on Catholicism and homosexuality in that same magazine in November 1994. It first appeared under the title, "Alone Again, Naturally,"[6] and then was reworked as "Virtually Normal" for Thomas Ferraro's *Catholic Lives, Contemporary America*. Though it was eventually expanded for a book, the essay form remains the most focused on issues of spirituality and religion and consequently fits nicely in this category.

Other anthologies of this type are dedicated specifically to the stories of gay priests and brothers, some of whom write their stories under aliases to avoid the obvious, potential ramifications to their ministries of publicly admitting their sexual activity. Jeannine Gramick's *Homosexuality in the Priesthood and the Religious Life* contains seven autobiographical chapters,[7] and James Wolf's *Gay Priests* contains two essays that explore the particular concerns of gay clergy through autobiographical recollections.[8] Some of the anthologies mentioned earlier in this category also contain contributions by gay priests, and several of them are by ex-priests or former seminarians. Indeed, many of the gay Catholics in this study considered becoming priests at some point in their lives. These details should not be surprising given the homosocial and implicitly homoerotic nature of Catholic clerical culture.[9] The fact that so many of these stories find a link to the "clerical caste" is indicative of how pervasively the issues I am addressing affect and are endemic to the highest levels of the church hierarchy. Furthermore, it signifies how much is at stake in the struggle between sexual and religious identities for many of these autobiographers. I will return to this theme of gay Catholics feeling pulled to the priesthood in later chapters.

In addition to the above kinds of spiritual autobiographies, I have gathered a significant number of short articles written for various magazines and newspapers. Brief and focused in first person on the most particular life issues, these are the most concise of autobiographical acts. Coming from publications as diverse as *Christopher Street*, the *Advocate*, *Equal Times*, *U.S. Catholic*, the *National Catholic Reporter*, *America*, the *Humanist*, *Dignity* newsletters, a university newspaper, and even the *International Journal of Sexuality and Gender Studies*,[10] they represent a range of singular responses to being gay and Catholic and are often written in response to particular issues or questions. Along this line, I have also gathered a number of published interviews with gay Catholics. Interview responses are usually somewhat spontaneous and do not undergo the same textual editing process normally given to written narration; hence, these are the most fragile of autobiographical acts, primarily due to the explicit editorial intervention of the interviewer. I draw on these in my analysis only for purposes of corroboration. Nonetheless, most of these fit in the "spiritual" category. These include three selections from David Shallenberger's *Reclaiming the Spirit*, Mark Thompson's interview with Joseph Kramer in *Gay Soul*, Thomas Stahel's interview with Andrew Sullivan in *America*, and Paul Crowley's interview with Richard Rodriguez in Ferraro's book.[11]

Of the many book-length autobiographies included in this study, the majority do not fit so neatly in this "spiritual" category. John McNeill's *Both Feet Firmly Planted in Midair*, however, is definitively spiritual and is as such reinforced by its subtitle: *My Spiritual Journey.* McNeill is a former Jesuit priest whose publications on Catholicism and homosexuality have been seminal in the field. This autobiography is his most recent book, coming after his trilogy of theological reflections on religious and sexual identities, and telling his life story through the prism of his spiritual struggles. Because of his career as a priest and then a psychotherapist, it could also be called a professional autobiography (a category I will soon address). A good portion of the text not only deals with the way his gay self-awareness influenced his vocational decisions but also recounts many of his struggles with church authorities over his ministry.[12] Fenton Johnson's *Keeping Faith* also belongs here because it focuses on his internal struggle to reconnect with his Catholic roots — via an exploration of Catholic and Buddhist monasticism — after years of anger and alienation.[13] Finally, Brian McNaught's *On Being Gay* and *A Disturbed Peace* fit largely in the "spiritual" category. These books, the first a revised reissue of the second, are not traditional autobiographies in the sense of mapping out a life trajectory. They are, instead, collections of essays organized around issues of growing up gay, coming out to friends and family, building relationships, and being gay in the church. His style, reflective of his experience as a motivational speaker, is to affirm his gay Catholic readers through the telling of his own life experiences.[14]

To the extent McNaught deals with gay culture separate from religious themes, his books might also be positioned in the next category: autobiographies centered around *cultural* concerns. I use the term "culture" in a deliberately broad sense, referring to a terrain of meanings and significations associated with specific communities or identities. Andrew Sullivan's *Love Undetectable* brings together three extended essays interspersed with autobiographical acts, which address ethical issues related to gay identity and culture, especially in light of what it means to be HIV-positive today. Because his work is involved with constructing an ethics for the gay community, his Catholic identity tends to be more explicit than in some of the other book-length autobiographies in this category.[15] James Morrison engages in a sort of gay cultural criticism in *Broken Fever*. A professional academic, he is most interested in the way his gay identity emerged in his childhood and how it continues to emerge and form in the narration of his childhood. His Catholic identity is almost incidental in the text, but present nonetheless.[16] This is also true of Patrick Horrigan's *Widescreen Dreams*, a project very much like Morrison's, but constructed around a set of movies and television shows that both influenced and now reflect his own life trajectory. Horrigan, an English professor, knows how intimately connected are the tasks of autobiography and cultural criticism.[17]

Frank DeCaro accomplishes the same sort of combination in his much more lighthearted autobiography *A Boy Named Phyllis*. His is a cultural criticism of the middle class American suburbia in which he was raised, through the lens of his current life as a New York fashion editor. Again, his Catholic identity is obscured, but integral to his life story.[18] Where DeCaro focuses on suburbia, the four Catholic contributors to Will Fellows's *Farm Boys* all come from a farming background. Like the Holtz anthology discussed earlier, Fellows converts their reflections on growing up gay in farm culture to text. Together, their stories reveal not only the difficulties of being gay in a rural community but also the lifetime impact of agricultural life and appreciation for the work ethic it instills.[19]

Richard Rodriguez also fits in the category of cultural autobiography because of the centrality of his Mexican-Indian-American identity. In *Hunger of Memory* and *Days of Obligation*, Rodriguez, a well-known media commentator, is primarily arguing in his books against bilingual education and affirmative action programs, which he feels work against people of Hispanic background becoming full-fledged Americans. His Catholic identity is configured in a much different way than many of the aforementioned autobiographies by white Americans. Rodriguez recognizes the cultural dimension of Catholicism and thus understands the imprint a Catholic upbringing leaves on one's personality. He knows this from his experience as an ethnic "minority" in America, and the close link between Hispanic ethnicity and Catholicism. A tension between Catholic identity and American identity, along with an ambivalence about what it means for him to be a successful American, underlie his autobiographies.[20] These themes and some of the same material are also reflected in an essay entitled "Irish Catholic," in which he articulates the influence of Irish culture on American Catholicism and the role it played in his own schooling.[21] In Rodriguez's texts, it is his gay identity that is obscured and, early in his writing, camouflaged. Although he has publicly acknowledged and claimed a gay identity, it is not ever mentioned in his first book and he only obliquely deals with it in his essay and the second book. He finally deals with his gayness more directly, but not without his usual nuance and subtlety, in his third book *Brown*.[22] As is true for those whose Catholic identity is obscured in their texts, his gayness and his relationship with his culture's machismo ideals still play an integral role in his life story.

Two anthologies address Italian-American heritage, a culture likewise intimately connected to Catholicism. *Hey Paesan!* features relevant autobiographical essays by Rob Nixon and Tommi Avicolli Mecca; *Fuori* contains a different essay by Mecca and a contribution by Philip Gambone. These are perfect examples of cultural autobiographical acts because Italian heritage is the central axis on which each of the narratives is assembled. Catholic identity is woven intricately into each story, though not as blatantly as it is with Rodriguez; but gay identity is at the fore, particularly in relation to gender concerns and Italian-American expectations of masculinity.[23] Rafael Campo's *The Desire to Heal* combines many of the themes traversed by these "ethnic" writers, in this case from a Cuban-American perspective: what is lost and what is gained in becoming a successful American; how that is affected by the mark of both an ethnic legacy and queer sexual desire; and how one negotiates these seemingly antagonistic identities. Campo is a physician and also critiques the culture of the medical field as he reflects upon his education and practice as a doctor. In addition, he has published three volumes of poetry which are autobiographical meditations on the same themes.[24]

Campo's book might also fit into the next category because he deals with some professional concerns. What distinguishes an *occupational* autobiography is the focus on the writer's professional career and how that career was altered by the acknowledgment of his gay identity. It is the same dilemma faced by gay priests, so these men are, in a sense, their secular counterparts. In some ways, these stories read like celebrity memoirs, but the emerging consciousness of gay identity over the course of their life trajectories makes them more complicated than simple memoirs. Catholic identity is, however, eclipsed by other pieces of their lives, as it is in some of the cultural autobiographies. José Zuniga's *Soldier of the Year* describes his fall from grace as a decorated sergeant in the U.S.

Army after going public with his gay identity. His Mexican heritage figures into the story, but not in any pivotal way except for his relationship with his father.[25] David Kopay's *The David Kopay Story* recounts his career as a professional football player (after a brief stint as a seminarian) and the saga of coming out in the culture of pro sports.[26] Similarly, Dave Pallone's *Behind the Mask* reports the fallout of his umpire career when his sexuality is discovered and he is falsely accused of sexual misdeeds.[27] I should note these latter two books are coauthored with journalists so they are not constructed in the strictest sense by the self about whom they are written. Even so, both Kopay and Pallone claim to have played primary roles in authoring and ultimately approving the final versions of their stories, and their locations as pro athletes lend an important range of experience to my study.

Two autobiographies stand in a category of their own because of their unique forms and the role of AIDS in their stories. The first, Robert Arpin's *Wonderfully, Fearfully Made,* tells his story from childhood to becoming a priest to being diagnosed with AIDS, and how his perspective is influenced by having to confront a fatal illness in himself and in his community. Arpin structures his ruminations in a sort of elaborated diary format, with each entry dated and addressed to particular persons. Most of the entries are addressed to a friend named "D" who, he says, "lives in Las Vegas and is a therapist to the stars." Others are addressed to family members and colleagues. The book then appears to be a series of letters written over six years, but covering his life history.[28] Fenton Johnson's *Geography of the Heart* is a memorial tribute to his partner Larry Rose, who died of complications from AIDS in 1990. Johnson, an extremely gifted writer, artistically weaves his own life story with that of his partner's to demonstrate how their relationship and its subsequent ending forever changed him. The very form of his autobiography acknowledges the way memory both affects and is affected by close interactions with others in our lives.[29]

The last set of autobiographies I examine fall under the heading of *coming out* stories. In a way, this is a problematic category to stand on its own because coming out, either to oneself, to friends or family, or in some public way, is a component in nearly all gay life texts. I will have more to say about the "coming out narrative" and its function in gay lives and communities later in this chapter; but for now, suffice it to say coming out is in reality a complicated journey in any gay life. When gay identity is made the focal point of a narrative, the coming out trajectory becomes isolated and appears more direct and predestined than is often the case. Many of the autobiographies I examine in this study are concerned with other identity markers in addition to gay identity, so the coming out narrative is either downplayed or problematized. Some, however, are explicitly about coming out, and this genre of stories has become extremely popular among gay and lesbian readers. Patrick Merla's anthology, *Boys Like Us*, is a collection of coming out stories by gay writers. The Catholic contributors to the volume are Andrew Holleran, Philip Gambone, Stephen McCauley, and J. D. McClatchy. Happily, all of them are professional writers, so their coming out stories are particularly compelling and creatively written.[30] Many of the best gay fiction writers have published compelling novels that are marketed as coming out stories, but are far from simplistic in their constructions of gay identity. This would be true of Andrew Holleran's *Nights in Aruba* and *The Beauty of Men*, David Plante's *The Catholic*, and Daniel Curzon's *The World Can Break Your Heart*, all of which I mention here because the writers have claimed in interviews that these novels contain autobiographical elements.[31]

These gay Catholic autobiographical acts provide the much-needed element of gay subjectivity that is at present so sorely lacking in the church's understanding of gay people. Taken together, they comprise a rich body of literature from which to theorize the important identity questions that need to be addressed in order to begin to overcome the problems in church teaching on homosexuality. First, however, it is necessary to understand some factors that make autobiography an appropriate, but not uncomplicated, source for this kind of analysis. Keep in mind the "limitations" imposed due to the nature of autobiography as a written genre: this is not a random sample of gay Catholics; it is a sample of gay Catholics who have committed their story to writing. Consequently, those who cannot write or be published, for whatever reason, are excluded. Yet even this limitation is at least partially overcome by some of these authors with the help of editors, in the case of anthologized autobiographical acts, and coauthors, in the cases of Kopay and Pallone. In any case, it should be obvious from the above survey that the life texts I am using in this study do represent a range of class, ethnicity, age, and experience.

Any one of these autobiographical acts on its own has certain things to say about gay and Catholic identity. This genre has, in fact, become one of the most popular ways of expressing and struggling with issues of difference and identity. But one gay Catholic life story is not adequate for seriously debating the kinds of problems I am addressing in this project. They tend to be inward and personal and less conclusive about the larger concerns of culture and society, except as these impact the individual. When these life stories are analyzed and theorized together, however, numerous conclusive possibilities are opened up. In the following section, I describe some of the theoretical implications of using the autobiographical genre as data. It would be simplistic and rather inaccurate to presume I am unproblematically bringing gay "lived experience" to bear on church teaching by using autobiographies. Yes, I am using lived experience (rather than scripture, tradition, or reason) as a tool of analysis and reflection, but it is experience as filtered through textual intervention. Certain conclusive possibilities may be foreclosed in this methodology, but the answers disclosed about identity and self-identification are eminently useful for building a more complex understanding of gay Catholic reality.

Using Autobiography/Surveying Theory

My mother's letter reminds me, too, that the figures I've used in constructing a mythology for myself about who I am and where I came from . . . exceed my grasp, don't do everything I want and need them to do for me, have a life of their own quite apart from the use to which I've put them, can in fact be used against me. And yet, without them, how else would I conceive of myself? What I've made of them is partly a fiction, but I can't live without *some* kind of fiction about who I am. For one thing, I would never be able to communicate my sense of who I am to anyone else without some amount of cutting, pasting, editing, quoting, sampling, shaping, framing — that is, without some kind of fiction-making.

—Patrick Horrigan, *Widescreen Dreams*

The focus in church teaching on sexuality as a "problem" has the effect of isolating and disconnecting one's sexuality from the rest of one's personality and life. Autobiography works against such isolation by revealing a self in context, connected to others in a complex web of personal relationships, living and working in particular places and situations over time. Personal narratives also provide a richer context in which to understand sexuality and sexual ethics. For example, while the public debate often frames the issue of homosexuality as one of "choice" (i.e., does one choose to be gay?), autobiographies reveal selves for whom issues of "free will" and "destiny" are much more complicated and nuanced than the public debate would imply. Indeed, these life texts function to disrupt such simplistic dichotomies and may help reframe the issue in ways which make more sense. Autobiography is also a useful resource for testing and evaluating the truth-claims made about the particular self by other agents. In the case of this study, church teaching can be evaluated in light of how gay Catholics write about their own lives and experiences. How valid, for example, is the split between homosexual orientation and behavior in these life texts? This same analytical eye can in turn be focused on claims made in other realms (political, psychological, societal, etc.), about gay identity.

What is the nature of autobiography and how does it function with regard to concepts of self, identity, truth and memory? Autobiography is an act of constructing both a world in which to make sense out of life events and a unique "self," so there is always a distance between the self of the text and the self who actually lives/lived (the life).[32] Figuring the relationship between the textual self and the life is the starting point of most autobiography theory: How much does the constructed self in the narrative resemble the flesh-and-blood person the narrative claims to be about? What can then be said about personal identity based on a self that is textually constructed? And ultimately, what are the implications of this theory on the position of the autobiographer as the privileged authority of his/her own life? If this self is a construction, what makes this rendering of the self any more authentic or authoritative than another author's rendering of the same character? Both readers and writers of autobiographies take the textual self/real life referentiality for granted; yet, it is helpful to expose these distinctions because we have direct access only to the text, not the person.

The notion of the constructed self in autobiography finds its origins in James Olney's groundbreaking work *Metaphors of Self.* Though each of us has a sense of self that we know privately and intuitively, it is only meaningful at an internal level. The task of the autobiographer is to externalize this self, to make it the subject of a text and impart a sense of that self to the reader through language. Internal consciousness and life experiences mean nothing until we supply a pattern and trajectory to make sense and meaning out of them. For Olney, metaphor provides this connection and meaning:

> The self expresses itself by the metaphors it creates and projects, and we know it by those metaphors; but it did not exist as it now does and as it now is before creating its metaphors. We do not see or touch the self, but we do see and touch its metaphors.[33]

Elsewhere, Olney discusses the complex interplay between the *autos* (self) and the *bios* (life), neither of which are complete or defined at the beginning of an autobiographical project. When the "I" shapes its autobiography, it "half discovers, half creates itself."[34] It is through the act of writing — producing written language — that the self and the life "take on a certain form, assume a particular image and shape, and endlessly reflect that image back and forth between themselves as between two mirrors."[35] When we read autobiography, we know the self not so much by the events and experiences narrated, but by the consciousness brought to that narration through the language of metaphor. For Olney, this process is reciprocal between the self and the life; the formulation of the textual self enables the life's own self discovery and creation.[36]

This separation between the textual self and the life is stressed over and over again by almost all autobiography theorists because it affects the kinds of conclusions we can make about the life behind its representation in the text. This is often depicted as an issue of truth vs. fiction. Some theorists want to disrupt the notion of autobiography as nonfiction and go so far as to insist there is no referentiality at all between the self and the life.[37] Others suggest the concept of a unified self as constructed in an autobiography is a fiction in itself based on modernist assumptions about personal identity.[38] These theories reflect postmodern critiques decentering the subject. One theoretical way around or through these debates is the concept of an autobiographical *persona*, something like a stand-in between the self and the life, which then functions as the subject of the autobiography and avoids conflating the subject and the self. This approach attempts to overcome the problematic terms altogether and still maintain a degree of subjective authority in the text.[39] For my part, I accept that the textual self is a construction and even a function of language, but I do not think this erases its reference to the life or diminishes its subjectivity; quite the contrary, I think it tells us a great deal about the life because the very act of writing one's life text is one of the most self-defining things one can do. My project obviously assumes and relies on the self-life referentiality of autobiographies: these textual selves represent real gay Catholics. These are stories of actual flesh-and-blood lives, most certainly constructed, but by no means fictitious.

So autobiography, as I use and understand it, is an act of representation: a signification of a real life. For Ken Plummer, the "life story" is precisely that: a story, limited by the language and metaphors available when it is constructed:

> *Whatever else the story is, it is not simply the lived life.* It speaks all around the life: it provides routes into a life, lays down maps for lives to follow, suggests links between a life and a culture. It may indeed be one of the most important tools we have for understanding lives and the wider cultures they are part of. But it is not *the* life, which is in principle unknown and unknowable.[40]

While Plummer is here reiterating the distance between the story and the life, he also recognizes the value of the story for getting "into a life." If the life itself is "unknowable," then autobiography provides one of the only points of access into a person's lived experience. I would further suggest it is a source to be privileged. The very creation of the autobiography is a moment of tremendous meaning in a life. Autobiography "does not show us the individual seen from outside in his visible actions but the person in his inner privacy, not as he was, not as he is, but as he believes and wishes himself to be and to have been."[41] Autobiographers present themselves as *subjects,* and their experiences as *they* assess them, in a world *according to them.* Far from being a limitation, this underscores the authority of these texts in relation to the lives they represent; and it makes them doubly

useful as sources of data: *how* one presents one's life story can be just as
revealing as *what* one presents.

But this still leaves some methodological questions unresolved. How
do we assess and apply the truth claims of these life texts since we are
dealing with subjective representations and constructed selves? Once we
accept the proposition that autobiography is not exactly fiction, in that it
references a real life, we need to come to terms with the fact that it is also
not simply an historical account of a life or the events surrounding a life.
Such historical accounts might be "verified" by a correspondence theory
of truth, which would suggest elements of the story can be documented in
other sources; but this simplistic approach does not account for the aesthetic dimension of autobiography, which could be said to reveal *narrative*
truth. While biography may be assessed using a correspondence theory of
truth, the *auto* is what marks these texts in a distinct way. In the words of
Philip E. Baruth, "A reader does not go to an autobiography for a referen-
tial history; a reader goes to an autobiography for a subjective perspective
by the author *on* the author."[42] The autobiographical narrative emerges
in a sort of reciprocal understanding between the author and the reader,
who both know the primary subject of the text is a self-identity that is a
product of the author's memory.[43]

Memory is a crucial factor in the production of an autobiographical narrative and an important consideration in a discussion of narrative truth.
To begin with, the mind simply cannot remember everything. It edits and
selects based on what matters in the context of one's life and it deletes that
which is seemingly irrelevant. Unlike a computer, however, which also edits and deletes, human memory is emotionally contingent and inextricably
linked with human imagination. In terms of the self, memory looks back
on a sense of self that has changed and continues to change over time. As
such, the self over time seems fragmented, as exemplified in the oft-heard
expression, "I'm not the same person I used to be." In the writing of a
life text, however, the autobiographer engages the memory to reassemble
the seemingly fragmented self. Yet memory is not static, and the way it
activates the past is dependent upon the present. As Olney notes:

> Memory, at least in part, is an adaptive function, with a self-adjusting
> and self-defining plasticity about it, turning back to the past so as
> to position itself and us for what is to be dealt with in the fu-
> ture: it adapts continuously to changing circumstances, external and
> internal, to constitute the self as it is at any given instant.[44]

If memory is thus filtered through all subsequent experience, what does
this say about concepts like accuracy and truth? Here again, Olney is useful. For him, these terms do not make sense because memory is by its very
nature indeterminate: "To indenture it to its own first perception of how

things are would be to deny memory's evident plasticity and its capacity for adaptation."[45] Memory is active. In constructing the life narrative, the autobiographer *remembers* — and reconstructs — the self, and narrative truth emerges. In a way, remembering is more revealing than first perceptions. Georges Gusdorf frames this in terms of truth: "In other words, autobiography is a second reading of experience, and it is truer than the first because it adds to experience itself consciousness of it."[46]

Concepts like truth and falsity become murky in this paradigm, but it is not adequate to simply cast aside concerns related to such concepts. After all, my project is addressing problems in doctrinal pronouncements by the church, and "truth," even with the contingencies I have noted, matters a great deal in the world of moral guidelines. By now, it should be clear it is best not to assess narrative truth in terms of accuracy and factual details; instead, we can shift the focus to other matters. Bregman and Thiermann use internal coherence requirements in their assessment of death and dying autobiographies. They expect consistency between the way characters in the story are portrayed and how their actions reveal them to be. Similarly, they ask for the narrator and the protagonist to bear a reasonable resemblance to each other. Ultimately, the story should not violate basic assumptions about how people behave.[47] In a sense, the life story should "ring true," and when certain elements of the text do not, it provides the opportunity to question why. Such instances of "falseness" can be the most revealing moments in an autobiography because they often signal divergences between ideals and reality. It can also signal divergences between the world views of the reader and the author. In any case, this leads to a complication and reevaluation of assumed perceptions and given truths. Making these divergences visible is one of my primary goals.

Narrative truth needs to be taken on its own terms and recognized for its own value. I tend to align myself with critics like Gusdorf who frame autobiography as a "truer" reading of life experience because it adds consciousness to the experience. It takes advantage of both insight and hindsight — the "If I knew then what I know now" phenomenon — examining one's life trajectory in light of current circumstances. The risk, of course, is the erasure — the forgetting, perhaps — of previously held perspectives and feelings that disrupt and complicate current consciousness; but these are precisely the kinds of divergences that make for a richer analysis. In Ken Plummer's sociological study of sexual stories, he shifts the focus from truth and falsehood to truth and consequence.[48] I want to follow this lead and focus on the implications of these narratives. For gay Catholics to tell their stories at this point in history is a bold challenge to deeply held, traditional beliefs about sexuality and sexual identity. It threatens not only the boundaries of what constitutes morally acceptable relationships but also the boundaries of Catholic identity itself. My hope is that my exploration of these gay Catholic autobiographies will make their truths more consequential by beginning to unravel the assumptions underlying problematic church teaching on homosexuality.

Autobiography, Identity, and Personal Meaning

I see identity now not as a fixed destination, but as the locus of all we've forgotten, all we know, all we'll never know. It's the site of imagination and desire, always on the verge of discovery and fulfillment.

— Rob Nixon, "Avondale"

Since identity questions, both sexual and religious, are central to my project, an examination of narrative identity is in order. In this section, I am interested in something more specific than the self, which I conceive as a collection of identity pieces. Identity here stands for the collective set of characteristics by which a self is known and recognizable as fitting into a particular group, in this case gay and Catholic. Even when an autobiographer's self-identity is presented as a given, the construction of the life text implies a concurrent construction of both self and identity(ies), which could be called the process of self-identification.[49] Let me start here by returning to Olney and his assertion that the self is only known, even to itself, by the metaphors it creates. In Olney's theory, there is a sense of narrative language as a doorway into the self, both realized and constructed. For identity, the pieces of which form the structure of the self, this can be pushed even further. Identity, at once singular and multiple, is formulated entirely through language, and narrative gives it its particular shape and substance.

Paul Ricoeur philosophically discusses narrative identity by distinguishing between two usages of the term identity: "identity as sameness" (*idem*), marked by continuity and permanence over time; and "identity as self" (*ipse*), marked by continuous refiguring and reinterpretation. Noting that human lives become more readable when transformed into narratives, Ricoeur states, "In the application of literature to life, what we transfer and transpose in the exegesis of ourselves is the dialectic of ipse and idem."[50] In Ricoeur's framework, autobiography is configured as a sort of "narrative hermeneutic of the subject," in which the self "cobbles together its identity by constructing a life-story that uses the resources of various narrative fragments."[51] This dialectical process gives rise to a self (con)textualized by narratively configured identity markers.

A key point here is that identity is molded and assembled in context, not only of the self's totality but also in relation to present and past circumstances. This follows Erik Erikson's admonition that autobiographical events need to be fixed in the moment of writing and in the history of the writer and his time.[52] The autobiographers I examine are narrating their stories in a contemporary context in which public discourse and media images have become increasingly sexualized even as Americans remain reticent to talk seriously about sex. It is also a highly politicized atmosphere, in which asserting and claiming a gay identity has become the basis of political action in the gay rights movement. Gay identity takes a particular shape based on expectations of the gay "community" and those who stigmatize it, and telling the story of one's sexual identity has become a way of coming to terms, so to speak, with difference. The availability of gay identity as it is conceived today is not unproblematic with regard to autobiographical narratives. On the one hand, claiming the identity (coming out) is a strategy of information control. By disclosing himself, a gay man no longer has to worry about managing the information of his sexual identity but rather his social situations and relations in light of his disclosed identity.[53] Coming out is, in this sense, a liberating gesture and the gay "community" applauds and almost requires the gesture as a mark of self-esteem.

On the other hand, it is often this coming out imperative which drives and defines the gay life story to the point where gay identity is "standardized." Gay people today can find readily available versions of gay identity in the proliferation of coming out stories and stage theories related to coming out. The whole process of coming out has taken on a mythic narrative structure of its own, with concomitant truth claims about the psychological benefits of doing so.[54] Goffman notes that the voluntary disclosure of a stigmatized identity is usually configured in autobiographies as the final, mature, well-adjusted phase in the self's moral career — "a state of grace."[55] While it provides a framework around which to organize the details of negotiating sexuality in one's life, this coming out narrative can intrude on individual autobiographies and act as a heavy handed interpretive force in the construction of narrative identity. "This model of coming out, by itself, exhibits little concern for how lesbian or gay identities are socially constituted, for how they are intersected by other arenas of difference, or for what sort of collective political action might develop from an assertion of one's lesbian or gay identity."[56]

Of course, people often try to orient their lives toward a model which is presented as an ideal possible "self." In many Christian conversion stories, for example, when the self is reborn with a Christian identity, he/she will strive to imitate the model of Christ. The autobiographer will construct the self after the conversion as close to this ideal as possible, even as the narrative as a whole reveals shortcomings toward the ideal. According to Karl Weintraub, "When a man's inner compass is set on the pursuit of such a model form of being human, ... The essential contours of his life and personality are prescribed. . . . The entire objective is to make his being conform, as fully as it can, to its normative ideal."[57] Weintraub's words can be especially applicable to the model of gay identity in the coming out narrative. Gay life stories can be "distorted" by the expectation to narrate a trajectory of coming out that matches the ideal model. Paul Robinson affirms this in his analysis of gay autobiographies. He observes how the narratives of the three contemporary gay autobiographies he analyzes are manipulated by the authors to conform to the standard model. He especially notices a "tendency to paint a blacker picture of the closet years than seems warranted."[58] This is similar to Christian conversion stories in which the preconversion years are painted as more hedonistic than warranted. For the gay "convert," the closet represents the period of time when he was "lost" before being "found." Robinson classifies this as a literary strategy, which it may be, but some writers may not perceive a choice to construct their story in any other way. This can be especially true when the writer comes from a Christian background in which these kinds of narratives have meaningful resonances.

The issue at hand revolves around narrating a unique and individual gay identity in an environment in which the communal gay identity is so powerful and articulated. Individual gay life stories are easily assimilated and subsumed into the story of the group. But this too is a complex matter. Yes, the gay Catholic autobiographies I examine do repeat some of the patterns of the dominant narrative, but they also disrupt the narrative in other ways. This is particularly true of the more gifted writers whose narrative technique overcomes linear models of finding sexual identity. Several of the authors depict a relatively happy childhood; some are still struggling with what it means to live a gay life; some of the writers simply do not fit into the expectations of the "community"; and many express some degree of ambivalence about it. James Morrison resists what he calls the myth of the collective because he perceives the collective as a false entity. His remarks about a gay rights rally he had attended are indicative:

> As much as I long to repeat experiences of collective transcendence such as those I associate with the time of my coming out, I'm suspicious of them, still and always, as the denial of genuine otherness. When you learn that I am gay, you still know nothing of my self, *even of my sexuality*, except what you think you know about gay people; and when I was in that life-sustaining crowd at the rally in Ypsilanti, I was not among people any more "like" me, necessarily, than I was in my sixth-grade classroom.[59]

Such ambivalence is to be expected. When a gay person finds himself in the company of other gay people, he will surely observe differences in himself that complicate his association.[60] If absolutely no ambivalence about the identity exists in the narrative, then it probably does not quite "ring true," and we need to ask why the narrative is ordered in such a way. While it could be construed as conforming to a gay ideal, it could also be interpreted as a resistive response to oppressive church teaching, which functions at the other end of the extreme by completely marginalizing gay identity. My analysis will uncover how normative ideals (both from the church and the gay community) are negotiated in the lives of gay Catholics, how they deal with "falling short" of the ideal, and to what degree these life stories are usurped by such models.

Despite these cautionary notes about communal identity and expectations, I do not wish to diminish the importance of the gay community in making the production of gay life stories and gay identities possible in the first place. For these narratives to be told and to flourish, there must be an interpretive community to hear them. The presence of a more visibly defined gay and lesbian community since the late 1960s has allowed for the creation of a shared history, identity, and politics. Life stories emerge from and contribute to this environment. As Ken Plummer puts it, "The one — community — feeds upon and into the other — story":

> As gay persons create a gay culture cluttered with stories of gay life, gay history and gay politics, so that very culture helps to define a reality that makes gay personhood tighter and ever more plausible. And this in turn strengthens the culture and politics.[61]

These stories represent the stories of a people whose existence was previously ignored. They reveal a communal reality and a set of beliefs about the meaning of gay and lesbian identity at this historical moment. In the words of Olney, "Autobiography renders in a peculiarly direct and faithful way the experience and the vision of a people."[62] This folklore of stories is transmitted from generation to generation, "complete with ritualistic days and marches — Stonewall, Gay Pride, Aids [*sic*] Awareness, etc. — which help to provide a sense of shared history."[63] In this respect, these autobiographies are sacred texts, canonized by the lesbian and gay community. Debates over the real cohesion of this community notwithstanding, the trope of communal identity is ubiquitous, powerful, and meaningful; and the existence of a gay culture — and by extension, a "people" — is undeniable in America today.

The church inadvertently contributes to the cohesion of the gay community by lumping all gay people into one marginalized category, as exemplified in church teaching that treats homosexuality as a singular phenomenon. Collectively, gay Catholic autobiographies depict the multiplicity within that community. They not only fill the void between church teaching and gay and lesbian reality but also replace the silence that would isolate gay Catholics from each other. When a gay Catholic writes his story, he is responding to a need for other gay Catholics and those who love them to know they are not alone. "The call of the human other, the neighbor, for justice and compassion secures the ethical and political aspects of forging a narrative identity."[64] Although the majority of the autobiographers I examine in this study are not aware of the many theoretical concerns related to this genre, they do have a sense that telling one's life story is vital to becoming a self and finding one's voice. In doing so, they challenge those who would marginalize them, and they do justice work for the entire community. "Storytelling from this vantage becomes a sacred act; authority is transferred from external figures and forces, to the newly discovered authentic and interior self."[65] They perform a service by bringing flesh and blood to church teaching that effectively disembodies them, and by giving life to otherwise theoretical moral arguments. In autobiography, they find the space to make personal meaning and express new forms of spirituality, and in the process help both the church and themselves to find their "soul": "To write a life, or to tell a life, is to wager that an exegesis of the self's untold story will pay rich dividends in one's quest for authenticity and integrity."[66]

The dividends of authenticity and integrity found in the narrative self will spill over into the broader Catholic community when we carefully attend to what these autobiographies have to say. These sacred texts collectively reveal what it means to be gay and Catholic in America at this time in history. In so doing, they also reveal how and why church teachings on homosexuality fall short. Examining how gay Catholics construct their life stories and author their own experiences restores a certain level of gay subjectivity to our understanding of sexuality and legitimates representations of gay Catholics as full human beings. The following exploration of sexual and religious identities as these autobiographers narrate them represents an exegesis not only of sacred texts, but of sacred lives as well.

Chapter 2

Narrating Gay Identification

But for another second the rock was still in midair, and it was *that* second when I knew that, whatever else, I thought Craig's *body* was beautiful; that I would have to find a place for such knowledge among whatever other knowledge I could forge; that my future life, which I could not before imagine, would depend on it; that in this way the lack I had perceived within me might yet be overcome.

—James Morrison, "Saved"

In Andrew Holleran's quasi-autobiographical novel *The Beauty of Men*, Lark, the protagonist, decides he needs "something very gay" after visiting his mother in a nursing home. He quickly drives to the weekly session of Gaytalk, a group forum for discussion of gay issues led by a variety of guest speakers. As he scans the mostly middle-aged group of men around him — in a chapter of the book aptly titled "Talking About It" — he ponders how difficult it must be for the facilitator to come up with a new topic every week: "What is there to say about being gay? Coming out is the central story, told over and over again, like people describing how they found Christ."[1] With that statement, Holleran lays down the central question this chapter will address with regard to these gay Catholic autobiographers: what is there to say about being gay? For Holleran's character Lark, there is nothing more to say about being gay. The repetition of coming out stories, each one bearing the "Once I was lost, now I'm found" theme, has become tiresome. The stories do not reveal anything original for him. He is bored and is probably disappointed not to find a young man in the crowd to pursue. After all, being gay is about sexual desire, is it not? What is there to talk about? Yet Lark still attends the meeting and seems to be seeking a different answer to his question than his cynicism would suggest. So, what *is* there to say about being gay? How *does* one talk about it? Is gay identity simply a repetition of the same story over and over, or is it something more complex?

This project is premised on the idea that sexuality can be configured as an identity category, so it is helpful to understand what terminology like *sexual identity* signifies. As I proposed in the previous chapter, "identity" represents the collective set of characteristics by which a self is known and recognizable as fitting into a particular group. A gay man labels himself as such because he *identifies* with other men who experience their sexuality in a similar way, even as he *dis*-identifies with those same men in other ways. This process of identification and dis-identification is a function of language in that it is a way of articulating and defining his erotic desires in relation to the rest of himself. The *self*, then, is comprised of various identities and fragments of identity, which are formulated and (con)textualized entirely through language. The autobiographical project brings this into sharper focus through the construction of the textual self via narrative identities. How gay sexual identity is "narrated" is the subject of this chapter.

At first, it may seem odd to use erotic desire as a factor around which to organize an identity. Why, for example, should men who like to have sex with men want to gather for intellectual discussions, or sing together, or play bridge together, or do any of the vast array of activities available in gay social clubs? The answer lies in understanding how such skepticism about sexual identity is actually reductive of what sexuality is and what it represents. Quite simply, sexuality is more than sex. Sexual *behavior* is usually a component and an expression of one's sexual *orientation*, which is "the preponderance of sexual or erotic feelings, thoughts, fantasies, and/or behaviors one has for members of one sex or the other, both, or neither."[2] Even the Catholic Church recognizes the difference between orientation and acts, as I have already made abundantly clear. The prevailing belief is that sexual orientation is relatively fixed and extremely difficult to change, while what one does with that orientation in terms of sexual behavior is completely a matter of choice. The missing link that helps to overcome this binary economy is found in the realm of sexual *identity*. According to Ritch Savin-Williams, sexual identity "represents an enduring self-recognition of the *meanings* that sexual feelings, attractions, and behaviors have for one's sense of self. This self-labeling occurs within the pool of potential sexual identities that are defined and given meaning by the cultural and historic time in which one lives."[3]

Sexual identity represents an integration of one's sexuality, both orientation and behavior, with one's sense of self. Claiming a gay identity is a way of making sense of and giving meaning to the erotic desires and the intimate connections experienced by men who have same-sex desires. It is first of all an insistence that sexuality is much more than sexual acts. A 1974 study of sexual identity concluded, "The [gay] community provides criteria for locating a sexual identity that differ from that of the stigmatizing society in that they do not specify acts of sex, but *feelings* of romantic or emotional sexuality as the basis of homosexuality."[4] This should not, however, be taken to imply that sexual identity is simply a different way of talking about a core sexual orientation, which is often perceived as immutable and inborn. Yes, a gay man may feel he was "born this way," and many of the autobiographers I study express such a feeling, but adopting a gay sexual identity is something much more and even different.[5] Barry D. Adam interviewed over a hundred men who enjoy sexual encounters with other men, not all of whom position themselves as gay or even bisexual. He concludes that "both gay and nongay men tend to locate themselves in relation to a language of emotional and relational engagement rather than to a sexual 'essentialism' per se."[6] This is significant in that the assertion of a sexual identity represents a moment of profound emotional subjectivity. A gay man locates his sexual identity not only in relation to his interpersonal affiliations but also in relation to available categories of sexual identity, which are invested with various meanings and social connotations.

Postmodern theorists like Foucault are quick to remind us that identity is not a stable category, and sexual identity categories can be restrictive of new pleasures and alliances. For Foucault, sexuality is "produced" through discursive strategies which reflect prevailing power structures. These constructed discourses give rise to "identities," which need to be policed and controlled. The shift in the discourse of sexuality to persons rather than acts is problematic for Foucault because it subjects the person (the "homosexual" and even the "heterosexual") to new regulations and expectations. Even if a gay man experiences his sexuality as a given, it is only because he has internalized the *discourse* of sexual identity.[7] While I find this theoretical framework convincing, I want to resist the tendency of postmodern theory to effectively erase gay subjectivity and agency. While we are all limited to a certain degree by the discourses of sexuality we inherit, we must and indeed do make self-narrative choices within that discursive framework. Deploying these identities may foreclose some possibilities for self understanding, but it also discloses others; narrative identification can be productive and revealing. Foucault remarks, "We must not exclude identity if people find their pleasure through this identity, but we must not think of this identity as an ethical universal rule."[8]

Foucault's words are cautionary because sexual identity might be useful as a descriptive mechanism, but it can too easily become prescriptive, and its effects are deep. In the words of Laurel Schneider, "Regardless of its origins, the individual's assumption of homosexuality as an identity has an effect on social organization and on physical bodies that is both real and enduring."[9] At the same time, identities should not be perceived as fixed entities. They are built upon, added to, fragmented, and even disposed of. I believe most gay people know this intuitively even if they would not theorize it quite this way. Most of these gay autobiographers spent part of their lives identifying as heterosexuals. Their self-definition shifted as they learned more about their sexuality and made different choices about their sexual identity. "Coming out" thus reveals the fluidity and partiality of all identities, and "unbinds us from any sense that we can establish a fixed identity completely and forever."[10] My goal is not to reify any single or static portrait of gay identity but rather to find what these gay Catholic men share in the way they narrate their individual experiences of gay sexuality. Against this backdrop, it will be clear that gay identity is not a singular phenomenon. As Jonathan Alexander says in reference to queer identity, "There remains the simple fact that we are obviously not all the same because we do not configure our specific sexual, emotional, and intimate desires in the same way."[11] And as Brian Utter says, "Categories become merely guide posts and the only definitions that are ultimately meaningful are self-definitions in which we affirm our own identity."[12] This represents a challenge for church teaching, which tries to paint all gay people with the same brush.[13]

Sexual identity is an articulation of the meaning of sexuality in the context of one's values and self-understanding. Some Catholics believe the church has a lot to learn about sexuality from gays and lesbians, who understand that "Sexuality includes interpersonal relations, emotions, our whole way of relating to one another as human bodies."[14] When understood in this way, it becomes clear why gay men would want to gather together in groups to do activities that seemingly have nothing to do with sexual orientation per se. It is important to note that heterosexual people do the same thing and likewise claim sexual identities congruent with the whole of themselves and their experience of sexuality. The heteronormativity of society masks the fact that being straight is as much a sexual identity as being gay — that the two depend upon each other for their definition. Some straight people may, in fact, question why gayness should be an identity at all — "why do you have to flaunt it?" — even as the "in-your-face" hegemony of heterosexual culture marginalizes those with different desires and forces the issue. Gay people are effectively forced into an "other" space in which meaning making and self-definition are a means of survival. This is even more pronounced in the church, where the heteronormativity of sacred texts and traditions leaves a void and thus creates a space for gayness where absence and reality collide.[15] Without a way to make sense of sexual "otherness," that space remains a vacuum. Sexual identity represents a way of making sense in that void.

In the epigraph to this chapter, James Morrison awakens to his emerging gay desire as a "knowledge" for which he knows he will have to find a place within himself. He intuitively knows, even as a fourteen-year-old boy, that the void he senses inside can only be filled with this "knowledge." It is a piece of himself, one of the identities that will form — construct —

his self. His future life "would depend on it." Rob Nixon similarly understands the way desire becomes a place within the self, so much more than
just a feeling, but a space where identity resides:

> There are places we visit. There are places we inhabit. There are
> places we can't go. There are places we can't leave. There are places
> that exist beyond our imaginings. There are places we dream. There
> is a longing so real it becomes a place, an identity, a home.[16]

For these autobiographers, being gay is an integral part of who they are.
Their sexual desire informs and completes their self-knowledge. It guides
them toward the kinds of intimate connections with others that will resonate in their hearts and occupy that place within themselves that feels
like home.

So, we are back to the same questions I raised earlier: What *is* there to
say about being gay? How *does* one talk about it? Is gay identity simply a
repetition of the same story over and over, or is it something more complex? In the world of these particular autobiographies, certain patterns
and themes do emerge, and the portrait of gay experience they provide is
often strikingly similar in important ways. It is not, however, a monolithic
experience, as the texture of their diverse lives reveals. I should reiterate
here that these gay men also share a common religious identity, which unavoidably colors the way they experience and narrate their sexual identity.
How these men experience being gay is deeply influenced by their Catholic upbringing and many of the examples I cite in this chapter reflect that
influence. In a way, it is artificial to isolate one or the other factor because
both sexual and religious identities resonate in the core of selfhood and
directly concern human fulfillment; and each of these men embody a host
of other identity pieces which make them so much more than any one of
these pieces alone. On the other hand, given the faulty assumptions about
sexuality in church teaching and the ignorance of so many Catholics about
the reality of gay experience, a focus on sexual identity is in order. That is
what I will examine in this chapter.

Being Gay—Coming to Terms

When the foreigner enters the native's terrain, the lesson *should* be
that whatever difference we think has thus intruded was really already there all along, in some other form, but unseen, effaced, or
denied. It is a lesson nobody knows as subtly, perhaps, or as powerfully, as the gay child: the child who longs, so deeply, to be like the
others, who is taken so readily to be like the others, since the crucial

difference is not "visible," but who sees reflected in the difference of others a difference that has already been gleaned, or discovered more fully, with terror, or with wonder, in the self.

—James Morrison, *Broken Fever*

For most of these narrators, any hint of being gay began with an awareness of feeling different when they were young. This sense of difference was not at the time necessarily linked in a conscious way to sexual desire, but many of them link it in retrospect to their emerging sexual identity.[17] Philip Gambone says, "Feeling different is the predominant experience of my childhood and adolescence. Most gay Americans can report the same thing."[18] He attributes this feeling not only to his gayness and his Italian Catholic heritage but also to a host of other factors in his personal history. Another Italian American, Tommi Avicolli Mecca, was convinced he was the only boy in his world who saw boys' faces in his sexual fantasies:

> If there was one word to describe my childhood, it is "lonely." An overwhelming, unbearable loneliness. Loneliness walked through my days, became my nightmares. I remember Christmas Days when I sat alone near the tree in the living room, looking into a kitchen full of relatives and family friends, feeling left out and thinking how unwelcome I'd be if they knew I was queer.[19]

Toby Johnson remembers when he was little feeling like he was "from outer space. I think that was the way I sensed my being different — not being part of the human race — being homosexual. There is something about being gay that just doesn't fit."[20] He eventually chose to enter religious life because he felt called to be an "alien" and that was the closest he could get. Frank DeCaro humorously configures his childhood difference in the context of his equally weird suburban family. He likens his family to *The Munsters*, who thought they were completely normal:

> In my mind, Frank and Marian [his parents] were Herman and Lily Munster, look-alikes for Frankenstein and Vampira; my grandmother was Count Dracula in a housedress. I was cast — by default — as Eddie Munster, the pointy-eared were-kid with fangs and a Little Lord Fauntleroy suit. But I felt more like Marilyn, the family's ugly duckling cousin. This unfortunate girl, golden-haired, with delicate features, was the blond sheep of the family — totally unlike her relatives, but bound to them nonetheless.[21]

In DeCaro's portrait, he is different, but he feels like the normal one in a strange environment. His use of the Munsters turns his difference back on those around him and affirms his own uniqueness. Patrick Horrigan uses Barbra Streisand in a similar way. He found himself drawn to her when he watched *Funny Girl* as a boy. Horrigan recreates his realization that there was something very special about her as he reviews the plot of the movie. He could tell this "ugly duckling" (Barbra Streisand as Fanny Brice) had an "inner life" that mattered more than what anyone else might say about her, and in fact, it seemed better to be her than anyone else in the world. "In that moment, she made it supremely okay to be cast out. Because of her, being rejected acquired beauty and dignity. She became someone to turn to, someone to emulate."[22] Even though he would still feel different and rejected at times, he had the sense that his difference could be distinctive and even beautiful in its own way. Mark, one of the contributors to *Reclaiming the Spirit* conceives of this "presence of difference, of not really fitting in," as a spiritual gift of being gay. He envisions a spiritual "ancestry" for gay people, through which the legacy of difference allows gay people to be compassionate ministers of healing.[23] While this legacy is certainly double-edged and can induce a sense of cynicism and bitterness, Mark's notion might explain why so many of these men wanted to be priests or join religious communities at some time in their lives.[24] As Fenton Johnson speculates, "Youngest of nine children, a loner in childhood, teased by my classmates...maybe that was the beginning of my consciousness of being a monk."[25]

Almost all of the autobiographers had some sense of their same-sex desire in their childhoods even if they could not name what they were feeling. Some of them date this awareness very early and link it to their feeling of difference. James Morrison explicitly understands how gay identity is socially constructed even as he maintains that this identity might "precede awareness, understanding, or experience of such desire." As such, he can not remember a time in his life when he was *not* gay.[26] Along this line, Frank DeCaro states, "I was *born* gay. It just took sixteen years for me to figure it out."[27] He ultimately "figured it out" in his junior year of high school when he fell in love with a boy from his geometry class.[28] Rafael Campo never allowed himself to fully explore his sexuality until well into his college years and yet he says, "I had been attracted to men as long as I could remember."[29] John McNeill knew he was sexually attracted to other males "even in early childhood," which made him feel hopeless and evil because he knew the church would not accept this.[30] Dave Pallone knew a career in baseball was in his blood — "it was something powerful inside me" — by the time he was in seventh grade; "But something else was in there, too. Something I didn't understand. Something I would later come to think of as 'the other me'."[31] William Hart McNichols felt his calling to the priesthood around age five, "not too much earlier than the time I began to experience a glimmer of my given sexual orientation."[32]

Similarly, Brother Jonathan knew he was attracted to men as early as five years of age: "I have a recollection of this, as well as an equally strong awareness that this was not something I could share. It was my secret."[33]

As a boy, Richard Rodriguez was embarrassed by his sexual imagination. His feelings made him suspect dimensions of the world existed for which he could find no precedent in his own sphere.[34] He learned early on that he would need to guard this part of himself: "For I knew nothing was so dangerous in the world as love, my kind of love":

> ...from an early age I needed to learn caution, to avert my eyes, to guard my speech, to separate myself from myself.... Or to reconstruct myself in some eccentric way.... My eyes looking one way, my soul another. My motive could not be integrated with my body, with act or response or, indeed, approval.[35]

Rodriguez learned to disguise his feelings and act in ways that would not betray his desires. When he had a boyhood crush on Billy Walker, he threw a rock at Billy's "beautiful face" because he loved him.[36] He did not have any context for dealing with or understanding his attraction to Billy, so he acted against it. Rodriguez wondered when his desire would match the images of love and family he saw depicted in the books he was assigned to read. He would study pictures in history books to find the persons who stood out or looked like they did not belong there. He read books about encounters between peoples in the old American West and read the proximity and convergence of races and continents as erotic: "I was looking for the precedent that made me possible.... I was looking for physical inclusion in the world. I was amassing an encyclopedia of exceptionalism for my own use."[37]

Fenton Johnson had known he was drawn to men from the earliest consciousness of his body. He perceived this as a curse by which he had been chosen by God, a sort of special temptation thrown his way to use as a means of proving his virtue. "I felt singled out in that way, except that where the saints always seemed confident that God was on their side, I was alone."[38] In high school, he tried dating girls and he tried to feel some of the heterosexual desire his classmates so vocally effused. "I decided passion was something other people felt. I concluded that I was an aberration, one of a kind, an emotional eunuch with a heart of stone."[39] As a teenager, he came face to face with the deafening silence surrounding the whole idea of homosexuality in his world. His family lived by a monastery in Kentucky and the monks would often visit them for fun-filled evenings of food, drink, and dancing. He was named for one of the monks, Brother Fintan, who abruptly left the monastery when Johnson was young. When Johnson was sixteen years old, however, Fintan (no longer *Brother* Fintan) returned with a male companion for a New Year's Eve Party at his family's home. They were received with the usual hospitality and Johnson eagerly looked forward to hearing more about Brother Fintan's "date":

> Afterward I listened for the customary postparty gossip. Had Fintan arrived with a woman, the household would have been abuzz: *who is she? Might they get married?* Had he brought a mere friend, there would have been idle chatter: *Nice man. Needs a haircut.* But: Nothing. My namesake and his companion might never have sat at our table.[40]

In that moment, Johnson understood why Brother Fintan had been asked to leave the monastery; and while the silence reinforced his sense of isolation, he felt a new kinship with his namesake that made him feel he was not alone.

The silence in childhood and adolescence around homosexuality was deafening in many of these gay lives, so much so that they had little or no context through which to understand and interpret their emerging feelings. For Johnson, he found nowhere to go and no one to turn to, no model of what his feelings might mean in terms of finding someone else to love: "Growing up gay in an isolated hill town, I had never encountered so much as a hint that others might share my particular landscape in the geography of desire. I understood this as the defining fact of my life: the utter invisibility of any resonant construct of passionate adult love."[41] When Lon Mickelsen grew up and heard stories of gay boys meeting in high school, he thought "it must have been on another planet." In his Minnesota farm community, he had no points of reference nor any role models for being gay: "It's not that homosexuality was frowned upon. It simply didn't exist."[42] But this vacuum of gay experience is not peculiar to farm culture and isolated American hill towns; gay boys in cities and suburbs often faced a similar void. Andrew Sullivan, who grew up in a town just south of London, echoes Johnson's experience of a sort of loud absence: "At school, the subject was everywhere and nowhere: at the root of countless jokes and double entendres, but never actualized as a reality or as something that could affect anyone we knew."[43]

Even schools and libraries were inadequate sources of information. Allen Barnett found only three relevant books in his local public library when he was sixteen years old, and the librarian made him feel very uncomfortable when he checked them out.[44] I remember going to the public library in my own home town to find information because there was no one in my life I felt safe asking. All I found were a few paragraphs here and there in books on sexuality in general, and I remember hoping I was just going through a phase because the alternative sounded too abnormal and marginal. For gay boys coming of age in suburban America before the advent of the Internet, the range of information on homosexuality available to children and teens was extremely limited.[45] Any information provided in schools before college usually provided no help at all and sometimes contributed to the unsafe atmosphere for gay boys. Frank DeCaro recalls his high school health class, taught by a male gym teacher who "possessed all the sensitivity of a pit bull with hemorrhoids."[46] When the class reached the chapter in the text on homosexuality, the teacher said, " 'I can't tell you what to think about ho-*mo*-sexuals, . . . Personally, I think they should shoot the bastards.' " DeCaro relates his predicament:

> I hated him, but did nothing. I never reported him to the superintendent or told my parents how his lectures made me feel. How could I? To do that would be to admit that I was gay . . . and I was not yet prepared to stand up and tell everyone. Instead, feeling like an alien in the most familiar of surroundings, misshapen and beleaguered, I suffered in silence.[47]

His teacher may represent an extreme example of blatant intolerance, but DeCaro's feelings are only too representative of the heartbreaking loneliness endured by so many gay boys in school.

Going to college afforded many of these men the opportunity to more freely explore their sexual desires, but their context was still limited and they struggled with what being gay meant in terms of one's identity. James Morrison captures the disparity between homosexual and heterosexual visibility: "What could I know of marriage, then, except what I could learn from all that daily surrounded me, or from every movie in the history of the world? But what could I *ever* know of the joining together of men, except what I might have gleaned from Laurel and Hardy, or else could teach myself?"[48] When Philip Gambone went to Tanglewood for a summer internship, he developed feelings for his roommate Andrew, who would talk about the church's "antiquated" teachings on matters of sex, including homosexuality. "All of this talk was academic, but my heart was pounding with excitement. If Andrew was sending signals in my direction, I didn't know it (after all, I had no context in which to read any signals)," he says. He later realizes in hindsight how full of gay men Tanglewood was that summer.[49] Rafael Campo similarly found himself feeling affection and desire for Jorge, his college roommate at Amherst; but the two of them danced around their desire for a long time:

> Sadly, we did not know enough about who we were from our own experiences even to know that we might call ourselves "gay." The few words we might apply routinely to ourselves, 'faggot,' 'homo,' and

'queer,' were like the few words I occasionally borrowed from Spanish: they felt lost and foreign in my mouth and did not even begin to describe what I hoped might make my life more comprehensible. Internally, we only guessed at the depth of expression available to us in the lost language of our hearts, a language that we knew painfully must exist, but for which we had no teachers.[50]

Campo was aware of his desire, but the terms he heard used to describe people with such feelings seemed to vulgarize something he sensed was deeply meaningful in his soul. He and his friend busied themselves all the more intently with their academic studies as a way of staying close but also to avoid a level of connection that seemed altogether dangerous: "We cultivated as vigorously as we could our identities as premeds — the one thing Jorge and I could be together that was accepted and normal, the one appellation we could safely share."[51]

The derogatory terms these men heard while growing up and even into adulthood made claiming a gay identity even more problematic. Dave Pallone never felt especially "different" as a boy because he enjoyed sports and a certain camaraderie with other boys, but he knew as a teen that boys who "liked" other boys were called names. "During the 1960s, when I was in my teens, those words were used as weapons. Getting labeled a 'faggot,' a 'queer,' or a 'homo' was considered worse than being called a communist."[52] Sadly, not much has changed since then, and these terms are still used to attack young men who are perceived as different. The climate of fear generated by these abusive terms, combined with a reluctance to feel anomalous and outcast, causes many men to resist acknowledging their deepest feelings and desires for a long time. Matthew Bartosik tried to think of himself as bisexual for a while in order to hold on to some form of heterosexuality, even though he did not feel any erotic desire toward women: "I was unwilling to identify myself as gay. I liked being with guys and having sex with guys, but I kept telling myself that I wasn't 'gay,' or a 'fag,' or any of that." He would tell himself he and the guys he was with were "real men." " 'Gay' was something else. I believed that if I didn't say that — even to myself — then I wasn't."[53] James Morrison likewise grasped the significance of naming his sexual identity. Unlike Bartosik, Morrison was always aware of being different from other boys and he never fit the "real man" category. Still, he was reluctant to claim a gay identity, even when the man he loved in college finally came out to him: "I know he wanted me to say that I was gay too, but I was not, in spite of everything, unless I said it."[54]

Many of the autobiographers recount a time when they resisted their gay feelings, even to the extent of trying to be heterosexual or at least appearing to be, and this was usually related to their fears of being perceived as gay. David Kopay found himself in a particularly difficult situation coming to terms with being gay as a professional football player. He had a few obligatory sexual relationships with women, but he never really enjoyed them and he often fantasized about his friend Ted. In fact, he and Ted had been able to have some sexual experiences together when they were drunk. Kopay did not even feel naturally aroused by the one woman with whom he felt comfortable enough to marry. When he was with her, he knew he would have been aroused by another man, "but the fact was I still didn't consciously know how to go about it. And certainly at the time I didn't think of myself as a homosexual any more than Ted did. Homosexuals were the effeminate 'fags' or 'fairies' of my teammates' curses."[55] He could not identify with his stereotypical impression of being gay, so much so that when a female friend of his took him to a gay bar, he reacted furiously at the implication that he might "fit in" there. In truth, he was frightened by the fact that his friend had obviously detected his homosexuality, and he was petrified he might be exposed.[56]

Rafael Campo was struggling to repress and eradicate his sexuality when he was visiting prospective college campuses. Though he tried not to be attracted to any of the handsome men he met, he felt drawn to some of them nonetheless. At Yale, Campo found himself attracted to the student who led the tour and made it a point to speak with him personally; but when the student casually mentioned the active gay and lesbian group and offered to send information, Campo was incensed: "I acted appalled. I told him, abruptly and in my iciest voice, that he was greatly mistaken and that I had long ago decided not to apply to Yale at all, but my parents were forcing me to take the tour anyway."[57] Like Kopay, Campo feared exposure of the sexual identity he was trying so hard to cloak. Andrew Sullivan also worked hard to guard that no one else in school would ever know the truth of his erotic desire: "I learned to kill off sexual yearnings for the boys I cared about and fell for, and to reattach sexual attraction to boys who would never know and never guess." Sullivan reasons this is why it remained so difficult for him to nurture meaningful intimate relationships for many years.[58]

When he was twenty-one years old, José Zuniga developed a brief sexual relationship with a waiter named Russell. It ended shortly after it began because neither of them wanted to think he was a "fag." Zuniga says he closed his heart to love the night their relationship ended. He "escaped" the identity he feared he was becoming by enlisting in the army.[59] While in the army, he fell in love with a fellow soldier named Alex; but the possibility of this kind of love was still too much for him. He was eventually transferred to a different unit and was relieved the relationship could not be pursued. He was determined to avoid his homosexual feelings: "I had shut the door to my heart when I signed my name on a dotted line, swearing my allegiance to the Army. I had made a conscious decision, a promise to myself, to repress any and all sexual and emotional feelings."[60] He was later stationed in San Francisco and allowed himself to begin exploring his same-sex desire behind the camouflage of a marriage of convenience with a lesbian. He hoped that by burying himself in his work he would keep his sexual feelings at enough of a distance to feel safe:

> But my attraction to men was continuous, and it affected me in so many disparate and confusing ways that I felt myself faltering. My life was in emotional upheaval. God, don't let me be wrong. At work I maintained the facade of a happily married heterosexual, wearing the snug straitjacket I'd worn in public since my high school days.[61]

Eventually, Zuniga would find his denial too much to bear, and he would risk his standing in the military in order to openly acknowledge his gayness and escape what he came to conceive of as self-hatred.

Lon Mickelsen dated girls all the way through high school and college, "mostly to be one of the gang." He had his last steady girlfriend in college. Though he dated her about two and a half years and actually loved her, he finally broke up with her because he could not bear the incongruence of his actions and feelings: "I was dating her, but fantasizing about my male roommates."[62] Even Frank DeCaro, one of the most flamboyantly gay of the men in my study, tried to be straight for a time in junior high school: "I would have been happy to make *anyone* my girlfriend. I was so lonely and wanted so desperately to prove to my classmates and my parents — if not to myself — that I could be straight, despite mounting evidence to the contrary."[63] Fenton Johnson fought so hard against his feelings that he believed he had no capacity to give or receive love:

> I had so deeply and profoundly accepted this given that I had no awareness of my own self-contempt. . . . I had never heard words to describe the desires that of their own accord visited me. A man loving a man — I had never read of this or seen images of it; I had never experienced it in any way other than in the recesses of my own desire, a place so ugly (I assumed) it was beyond the pale of words. To defend myself against my desire I constructed an elaborate wall around my heart, so high no one could see in and I could not see out.[64]

Like so many of these men, Johnson tried for a time to be straight but did not succeed.[65] He spent his teen years avoiding physical contact with anyone of either gender. He hoped his first sexual encounter would feel like a gift from God; instead, he felt anger and shame: "On the morning after I first had sex — a few months after my twenty-first birthday — the man with whom I'd gone to bed put his hand on my arm. I shook it off. 'Touch me again,' I said, 'and I'll break your neck.' "[66]

Andrew Holleran relates the push and pull of desire and resistance in a short coming out story. Drafted into the army and stationed in Germany in 1968, he remained sexually inexperienced even though he was surrounded by men who were living gay lives. "Denial is always astonishing in retrospect, that one was able to compartmentalize oneself, to proceed with one part while putting another on ice."[67] On the night he finally allowed himself to have his first homosexual experience, he found himself subsequently washing his mouth out with soap in the shower room, where he would also be likely to see another man's body. After telling his roommate about his experience, he went back to the shower room:

> In truth to wash my mouth out again and wait for somebody else to come in and take a shower; the two instincts (desire and remorse) that would characterize much of my homosexual life to come — a life, I would discover, that was, just as my teenage self had suspected when it retreated into books, easier to read about than live.[68]

This dynamic between desire and remorse, acceptance and resistance, avowal and disavowal, is a recurring theme in the lives of these gay men as their sexual orientation emerges and they try to integrate its meaning into their selves. In large part, the struggle for these men as they come to terms with their sexual identity is how exactly to "be gay" in a world designed for heterosexuals. Feeling odd and alone, they find little guidance, a fragmented context, and no easy answers. Holleran describes the feeling through his character Lark, who finds himself trying to connect with someone (anyone) at the Gaytalk meeting. He wonders why gay men keep trying against all odds:

> Because, he thinks, being a homosexual is like trying to climb Niagara Falls. Eventually you have to admit: The water is going the other way. If you would only go in its direction, Life would take you right along downstream. Heterosexuality is like having a room ready for you at a hotel: The staff is expecting you — everyone knows his role. The homosexual shows up and has no reservation; he ends up outside, quite literally in the bushes.[69]

In narrating his sexual identity and how it has taken its present form, the gay man reserves a space for himself. Together, these autobiographies represent a river going upstream, following a path of new stories by which to navigate one's direction.

Being a Man —Gender Expectations

> ... Before too long, I'd dance and twirl,
> turn diva in my bathroom mirror, ...
>
> . . . .
> I didn't care. I knew the melody
> would never really set me free, I was
> so utterly bereft. Yet *not* alone—
>
> I knew a woman's voice was saving me.
>
> —Rafael Campo, "Diva" in *Diva*

The feeling of difference I explored above is often configured as a failure to live up to masculine gender expectations. It is no surprise gender should play a primary role in narratives about sexual identity given that gender role subversion is an issue in debates about sexual orientation and identity. Heterosexual norms buttress a paradigm in which all same-sex activity goes against what is considered proper and natural for male and female bodies. For example, male bodies have traditionally been understood as active agents and female bodies as passive recipients in sexual acts; but same-sex acts seem to subvert this paradigm and thus become a perceived threat to the moral order of sexuality. So, "men behaving like women" becomes as much of an issue as the fact that men are having sex with each other. Most theorists today separate the construction of gender from the category of "sex," which is the anatomy of bodies as male or female.[70] Gender, which relates to concepts of masculinity and femininity, is a social construction built on top of bodies. This is why we can speak of the concept of *gender identity:* how a person experiences his/her gender and makes meaning out of it in relation to his/her body. The traditional assumption has been that "normal" gender identity occurs when one's expression of gender matches one's anatomical sex. This has, of course, been called into question by those who project gender markers that differ from what is traditionally expected. This conception of gender as a construction on the body casts gender as something people do, rather than something essential about who they are.[71]

The separation of sex and gender allows for a more meaningful understanding of concepts like masculinity and femininity, the performative aspects of gender. As such, being biologically male and "acting like a man" are two very different things. *Masculinity* is the culturally contingent and temporally varied configuration of practices that represent manhood. Though it is often mistaken as natural and given, the content of this category is not monolithic. In our patriarchal culture, masculinity has been associated with practices and attributes that seemingly uphold male dominance in society. Aggression, strength, toughness, power-over, control, muscles, etc., could all be said to be elements of masculinity as conventionally understood. Theorists sometimes refer to this as "hegemonic masculinity," because it exalts and upholds one vision of manhood to the exclusion of all others.[72] This is precisely where gay men encounter trouble: hegemonic masculinity in today's popular American culture relies to a great extent on the repression of male-male eroticism. Gayness then becomes whatever is expelled from hegemonic masculinity. Men who demonstrate enough qualities or attributes that are considered "feminine" — "men behaving like women" — are suspected of being gay, whether they are or not. Gay men then experience any "nonmasculine" traits as doubly marginalizing.[73]

Almost all the autobiographers in my study encountered "trouble" because they failed to live up to masculine expectations. Interestingly, their "feminine" traits (all the ways they were not conventionally masculine) often revealed themselves at an early age, well before these boys were "sexual." This had the effect of alienating them from other boys at a time when they were just beginning to sense an inner attraction for them. The recurring patterns of traits perceived as feminine and the strategies these authors recall for dealing with their resulting alienation are strikingly similar. Patrick Horrigan notes about his school days, "As a rule, guys hated me because I had female friends, I was a sissy, and I was a top student." He also suspects there was something about the way he inhabited his body that made him fodder for other boys' hatred.[74] Like so many young gay boys, he had to face daily insults being shouted his way — "you faggot" — and the embarrassment of it all prevented him from confiding his pain with anyone else. Yet he knew he identified more with girls and women than other boys:

> I resented my effemininity and hated the masculine entitlement other men and boys seemed to flaunt at my expense. . . . I sought revenge in being an excellent student, and I comforted myself by playing the piano with aching sensitivity. But in the tough world of boys and masculinity, those things counted for almost nothing.[75]

Horrigan hits on the key issue here: what counts and what does not in the world of boyhood and adolescent masculinity. Being good at sports and excelling in physical education classes definitely counts; being a good student and preferring aesthetic endeavors usually does not.[76]

Horrigan relates a very telling story from when he was thirteen years old. It was 1976 on the night of the television premiere of *The Sound of Music*. Horrigan had already seen the movie three times in the theater and he could not wait to see it again. That day, however, his family had gone to a Philadelphia Phillies game and got stuck in traffic on the way home.

Horrigan was out of his mind at the thought of missing even one minute of the movie, especially because he had been dragged to a baseball game he did not even really enjoy. Sitting in the car, his mother became exasperated with him. Here they had superbox seats at the stadium — something most boys would love — and all he could do was think about *The Sound of Music.* "All of this meant, somehow, that I wasn't learning to act the way a boy ought to act (preferring Hollywood musicals to baseball games and making a big fuss over it),"[77] Horrigan observes. Boys who would be men were always supposed to be sports fans. Otherwise, something seemed "wrong" with them.

P.E. class was the site where one's "manhood" was put to the test. Several of these autobiographers recall the "Darwinian atmosphere of gym class,"[78] where their masculine inadequacies would be fully exposed for the taunting of their classmates: "Gym entailed games, but its atmosphere could never have been mistaken for that of play. The games were brutal and primal."[79] Frank DeCaro, an otherwise straight-A student, was called a "faggot" every day of school through junior high. He remembers gym class being an exercise in forced humiliation with no remedial help available, especially for an overweight "sissy":

> In English, if you were a nimrod and didn't know that "a lot" is two words, you could get all the catch-up help in the world. But if you couldn't slam-dunk anything but a doughnut, you and your incredible shrinking self-esteem were made, time and again, to prove just how bad you were at balls — kick-, soft-, basket-, and dodge-.[80]

Robert Arpin was also a "fat" kid, so it made playing sports that much worse: "Teasing and being laughed at were part of my life from a very early age."[81] Brian McNaught recalls feeling "paranoia" in gym class, especially in the locker room — "the sacristy of straight male machismo" — where one's masculine "fitness" or lack thereof was on full display. Whenever he goes to the gym as an adult, McNaught thinks about how many upset stomachs he had as a kid, "fearing that I would strike out at bat, drop the fly ball, cry in front of other boys when I hurt myself, get into a fistfight, cross my legs or look at my fingernails in an 'unmanly' manner."[82]

Although most of the autobiographers in my study who discuss their experience with sports and P.E. share this sense of dread and failure, there are a few exceptions — enough to dispel any bizarre notion that sports can "cure" homosexuality. Dave Pallone, for example, fell in love with baseball from an early age. José Zuniga says he "detested sports," especially "battleball" (dodge-ball), and he felt himself an artist at heart, but he was never the stereotypical outcast on the sidelines. By the time he went off to college, he had become a real fan of football.[83] Rick Noss enjoyed track and was captain of his high school basketball team in his senior year.[84]

David Kopay always loved sports, especially football, and he insisted on playing even when his parents discouraged him from doing so because of a knee problem. Kopay's experience on the other side of the sports divide, however, illustrates how tightly interwoven masculine expectations are in games like football. Kopay says from grade school on, "the curse words on the football field are about behaving like a girl. If you don't run fast enough or block or tackle hard enough you're a pussy, a cunt, a sissy."[85] Even more revealing is his discussion of the imagery used to coach the team: "The whole language of football is involved in sexual allusions. We were told to go out and 'fuck those guys'; to take that ball and 'stick it up their asses' or 'down their throats.' "[86] The overt implication is to emasculate the other team by metaphorically making them the passive recipients of homosexual acts. For gay boys who do enjoy sports, this kind of imagery and language only reinforces the fear of appearing feminine or being perceived as gay. The "protection" sports provides in terms of masculine appearances feels thin and contingent on their continuing to follow the "rules." Young gay men intuitively understand their desires are literally dangerous in a world of sports that is constantly policing the boundaries of masculinity.

No wonder so many gay boys find solace in aesthetic and intellectual interests, even as this increases their risk of being perceived as "feminine." Richard Rodriguez would withdraw with five or six "intelligent" but physically clumsy classmates to a distant corner of the field during his high school P.E. classes. From that vantage point, they could engage in witty, sarcastic conversation to scorn the "animal" games being played around them.[87] John McNeill felt very different from his peers when he was a child because of his "total captivation with the beauty of classical music" and his general "sensitivity to the beauty of music," which he interprets in retrospect as God's special gift to him in his gayness.[88] Drama class and theater were Frank DeCaro's salvation in high school, for he finally found a place where his effeminate traits could be applauded as "acting." In the school musical, he was part of an "in" group, and he even found himself abandoning other outcasts who had previously been his friends.[89] He saw in flamboyant performers like Elton John, Charles Nelson Reilly, Liberace, and Paul Lynde the opportunity to take his effeminacy and sell it back to the world as "fabulousness."[90]

Aesthetic interests offer some gay boys and men the chance to turn their difference back on itself and find a niche. Patrick Horrigan's interest in movies offered him an escape from the ordinariness and loneliness of his world. He could imagine possibilities for himself to be transformed from a misfit into a "star." In acting out a role, he could try on different identities and explore who he really was. For Horrigan, drama is a hiding place where one finds oneself: "And once your solitude has turned into drama, in a way you're no longer alone; someone is always bearing witness to you, even when no one else is around, because at least *you* are bearing witness to you. You become your own best friend."[91] Horrigan's words express how the artistic life overcomes loneliness but also relies on it. Clearly, the aesthetic realm provides not only liberation but also a hiding place for some of these autobiographers, even in adulthood. Sometimes the line between finding and avoiding oneself is quite narrow, as James Morrison so eloquently writes:

> The more undeniable my sexual identity became, the more aestheti-cized I willed my intellectual or emotional or cultural identity to be. It was like so much in my boyhood, a way of asserting and disavowing a gay self, at one and the same time.[92]

Claiming an "artistic" identity is a way of defining oneself as "creative" rather than "weird," and it offers a way to live on the margins of masculinity and still find some level of acceptance and self-empowerment. Richard Rodriguez discusses this rather cynically in his assessment of gay life in San Francisco, where he has made his home as an adult. He reasons that since society condemns homosexuality as being a sin against nature, homosexuals have been forced to find their redemption — a way of ordering their existence — outside nature, in the aesthetic realm. Society has also assumed gays are always childless (increasingly not always the case), so Rodriguez configures the aesthetic impulse as a way for gay people to arrange "a decorative life against a barren state." But he is not sympathetic with this impulse and he makes a point to trivialize the aesthetic, comparing it to a list of ornamental and decidedly unmasculine pursuits: "Homosexual survival lay in artifice, in plumage, in lampshades, sonnets, musical comedy, couture, syntax, religious ceremony, opera, lacquer, irony. . . . The impulse is not to create but to re-create, to sham, to convert, to sauce, to rouge, to fragrance, to prettify."[93] Rodriguez scorns gays who invest themselves in the aesthetic, even as he engages in the aesthetic project of writing his own intellectual autobiographies.

In fact, Rodriguez hides himself to a great extent behind beautifully written literary criticism, flowing rhetoric, and an ever-present preoccupation with the line between public and private selves. Though he has publicly acknowledged his gay sexual identity, he never directly identifies as gay in his first two books.[94] His allusions are always indirect and couched within external observations and related concerns. Just as the content of much of his writing deals with his struggle to balance his Mexican and American identities, his narrative identity reflects his struggle to write intellectually and creatively and still live up to masculine expectations — "machismo" in his cultural background.[95] He discusses the three F's that were expected of Mexican men: *feo, fuerte, y formal* (which he translates as rugged, strong, and steady), and ponders how he may or may not have measured up to the nuances of this definition of manhood. He was often concerned that his education was making him effeminate: "And it seemed to me that there was something unmanly about my attraction to literature."[96]

At the end of his chapter on gay San Francisco, Rodriguez seems to moderate his cynicism about gay aesthetics and shifts it toward himself as he sits in church during a roll call of AIDS support group volunteers. He notices a gay man in his seventies stand when his name is called and we get a glimpse of his own insecurities about how he may be perceived: "Something of the old dear about him, wizened butterfly, powdered old pouf. Certainly he is what I fear becoming."[97] Then, he seems to have a realization as he views these "saints" at the front of the church:

> These learned to love what is corruptible, while I, barren skeptic, reader of St. Augustine, curator of the earthly paradise, inheritor of the empty mirror, I shift my tailbone upon the cold, hard pew.[98]

Perhaps there is more to the aesthetic impulse than Rodriguez first expressed. Yes, it may be a survival strategy that provides a veneer of acceptability for a marginalized position; it may be a way of reordering or reinterpreting reality; but it also reflects the human capacity to make life meaningful and to embrace beauty — a love of the "corruptible" in the face of death-dealing circumstances.

Besides the aesthetic and decorative, it is amazing the number of traits and interests that become linked to the feminine in these narratives because of the rigid code imposed by hegemonic masculinity. Gay boys who already know they are "different" become almost hyper-sensitive about the ways they do not meet the code. James Heckman wished he could be at his mother's side to cook, bake, and sew, but "only girls did those things." He had to avoid most of the things that really drew his interest:

> Needlework, knitting, and crocheting fascinated me, and I really wanted to do them. But had I done them, I would have been ridiculed for being such a sissy. My uncle would have started it and it would have spread out from there. Even my grandfather would say, "Oh, you don't want to do that. That's girl stuff."[99]

Violations of the masculine code can be found in the smallest details. Both Patrick Horrigan and Brian McNaught recall the requirement for boys to hold their schoolbooks at their side on their hips, even if it was much more comfortable to hold them in their arms.[100] I remember balancing ridiculously large stacks of books on my hipbone in order to meet the code because I did not want to be late by going to my locker between classes, not realizing until later I was violating a different code by carrying around so many books. The boys in these life texts came to understand very early what was okay and what was not. Boys should: maintain emotional boundaries between themselves; always appear in control; enjoy and be good at sports; like to go to camp; not have too many female friends; not enjoy home ec classes; never cry; not be too neat; and most importantly, never appear weak. Violators were sissies.

One of the illusions of hegemonic masculinity is that real men are "perfect men" — tough, sturdy, strong, and most definitely at the top of their fields. While most men do not live up to the ideal, they find ways of accentuating the ways they do, and they can reap the benefits of the ideal by proving their heterosexuality. Since gay boys are constantly told they fall short of the masculine ideal, they often strive to be "perfect" in other ways. Many of these Catholic autobiographers spent their boyhood doing well in school, overachieving, or just being "good boys" in order to please their parents and teachers, to be "on top" in some way, and to redeem themselves from the fate of total ostracism and church condemnation.[101] Andrew Sullivan describes this as being "driven inward." He says many intelligent gay boys harbor grandiose ambitions or display precocious scholarship not because of any intrinsic nature, "but as a form of protection against the taunts and weapons of the people around them."[102] Gerald Allen was an exemplary high achiever: "I got A's in school. I was an altar boy *par excellence*. I was a liturgist and was master of ceremonies for big events. I was active in CSMC (Catholic Students Mission Crusade), Holy Name Society, Boys Club, and 4H Club. I did what the family expected of me and did it well. I did what the church expected of me and did it well."[103] Dan, one of the profiles in *Reclaiming the Spirit*, says, "I was always a good boy. I always did what they told me to do, and never got in trouble."[104] Mark, another of those profiled in this volume, was the one in his family everyone thought should become a priest, which he attributes to winning the admiration of his nun teachers by being a perfect student and always getting straight A's.[105]

The drive to please and be perfect is not without its costs. For many, it was a way of blocking their feelings. For Rafael Campo, it was his way of trying to contain and decipher his "discordant inner reality": "My cardboard report cards, like my bed and all windows and every classroom, were each another in a series of squares that contained me. My parents rewarded me generously for all the A's that were neatly held, like me, in tiny square boxes, and I pretended to be happy."[106] Philip Gambone sublimated his erotic desire for other boys throughout his high school years by busying himself with school work and lots of after-school activities.[107] James Abdo looks back at his own adolescence from his standpoint as a psychologist at a student health center. He fell into the same pattern he frequently sees: He cut himself off from his adolescent energy by doing what everyone in authority hoped he would do. Thus he was a real hit with his parents and teachers, but he suffered the rejection of most of his peers.[108] Similar stories abound. Toby Johnson and Tom Cunningham both talk about being "good boys" in school, doing everything right and developing workaholic study habits.[109] These habits also work effectively to subli-mate erotic desires as adults. Joe Izzo and Larry Sullivan both believe they dove into their careers in such a big way because they were avoiding their homosexual desires and trying to live "normal" looking lives. Eventually, both of them found the "normal" lives they had fashioned for themselves were quite fragile when they acknowledged their erotic attractions.[110]

The drive to be perfect is a running theme in many of Brian McNaught's autobiographical essays. Throughout his life, he was always a "good boy," getting A's in school, doing everything expected of him, and never giving his parents any trouble. He was always trying to prove himself worthy of love and respect. He even tried dating girls in high school and college and "seriously considered getting married on three occasions,"[111] because that's what good, successful Catholic young men should do. When he went to Marquette University, he was a daily Mass-goer and was labeled the "saint." He did not have a sexual encounter of any kind until he was twenty-one. As McNaught reflects on his life, he wonders how much of his life "is an attempt to prove to my folks that they didn't fail. How much of my life is an attempt to prove to the church that I am still worthy of its praise?"[112] McNaught ultimately realizes it did not matter how much he tried to be perfect throughout his life; he would always feel discounted in some way because of his sexual identity. It is tremendously frustrating for him:

> I am a good man, a loyal and loving son and citizen. I smile a lot, say please and thank you and give money to people in need. My home is wonderfully embracing. My relationship with my lover is nourishing and inspiring. My bills are paid; my dog is well-trained; my lawn is mowed; my flowers are the envy of the neighborhood and I always put down the toilet seat when I'm finished, so why do I sometimes hurt so badly? And why am I so angry?[113]

By emphasizing the quotidian ways he is a "good boy," McNaught demon-strates how much he simply wants to be considered "normal." He does not want to be defined solely by his sexual identity and he does not want to be excluded because of it: "My hurt resulted from wanting to be part of the group and knowing that no matter how good I was, how smart, how kind, how generous, I would never really fit in."[114] Although McNaught has now happily claimed his gay identity, there is clearly a part of him that wishes things could be different; but he knows he cannot change who he is and being "perfect" will not change how society views his sexuality. This disen-franchisement in the face of trying so hard to be fully accepted is what drives so many gay men to find spaces where they will fit, as I will discuss shortly.

Richard Rodriguez was also an excellent student and a high achiever. He was an obedient, organized Catholic schoolboy who by the fourth grade shelved his books at home alphabetically.[115] He uses Richard Hoggart's *The Uses of Literacy* to describe himself and to interpret the gains and losses of his academic success. The "scholarship boy," like Rodriguez, comes from a working class, "illiterate" background and finds himself increasingly distanced from his familial and cultural (Mexican-Indian) roots as he attains mastery of his education. The more he achieves at school, for which he is then mocked, the more he keeps to himself at home. The more he pleases his teachers, the more foreign he becomes within his own family and even to himself: "Here is a child who cannot forget that his academic success distances him from a life he loved, even from his own memory of himself."[116] Rodriguez frames this experience entirely in a cultural paradigm (what it means to become an "American"), so he does not consciously link his drive to be a "good boy" to his emerging sexual identity; but he does not ever directly narrate his sexual identity. The similarities of his experience as a "scholarship boy" to other gay "good boy" stories are striking. The quest to prove and find oneself involves the same search for affirmation and subsequent alienation from one's familiar world. For Rodriguez, the world he "lost" in his personal journey was culturally determined, but it was also heterosexually defined. Surely this was also an element in his feeling of difference at home — a factor that would make the divide between him and his parents all the more palpable.

Being at Home —Relating to Parents

My father is another man I love.
I love another man. My father is
A man who loves his parents, wife, and kids.
I am his son. The other man I love
Is someone very much like him, a man
Of honest words. And strong commitment....
. . . .
. . . My father knows I run
Away in his direction. That I love.
That words I make are only words, that sons
And fathers love enough so that a knife
Can grow between two men, and take one's life.
I love my father. I am not alone.

—Rafael Campo, "Love Poem"
in *The Other Man Was Me*

Relating to one's parents as a gay child can be challenging, especially in a Catholic context. The parents in these autobiographies were almost all reared in the pre–Vatican II Catholic generation, when gay people were not as visible in society, much less the church; and when even the pastoral acceptance of celibate homosexuals was unimaginable. A gay boy grows up knowing his parents' feelings about homosexuals and usually believes coming out will cause a rift in his family. The implicit knowledge that his parents will perceive him as "flawed" if he is gay sometimes fuels the drive to compensate by trying to be "perfect" in other ways. In any case, parents may sense something different about their son, and this difference sometimes makes it difficult for one or both of them to connect with their son. As Joseph Kramer says, "We are outside of their frame of reference even before we are explicitly sexual."[117] This in turn may cause the gay son to pull away himself, creating a gradual cycle of ambivalent alienation.[118]

Sometimes parents already know their son is different, and they may even "know" he is gay, but they will not think of him that way until the word is spoken. Once again, sexual *identity* is about language and identification. J. D. McClatchy kept his sexuality a secret from his family until he was in his late twenties and in a relationship. He announced at the dinner table that he had something important to tell about himself, to which his mother replied, "Don't bother, I know what you're going to say." McClatchy's narration of his subsequent realization is so relevant to the material in this chapter, it is worth quoting in full:

> Of course she knew. What else could she have concluded, years ago, from all those afternoons I'd spent listening to Brahms in my room while my father took my sister to the football game, from my want- ing to play house with the neighborhood girls when I was young and later insisting on late-night pool parties with the classmates in my all-boys prep school, from my acting out Eve Arden roles in our liv- ing room, from the too-glamorous dates I found for the proms — oh, from hundreds of things done and not done, felt and not felt. My parents could see as well as I the texture of my life, like a cobweb on the lawn that if touched anywhere trembles all over, so tender that it feels everything. But what was more important even than my "orien- tation" was that it not be spoken about. That was what my mother's interruption meant: *Whatever you do, don't put it into words.*[119]

For McClatchy, "Not-speaking-about meant not-dealing-with,"[120] and he wanted the feeling that his identity was no longer disguised; but his par- ents maintained their silence about it even after his revelation, implicitly refusing to embrace his sexual identity and all that meant for him. His parents preferred the illusion silence gave them; McClatchy wanted revela- tion and redemption. Yet from that night on, he felt a certain ambivalence about the whole thing and wondered if he had spilled the secret as a way of manipulating what his parents felt.

When Stephen McCauley's mother seemed to figure out the nature of his relationship with an older man who was his lover at the time, she raised the question. His affirmative response was all it took to send her into an emotional frenzy, after which she implored him not to tell the rest of the family. Later, after his father had learned the news and reacted similarly to the point of suggesting he should leave, McCauley wonders whether lying would have been better — if that is what his mother wanted him to do all along — and forever feels a disjunction between who he had been before he named his identity and who he was after.[121] Brother Jonathan felt his relationship with his parents would forever be shallow if he did not disclose what he felt was a vital part of himself. His parents accepted him but never spoke of it again, and he knows they never will have to talk about it as long as he remains in religious life and maintains his vow of celibacy.[122] Paul Albergo states, "My parents' approach to my gayness is denial. If we don't talk about it we don't have to deal with it."[123] The only time his parents did talk about it was when Albergo was president of the Washington, D.C., chapter of Dignity and appeared in a television interview. His parents saw it and told him he should be careful. My own parents stayed silent on the topic in spite of my work in the field. When I was on the board of directors of Dignity Denver and appeared frequently in the news, they never said a word to me about it; but then I never discussed it with them either.

Based on the accounts of the autobiographies in this study, there is no single way to characterize the relationships these men have had with their parents.[124] Growing up Catholic before Vatican II, most of the parents grew up in a church and societal climate that maligned and condemned homosexuals; but Catholic parents are as diverse in their opinions as the general population. Not surprisingly, some parents are supportive and some are not; some need more time than others to come to terms with their son's identity; and some never come to terms with it. Rick Noss came out to his parents in a note he wrote for them to read on their way home after visiting him for Labor Day. "My dad called me at 6:30 the next morning to make sure he caught me, to tell me he loved me and he didn't care." Even with such a positive attitude, there were great periods of adjustment between Noss and his parents. At first, they did not seem to want to meet any boyfriends; but eventually, they made a special trip to meet his boyfriend for Christmas. Today, Noss feels loved and supported by his parents, and knows he always has a home with them: "I can't describe how much they mean to me because of that."[125]

Other stories are not so easy. José Zuniga's father was an officer in the army and ran their home like boot camp. As a boy, Zuniga's toys had to be arranged by height, and no infractions against any of the rules were tolerated.[126] Though he believed his father loved him, Zuniga's father was emotionally unavailable throughout his life; and his rigidity inspired fear. Zuniga tried desperately to please his father, especially in his teenage years. The only time his father ever said "I love you" was when Zuniga was going off to serve in the Gulf War and his mother was gravely ill.[127] Though Zuniga had always felt closer to his mother and he suspected she knew his sexual identity on some level, she died before he came out. When Zuniga did come out and made a splash in the media for being discharged from the military, his father was quoted in the newspaper as saying, "I have no son named Joe."[128] Zuniga felt abandoned and did not speak with his father for over a year. Time, however, has an inevitable way of changing circumstances. In his epilogue, written just two years after coming out, Zuniga reports that he and his father were speaking again — on trivial matters, but speaking nonetheless.

Robert Arpin's parents had a hard time with his coming out. The only thing that moderated their loathing was Arpin's diagnosis with AIDS and their concern for his health.[129] David Kopay's mother became hysterical when he came out to her. In the height of her frustration, she told him, "I created you and I can destroy you, . . . I never want to see you again."[130] They did see each other again and had reached a point of "respect" for each other's positions as of the writing of his narrative.[131] Tommi Avicolli Mecca's experience is illustrative of how parents feel when they too have to "come out." Mecca dealt with his femininity by embracing it and flaunting it. After he came out, he began wearing makeup, dresses, and heels. He walked the streets of South Philadelphia in drag and heard the little old Italian ladies shout, "Don't you know you're killing your mother?" Their husbands would mutter, "If you was my son, I'd give you a good wallop to the head — that'd straighten you out."[132]

Mecca's parents had to face their friends and neighbors who saw their son dressed in drag every day. His father never really got over the shame he felt, but father and son seemed to reach an unspoken truce before the former passed away. Mecca's mother was always more open to learning about her son, but the two of them really became close only after his father died. Eventually, on her deathbed, she took steps to really make peace with him. She revealed a secret that speaks volumes about his father and his own masculine negotiations. His parents and uncle were driving one day and saw Mecca walking in drag on a downtown street:

> My uncle told my father to pull the car over, because he wanted to get out and beat the hell out of me. Momma had to physically restrain him. Poppa did nothing. As she told me this story, I was devastated. The rage I felt was unbearable. I wanted to run out of that hospital and cry, scream, anything. But I sat there listening to her

talk, knowing she had to get it out before she died: the final Mecca aria, that her father sang, her sister sang and I will one day sing.[133]

Mecca constructs this story as the final scene of an Italian opera — with all the passionate emotion of an old Requiem Mass — to convey the drama and tragedy families needlessly face because homosexuality is so stigmatized. In this case, family divisions were only bridged when death finally put everything in perspective.

It was easy for Frank DeCaro to love his father when he was a little boy and masculine differences did not matter so much; but as he grew up, their differences began to matter. DeCaro found more in common with his mother, and the two eventually became quite close. When he finally came out, his mother reacted coldly and became depressed until one of her best friends reacted neutrally to the news her son was gay. With "permission" from her friend to feel okay about it, she ultimately became "gay-positive."[134] His father was yet a different story. When DeCaro came out to him, his father ranted, "You mean all those kids were right all those years!" This hurt DeCaro because his father had always yelled at him for not fighting back. "Now it seemed he was joining my tormentors' ranks, doing to me what they'd always done."[135] Frank, Sr., never understood why his son had to be so open about his sexuality — he preferred that it remain a secret. For years, they found ways to hurt each other:

I could no longer see the goodness in his heart or the reasons we'd nicknamed him St. Francis when I was a kid. It would be years before we became close again, and by that point, neither of us thought that day would ever come.... It turns out my father and I are a lot alike...both self-centered, both believing we were always right; each unable to say "I love you" even though we both knew it was mutual and true.

The fruit *didn't* fall far from the tree after all.[136]

Once again, the stigma of homosexuality added unnecessary walls in a family. Because of the way gayness becomes overdetermined rather than situated among a variety of identity factors, other commonalities among family members get lost. Sadly, these divisions can persist and may only be bridged in times of crisis, if they are at all.

Being Oneself — Finding Home

Coming out, or rather coming *into* a gay identity, involves a sort of reinvention of oneself in response to shifts in one's sexual self-awareness. I want to resist the language that portrays coming out as "finding" oneself;

instead, I like to think of it as a re-narration of the self. For these auto-biographers, coming out represents planks in the reconstruction of their narrative identities. In the process of building their life stories, they fashion a description of sexual identity that makes sense with the whole of their feelings and experiences. They narrate themselves into gay identities that reflect both their own unique qualities and definitions of sexual identity currently available to them. If there is a sense of inevitability in their sexual stories, it is revealed only in retrospect through memory; but as I discussed in the previous chapter, that is the form and function of autobiography. In rereading the past, the autobiographer brings a second consciousness to bear on it. The autobiographer refashions his identity puzzle pieces in a new way that makes more sense with who he has become.

Part of assembling this puzzle is figuring out where he fits. For several of these authors, this quest is literally geographical. A recurring theme in these narratives is the idea of "belonging" somewhere other than his place of origin. This is not surprising given how many of them felt they did not "fit in" while they were growing up. Usually, the geography is configured as a difference between cities and suburbs or small towns. Gay "communities" in America have emerged for the most part in large cities and a few "remote" tourist destination spots,[137] so other gay people are not usually as visible outside of these areas. Frank DeCaro fell in love with another boy in high school, and the two of them became schoolboy friends and lovers. Of course, they kept their relationship a secret and did not even really think of themselves as homosexual: "We had no gay identity then, no sense of a gay community existing beyond the world we knew in Little Falls."[138] He also recalls his boss at an after-school job and the neighborhood postman, who were both thought to be gay in his suburban town. Both men ultimately committed suicide — casualties, as DeCaro says, "of time and place, and the inhospitable nature of the suburban environs we call home."[139] DeCaro would eventually escape his suburbia and reinvent himself in the big city. Rafael Campo's moving away to college in Amherst is comparable to DeCaro's feelings about the suburbs. Campo talks about leaving "the confines of suburbia" and becoming someone else, a different person: "The sun seemed a bit less out of reach."[140]

A remarkable number of these autobiographers extol New York as the place where they feel most at home. In Ric Burns's PBS documentary *New York*, the narration consistently refers to New York as the place to come and reinvent oneself, much as the city has done throughout its history. No doubt many of these autobiographers would understand that message deeply. Andrew Holleran, whose novels offer a portrait of gay "circuit" life in 1970s New York City, says of New York: "It was a place where you could just leave everything behind and create yourself anew." He adds that the thing that makes gay culture possible in cities is "that kind of anonymity and freedom, that detachment from your origins."[141] Frank DeCaro also mentions the "comfort of anonymity" he feels in New York.[142] This has all the sound and feel of "escape" or even "running away," and to a certain extent it is; however, it would not be accurate to dismiss this migration to the city as a shirking of responsibility or abandonment of one's family. Some of these men lose touch with their families of origin, but this is far from a dominant trend in this set of autobiographies. For most of them, the city atmosphere provides them with a place to feel at "home," which in turn gives them a better vantage point from which to view their families of origin more clearly, without the angst of feeling like the odd man out. Most of them continue to take family relationships seriously, albeit in different ways.

The city represents freedom, community, and refuge for gay men. For Tom Cunningham, choosing to remain in his New York assignment (as a Dominican priest) rather than accept a transfer to South Carolina meant "the end of the good Catholic boy who always does what he is told." It also meant the end of his active ministry as a priest.[143] Joseph Kramer felt liberated in New York: "My authentic self was terrified to express itself until I traveled to New York City at age twenty-eight and met men who were kindred spirits."[144] When Rob Nixon was young, his family moved from their Italian neighborhood in New Jersey to Florida, where he was the only Italian in his school class. In New Jersey, he was "weird"; in Florida, he became "exotic": He was The Italian. Nixon took comfort in being able to "hide" in this identity: "It became my mask, a cover for my oddness, an excuse for my theatricality, my strange way with a gesture or turn of phrase. I mythologized my difference. . . . Even the kids who disparaged me did so, not because I was queer, but because I was from New Jersey. Italian became the lie that saved me from the truth I dared not speak."[145] As an adult, Nixon moved back north to New York and let go of the identity he had fashioned to feel safe in Florida:

> I no longer needed to be a dancing minstrel show of Italianness to be accepted. I had achieved the gleaming city at last. Fully out on the streets of New York, I felt I had arrived somewhere, a destination where what had been hidden, disavowed, was given a name and a public face. . . . I found a physical site to inhabit, an architecture for my existence as a gay male in late twentieth century America. . . . I was gay, and the identity fit like a glove.[146]

Nixon's words reveal much about the relationship between migration and reinvention of the self. His experiences in both Florida and New York represent various strategies of identification — ways of constructing himself in order to feel safe and at home.

New York figures prominently in so many of these stories because of its size and ethos, but it is not the only city, of course. Other cities like San Francisco and Washington, D.C., also figure in these stories and these are described when the geographic move is meaningful to the author. In some cases, the movement is away from the city, and gay people by now have established a variety of lives in a variety of locales across the country. Fenton Johnson, for example, found gay life in 1970s San Francisco (where he too had moved to chart a new arrangement of himself) a bit too fast for him. He escaped to a small Midwestern college town in the early 1980s and remained there for a few years, only to return to a San Francisco changed by AIDS.[147] Some writers remain in surroundings similar to their origins and find other ways of refashioning themselves. James Heckman, for example, grew up on farms in Indiana and still lives among farmers in Wisconsin. He loves to go to New York periodically and knows he could have a "gayer" social life if he moved there, but that is not his home. As he puts it, "Agriculture is my life." For Heckman, farming actually helped him understand his sexual identity: "On the farm, I learned to appreciate nature, and for me being gay is a very natural thing. Some cornstalks do not bear ears of corn, some gilts do not have babies.... On a farm, you accept that some things are out of the ordinary. That has helped me to accept being gay."[148]

Richard Rodriguez moved from his boyhood home in Sacramento to go to college in Stanford — not too far, but far enough to make a difference. More significant to Rodriguez than the actual geography, however, is what his migration represented: "My departure would only make physically apparent the separation that had occurred long before."[149] Couched again in cultural differences, Rodriguez still understands how the migration from home begins before the physical geography changes. In his final chapter, aptly titled "Mr. Secrets," Rodriguez declares that the new version of himself — what he calls the "public person," the successful writer — that he fashioned in the "liberation of the city," would remain "distant and untouchable" to his parents.[150] Inevitably, the public self Rodriguez created when he moved away would also maintain some "private" dimensions, such as his sexual orientation, which would contribute to his feeling of distance.

A Gay New World?

The inner movement to reshape oneself with a gay identity begins prior to and apart from any geographical change that may or may not occur. As these life stories testify, most gay men experience an incongruity between who they are and who they are expected to become well before they can name this difference as something sexual. Claiming the gay identity ultimately becomes a matter of integrity. Though it is often framed and perceived as finding oneself, it reads more like an acknowledgment of an identity piece that has been hidden for some time; hence the imagery of being in the closet and coming out. Though it inevitably causes some pain and entails loss as any change would, coming out is usually narrated as a healthy decision. I suspect this is not only because it feels "true to oneself" — a question of integrity again — but also because it takes more energy to conceal one's sexuality and the relationships that result from it. Concealing it feels deceptive and honesty is freeing. As Brian McNaught says, "I no longer fear being discovered."[151] For McNaught, coming out was more than an issue of integrity; it was a matter of life and death. Hiding himself nearly cost him his life in a suicide attempt, a literal way of undoing the self he had become according to external expectations. He pledged to live according to the geography of his own inner compass and found it liberating: "My freedom began only after twenty-five years of hiding, of keeping my secret, of being what others thought I ought to be."[152]

Coming out and naming oneself as gay is a strategy that takes many different forms in these autobiographies, and an entire book could be written about the choices involved in taking that step. José Zuniga, David Kopay, and Dave Pallone each sacrificed their careers by telling their stories publicly. Though each of them paid dearly for their coming out and express bitterness about what happened to them, they all feel "healthier" and say they do not regret their decision. This says a lot about the centrality of this piece of identity. Coming out need not be a grand and public act; however, it is usually felt most deeply within the dynamics of one's most important relationships. Recall the poignant instances of coming out to parents I discussed above. Fenton Johnson's coming out to his mother is indicative of how significant and transforming these personal interactions can be. When he told her he was gay, when he spoke the word, she responded positively; but even if she had not, Johnson would have been forever changed by naming and claiming his sexual identity: "In that moment I felt our relationship transform itself from parent/child to that of peers. In that moment I acquired a sexual and romantic life. At thirty-two years old I became an adult."[153]

Johnson may have come out in the sense that he revealed a piece of identity he had been hiding, but his mother had already suspected it. Johnson's narrative moment is better described as a *coming into*, as I suggested earlier. In revising his self-image to include a gay identity, he also became a man, despite what hegemonic masculinity might otherwise suggest. He established the geography within himself on which to chart his sexual identity. These inner movements toward being gay are profoundly meaningful. Rafael Campo also uses geographic imagery to depict the inner movement to his gay identity. He writes of his thoughts during a medical lecture about people and diseases in foreign lands, and imagines a homeland for gay people:

> I began to daydream more deeply, instead, about the possibility of a kind of homosexual country of origin, a different and fabulously free New World, a place whose existence seemed plausible to me after so many long and tortured journeys I had made across oceans of disavowal to the deepest reaches of my heart. On each of these journeys, a vast and unexplored continent stretched before me there, in the shape of a man's body. I had the feeling that I was searching for something of tremendous value.[154]

Campo's quest is to find the space where he fits: his home, the place where the puzzle pieces of his identities come together to form himself. One of these pieces is his sexual identity, his desire for other men, which he has denied like "oceans of disavowal." This desire is physical and sensual and is located on the beautiful expanse of the male body.

The core of sexual identity lies in the heart of this erotic desire. For some of these autobiographers, it is in the moment of sexual connection with another man that they know they have arrived in a place where they fit, where the pieces of identity make sense. Philip Gambone experienced this consciousness when he was a boy messing around with another boy: "In some unverbalized way, I understood that erotically touching another boy — being with another boy that way — was going to be a fundamental, inescapable aspect of who I was."[155] Dave Pallone put off having a sexual relationship with a man until well into his adulthood. When he finally found an opportunity and allowed himself to do it, it was a breakthrough moment for him. "And I knew it was the real me touching him: the excited boy who groped with other boys in the shed, not the tortured guy behind the mask with women." Pallone felt in that intimate moment with another man that he was the person he had always imagined himself to be, and for the first time he felt love would be possible for him in the future: "Because now I knew who I was. For the first time in my life, I knew absolutely: *I was gay.*"[156] Peter Krask had his revelation the first night he shared another man's bed. He intuited a new inner harmony when the man kissed him gently on the ear and fell asleep beside him: *"You have changed your life."*[157]

Rafael Campo wrestles throughout his life text with the same-sex desire he had tried so hard to deny, and with its consequences. He spent many years afraid of it, wanting to be "normal," but he was unable to extinguish the desire he felt. When he was drawn to Gary, a flamboyant gay black man on campus, he found ways of dismissing his attraction by stigmatizing Gary: "I had neatly and efficiently converted his campiness into effeminacy, his raucous humor into poor taste, and his sexual confidence into a self-destructive addiction to promiscuous sex."[158] He eventually realized he was mostly afraid of how Gary and he were alike — he was afraid of himself: "Now I realize that for a long time what I had feared was my own humanity. . . . There is no medication to cure me, and only boxes of my own construction to contain me, whose walls allowed me to smash against them my own head."[159] He needed to find space for his desire within himself, not in some exterior landscape that would feel safer. Once he embraced the erotic attraction he already held inside, the puzzle pieces started to fit, and he could know the pleasure of desire: "Being gay was joyfully not to have a country of origin at all, only a place in my heart where a man was extending his arms toward me."[160] Campo comes upon this revelation in the poetry and stories he writes. He finds in the written word the power to reinvent himself with an identity that reflects his desire. He "finds himself" by narrating himself. It is the same revelation for each of these autobiographers when they finally say the words, even within themselves: *I am gay.*

But being gay also means figuring out where one fits in terms of communal identities. Like Richard Rodriguez, Philip Gambone explores the ways American identity pulls him from his cultural roots. Gambone, however, is more direct about the ways ethnic and sexual identity converge and play upon the person in analogous ways. Gambone writes at length about his Italian background and his Italian American identity, trying to sort out what distinguishes this category and what about it makes him unique. "What part of the whole person I am today is the "real" me, and what part is just the *bella figura* I was taught to present to the real world?" As he grows up and charts his own landscape as an Italian American, different from the path of his parents, there will be some inevitable disconnection from them. He ponders how his sexual identity is also a catalyst in this process:

> And what is it like when the world you're being prepared for —
> yes, isn't this exactly where the experience of many third-generation
> ethnic Americans and the experience of gay Americans intersect —
> when the world you take your place in as an adult is not a world your
> family can follow you into?[161]

While it is expected that every person will chart a path at least somewhat different from his/her parents, this is further exacerbated for Gambone because of his gayness. He understands, moreover, how this path moves him even farther away from his people. In the process of becoming more "American" and "gay," he will explore a geography not only different from, but

largely unfamiliar to the people he has known before. He will effectively
find a new people, a new tribe.

One's inner geography is mapped in conversation with the gay communal landscape and all that being gay means — and this is the ultimate
coming to terms. For almost every one of the autobiographers in this study,
it meant and continues to mean coming to terms with his own difference
from the "norm." It means an acceptance of the ways he is not masculine,
of the ways claiming this identity will be liberating even as it reinforces his
marginalized position. It means identifying — and dis-identifying — with
others who are gay. Some gay men experience a certain amount of cognitive
dissonance finding their position within the landscape of gay communal life and expectations. Other than the common bond of their sexual
identity, they may have little else in common. Several of the autobiographers I examine express reservations about their fit in this larger puzzle.
R. Roberts, for example, does so by criticizing gay subculture. When he
was first coming out and exploring gay life, he visited bars, bookstores, and
dance clubs. "I was struck with two impressions: first, I was very much
attracted to the men and being with them; second, there was a subculture
that was not attractive. I noticed a superficiality, a slavish conformity, a
painful impersonalism."[162] I suspect Roberts was responding more to the
ethos of the types of establishments he was visiting, which would feel that
way even in a heterosexual setting, than anything endemic to gay culture
per se. Larry Ebmeier echoes Roberts's sentiment when he describes "the
outgoing, outspoken, socialistic, activist, flamboyant and fast-paced, dish-
ing, camping-it-up type of people who seem to dominate when gays come
together in urban areas." Much more the introvert, Ebmeier prefers a less
visible segment of the gay community — the people who enjoy staying
at home.[163]

For each gay man, the foray into the "gay ghetto" represents another
step in the process of locating himself in the larger framework of gay culture. The process of gay identification involves a struggle to both claim the
identity, which in some ways feels so right and seems to "fit like a glove,"
and not be trapped or limited by it. This echoes Foucault's cautions about
the traps of identity and the way it can police and control persons. James
Abdo seems aware of Foucault's theory and expresses his frustration over
the current available descriptions of sexual identity. He notes the lack of
definitive content in the categories of "gay" and "straight": "People self-
select, and nobody knows on what criteria. . . . But when it comes to their
individual identity inside, there is a lot of complexity involved."[164] Rob
Nixon felt confined by the available sexual identity categories when he
was just an adolescent: "As yet only dimly aware of the traps of identity, of the unnatural suffocation declared by 'us' and 'them,' I straddled
worlds, negotiating rules and rites, searching for a geography that could

welcome and contain all that I was."[165] Philip Gambone, always the good boy who tried to do everything right — like so many gay Catholic boys — hopes to find the geography that will contain him as he grapples with the expectations of gay identity:

> I still sometimes get too concerned about whether I'm gay enough, too concerned about whether I'm doing the queer thing the way I'm "supposed" to, still too anxious that the boat that will transport me to the fabulous Gay New World is leaving and I'm not on it.[166]

And so we come full circle. The metaphorical search for "home" brings us back to the questions first raised in this chapter. What is there to say about being gay? Is it just the same story told over and over again? The answer appears to be both yes and no. In this chapter, I have explored some recurring patterns and themes that emerge in these narrations of gay identity. These include the feeling of difference while growing up; some sense of sexual attraction at a very early age; the experience of silence on the subject of being gay; being objects of derision in school; the struggle between denial and avowal of sexual desire; various negotiations with masculine gender expectations; stormy relationships with parents, particularly around coming out; and finding a new geography through which to narrate oneself, both literally and figuratively. Yet no single portrait fits everyone. These narratives of gay identity unavoidably complicate simplistic and reductive conceptions of what homosexuality is all about. The fact that the content of American gay identity is amorphous is compounded by the way it continues to shift and change in response to historical circumstances. After all, it has only been some 130 years since "homosexual" was first applied to persons; and it has been less than 100 years since "heterosexuality" attained its popular normative status.[167]

At present, gay identity is marked by particular meanings and contexts, which may or may not resonate with all men who experience same-sex desire. Even so, it is an identity label embraced to some degree by all of the autobiographers whose life texts inform this study. They do so because they live in a cultural context in which powerful forces like the church and lawmakers tell them their erotic attractions matter. They do so in response to societal attitudes and messages designed to marginalize them. As William Glenn says in his reflections on being gay in a Catholic school, "My story is a version of the 'coming out' story of every gay boy or girl, and these stories will continue until the dominant culture, which suffers exquisitely from its own homophobia, withdraws its enormous and blinding sexual shadow."[168] I would like to think we will reach a point when sexual identity does not "matter" as it does now, by which I mean gay persons will be able to celebrate their sexuality and forge their relationships without societal stigma and church condemnation overwhelming them. Perhaps we are seeing movement in that direction as laws change and AIDS becomes less fatal; but the progress is uneven and contingent, so being gay still "matters."[169]

Based on these life texts, being gay is not just about men having sex with men. Yes, it is about erotic desire; but it clearly means so much more and it is performed in myriad ways, not just through erotic activity. It is deeply linked to constructions of gender and informed by a range of normative expectations. These autobiographers show how being gay is deeply embedded in their sense of self, emerging before they become sexual. Indeed, an astonishing number of these men never even had gay sex until well into their adulthoods, yet they recall performing in gay ways throughout their childhoods. The church would like to separate *being* gay from *doing* gay, but it is not that simple according to the life texts examined here. For many of these men, they were "doing gay" before they really came to terms with "being gay." Gay identity bridges the enforced chasm between orientation and acts. It encompasses feelings and behaviors that happen across lifetimes. Gay identity involves relationships, secrets, honesty, fears, hopes, decisions, love, and desire. In the words of Andrew Holleran, sexual identity "is also the thing around which our deep wishes coalesce: the desire for love, trust, fidelity, stability, a home, a companion, a future, all of that."[170]

For men who claim a gay identity, being gay and doing gay are inseparable. The church's monolithic vision of homosexuality seems sorely inadequate to capture the rich experiences of these authors. In the next chapter, I will take up the Catholic piece of these gay lives. My analysis will shed light on the ways being Catholic and being gay intersect and complicate each other. By surveying the way gay Catholic identity is performed in these narratives, I will provide a framework through which to understand how these identities are worked out in reference to each other. Here again, being and doing are not so easily separated.

Chapter 3

Orbiting the Catholic Axis

My mother worries about my association with Larry Faherty.... My mother has no reason to fear. I will always be attracted for the same reason that I will never become. Because I am a Catholic.
— Richard Rodriguez, "Irish Catholic"

Talking about religious identity is no less complicated an endeavor than talking about sexual identity. The same theoretical concerns with regard to the concept of identity in general apply. Like sexual identities, religious identities are not fixed but rather are dependent upon available categories which change according to historical and cultural circumstances. Religious identities are similarly worked out and articulated in relation to both self-understandings and communal expectations. This communal dimension, however, is particularly strong with regard to religious identity. Among its many roles and functions, religion is often concerned with boundaries that differentiate insiders from outsiders. Much as with ethnicity, members of religious groups learn what makes "us" distinct from "them," and this consciousness enhances the definition of their religious identity. The idea that religion is also partially a belief system further amplifies this sense of boundedness and consistency, to the point that words like "heretic" and "dissident" are deployed in some religious systems to marginalize those who do not adhere to the prevailing creed and/or code of ethics. But this ideological cohesiveness is illusory and is usually asserted when the boundaries of religious identity are contested by different interpretations of what it means to be a member. Such contestation is further exacerbated by the reality that religion is also deeply "cultural," replete with a variety of socially transmitted practices and customs that inform the way members interact with the world and with others.

For Catholics, the communal identity is reinforced by the strong and visible hierarchical structure of the church, with watchdogs like Cardinal Ratzinger who try to police the boundaries of Catholic identification. Ratzinger would point to ideological factors, such as adherence to certain doctrines or allegiance to the Pope, to define what it means to be Catholic; but this does not take into account the various cultural, political, and psychological factors which also contribute to the formation of Catholic identity. These factors are much more difficult to control and act on persons in subtle ways. This is the Catholicism that is less about adhering to specific beliefs, and more about a living system into which one is born. At this level, Catholic identity is not constructed by those who make the "rules" (i.e., Roman officials and the bishops) but rather is passed on and "learned" through particular Catholic communities and families. It is experienced more than taught. This is the Catholicism that permeates the lives of these gay men. That being said, I do not mean to overdraw a dichotomy between Catholicism that is directly "taught" (i.e., doctrinal) and that which is "passed on" (i.e., cultural). Though not always perfectly harmonized, these aspects are not mutually exclusive. Indeed, it is difficult to imagine one without the other, even for adult converts who study church doctrine but learn Catholic practice and culture within the context of particular parish communities. The question is, how do these aspects inform American Catholic identity today?

It might be helpful to begin this discussion with a dichotomy that is more familiar in the Catholic landscape today: the split between "liberal" and "conservative" Catholics. Although these terms oversimplify more complex positions, they are used and claimed by a wide range of Catholics and those who write about them.[1] The words denote ideological stances, and as such would seem to relate most closely to the doctrinal dimension of Catholicism. "Liberal" Catholics are usually cast as the ones who diverge from church teaching, especially on sexual, reproductive, and gender matters, while "conservative" Catholics are cast as holding to the "party line." But this construction is misleading because "conservative" Catholics are just as likely to dissent from church teachings, often in the seemingly different arenas of socioeconomic justice and liturgical reform. The problem is that the terms are predefined by the bipartisan political atmosphere and are then unevenly applied in the context of church teachings and tradition.[2] Michele Dillon recently studied Catholic identity in relation to members of three groups she calls "pro-change Catholics" because they challenge particular aspects of church teaching: Catholics for a Free Choice, Women's Ordination Conference, and Dignity.[3] Although usually identified as "liberal," these Catholics demonstrate a remarkable variety of positions and opinions, conservative in some ways and liberal in others. Dillon's study demonstrates not only the inadequacy of labels like "liberal" and "conservative," but also the fallacy of assuming pro-change Catholics fit neatly in the liberal category. Some gay and lesbian Catholics, for example, are fiercely conservative regarding church and/or social issues.

In terms of identity, one might be tempted to align "conservative" Catholics more closely than "liberal" Catholics with the doctrinal aspect of Catholicism, but both camps evidence complicated positions in relation to the Catholicism they have been "taught." Consider Supreme Court Justice Antonin Scalia's public dissent from the church's teachings on the death penalty in early 2002. He did not justify his right to dissent based on a notion of individual rights or a uniquely personal faith but rather on the doctrinal technicality that these teachings have not been proclaimed *ex cathedra.* [4] Although Scalia would definitely describe himself as conservative, he uses an argument more often associated with liberal Catholicism. Similarly, in Dillon's study of "pro-change" Catholics, she found that even though they have disagreements with Catholicism as it is officially "taught," they still draw on traditional church teachings (like baptismal equality) to justify their stance:

> Importantly, it is these doctrinal rather than nondoctrinal cultural resources that pro-change Catholics use to legitimate their pro-change projects. Rather than using distinctively American arguments, such as appeals to individual or group rights . . . , the respondents in this study reflexively engage the Catholic tradition. [5]

Despite these efforts to remain in some way aligned with doctrinal Catholicism, these kinds of disagreements inevitably disrupt Catholic identification. It would imply a sort of Protestant fragmentation were it not for all the other ways one "learns" to be Catholic. Catholics faced with the paradox of being Catholic and being at odds with aspects of its ideological dimension usually lay claim to the cultural, "passed on" dimension as a way of getting around what others might perceive as an insurmountable contradiction. Appealing to that aspect of Catholicism provides a way of holding it all together, even when the ideal of a unified Catholic identity is no longer a reality.

Another complicating factor is the way generational differences inform how Catholic identity has been and is negotiated. To understand this facet of the Catholic equation, it is important to situate this discussion within a particular historical context. American Catholicism, though closely tied to and technically governed by the global Roman Catholic Church, has its own unique history and assumes its own kind of identification. [6] Underlying most discussions of American Catholic history is the prevailing understanding that the United States is historically a Protestant country, so Protestantism operates hegemonically in American religious discourse. From this perspective, American Catholicism developed as a religious "outsider" and American Catholic identity has been formed through the mind-set of being different from the Protestant Christian "norm." The theory, as articulated by R. Laurence Moore, is that to be a true American, one has to be an "insider," so the story of American Catholics is a story of struggling to be accepted as insiders — true Americans — while in some way remaining distinctive. At the same time, however, "outsiderhood" is a characteristic way of constructing American identity, so having a unique identity turned against the dominant culture is in itself a mark of being American.[7]

This insider-outsider dialectic is borne out in varying degrees in most surveys and studies of American Catholic history. In this theoretical framework, Catholic identity becomes a strategy for remaining distinct in the face of an inevitable Americanization that threatens to make the boundaries between Catholics and non-Catholics nebulous. For example, beginning especially with the influx of immigrant Catholics in the mid-nineteenth century and lasting until at least Vatican II, hallmarks of Catholic identity included attention to sin, an emphasis on ritual, Marian piety, belief in the miraculous, close contact with the communion of saints, and adoration of the real presence of Jesus in the Blessed Sacrament. Though varied because of the many different cultural versions of Catholicism, such instances of devotionalism and supernaturalism thrived in America precisely because they distinguished Catholics from Protestants.[8] Rather than moderating Catholicism for public consumption, most Catholics chose to assert a distinct identity in the private sphere of devotional life and in particular cultural traditions associated with sacraments and feast days. This dialectic was not lost on church leadership. Robert Orsi and Ann Taves both note how leaders in Rome used their approval and regulation of private devotions as a way of combating Americanist and modernist tendencies in the church of the late nineteenth and early twentieth centuries. This in turn buttressed Roman control and safeguarded Catholic identity against Protestantization.[9]

As time went on, more and more Catholics began to move into the middle class and they began to fashion a sort of Catholic Americanism to replace their ethnic consciousness.[10] This amounted to a sort of Catholic subculture within the dominant American norm. As they began to embrace typical American middle class values, Catholics had to find other ways of maintaining a distinct identity, and scholars have revealed multiple strategies which functioned to that effect. Paula Kane finds Catholics of the early twentieth century achieving mainstream success but also asserting a code of conduct designed to avoid the individualistic philosophical implications of that success. Their efforts to preserve rigid communal boundaries found symbolic representation in church buildings designed to imitate old medieval cathedrals.[11] William Halsey finds Catholic intellectuals sustaining American optimism and innocence after the devastation of the World Wars through the resurgence of Thomistic rationalism.[12]

James Terence Fisher finds Catholics in the same time period identifying with a counterculture based on self-abnegation, the romanticization of the collective, or alternative aesthetics.[13] The diffusion of Catholic identities was further compounded and complicated by other identity components that became increasingly contentious in the American context, such as race and gender.[14]

The establishment of the highly successful parochial school system played a major role in the maintenance of Catholic identity, even as education moved more Catholics into the mainstream. Born in 1945 and coming of age in the 1960s, Richard Rodriguez's life story parallels this broader Catholic movement and reflects the ongoing dialectic of being both American and Catholic, which he constructs in comic/tragic terms. In his Catholic elementary school, the Irish nuns who were his teachers assumed their students' eventual success as Americans. Ambition and optimism were expected in the pursuit of worldly knowledge, in the learning of reading, writing, and American history; but in religion class, the students entered a different world — the "cold bath" of Irish Catholicism:

> The dagger in Mary's heart was sorrow for man's sins. The bleeding heart of Jesus was sorrow for man's sins. . . . *That cross you wear isn't a pretty bauble, Patsy, it's like wearing a little electric chair around your neck.* Christ had instituted a church — a priesthood, sacraments, the mass — and man required all the constant intercession of the saints and the church and the special help of Mother Mary to keep the high road. . . . The nuns never reconciled the faces of comedy and tragedy, and they never saw the need.[15]

Rodriguez's teachers inculcated the necessity of Catholic identity in light of humanity's continual need of redemption. Even American success, by then a given possibility for Catholics, could not obliterate sinful human nature. Besides, the church had consistently been wary of modernity and progress, key factors in the American imagination.

Vatican II and the 1960s, however, brought significant changes in the landscape of American Catholicism. The election of John F. Kennedy to the presidency is often deployed as the symbolic marker of the arrival of Catholics as true Americans. As Catholics attained American insider status, Catholic identity could no longer rely on "ghetto" churches and communities for its maintenance. It could no longer be assumed that Catholic children would attend Catholic schools. As Rodriguez states, "My generation would be the last to be raised with so powerful a sense of the ghetto church."[16] Part of this movement toward American insider status was manifested in the mass movement of Catholics from their urban ethnic enclaves to the suburbs, which began in the 1950s. Though not as quick to make this shift as other middle class Americans, Catholics slowly established themselves in the suburbs where Catholicism was no longer the dominant presence. And they did so in large numbers. In fact, the majority of the autobiographers in my study who are in their forties and younger grew up in the suburbs, which played a definitive role in the way they apprehended their gay identity, as I discussed above.[17] It also influenced how they experienced being Catholic. Anthony Smith theorizes that the mass movement into the suburbs already occurring by Vatican II actually enabled many of the changes of the Council to take hold. He asks, "Did the impact of Vatican II depend as much on the ranch-style housing American Catholics were moving into as it did on *Gaudium et Spes?*" Smith believes these Catholic suburban "pioneers" were already engaging themselves with the changing world and were thus more receptive to the task.[18]

Vatican II's openness to the modern world was marked in several symbolic ways. Church architecture shifted so that Catholic churches became less distinguishable from Protestant ones. The switch from Latin to the vernacular made the liturgy seem less mysterious; communal participation became one of the central features in the celebration of the Mass. Though he mourns the loss of mystery and transcendence in the new liturgy, Rodriguez interprets this change as a necessary permutation in the maintenance of American Catholic identity:

> It reflects and attempts to resolve the dilemma of Catholics just like me. The informal touches; the handshaking; the folk music; the insistence upon union — all these changes are aimed at serving Catholics who no longer live in a Catholic world. To such Catholics — increasingly alone in their faith — the Church says: You are part of a community of believers. You are not single in your faith. Not solitary. We are together, Catholics. *We* believe. We believe. We believe. This assurance is necessary because, in a sense, it no longer is true.[19]

Rodriguez is on to something very important about American Catholic identity today: the boundaries between "us" and "them" have become diffuse; the borders are harder to identify and negotiate. This does not mean, however, that Catholic identity is no longer a component of self definition. It merely means the terms have shifted and Catholic identities have become more varied and less monolithic. Indeed, what Rodriguez mourns throughout his life writings as a loss of contact with his ethnic roots is also a loss of a more defined and distinct Catholic identity.[20]

Rodriguez's experience points back to the way generational identity is an important consideration in the formation of Catholic identity.[21] As American Catholicism has grown and changed throughout its history, so too have the strategies for Catholic identification shifted. Though most of these autobiographies reveal common threads in their experiences of Catholicism, this should not obscure the fact that their life stories do not all follow the same trajectory with regard to American Catholic history. During Vatican II, some were middle-aged, some were growing up, and others were not yet born. Consequently, their experiences of Catholicism varied. As Leslie Scanlon states, "For American Catholics, the church they know now, the church that's emerged from the nearly 40 years in the stewpot with the teachings of Vatican II, embodies a much different kind of Catholic culture than that of their parents' or grandparents' generation."[22] While this is probably an obvious insight, given the rapid changes in American Catholicism this century, it is important to reiterate and explore it. Note that Scanlon says Catholic culture is different; it has not dissolved but rather morphed into something less uniformly definable. There is still something being "passed on."

Some of the differences are born out in a recent article about two Catholic nuns: "fifty-something" Carolyn Osiek and "thirty-something" Laurie Brink. Osiek was raised with the rigid Baltimore Catechism and became a nun at the cusp of adulthood before Vatican II. Like many of her religious sisters who have remained in their orders, she wholeheartedly embraced the promising reforms of the Council. Brink, on the other hand, was raised reading "comic books about St. Francis" and coloring "endless pictures of Jesus in various cardboard settings." Her spirituality sprang out of the folk tunes she learned at Saturday evening Masses, and her decision to join a religious order came well into her adulthood. Many of Osiek's generation were happy to jettison older practices which they had experienced as restrictive or even oppressive, and many of them feel betrayed and angry the reforms did not go as far as they would have liked. Brink, on the other hand, does not understand her older sisters' anger. Her formative experience took place in a church that was already in flux, already embracing new practices and revising older ones. As Brink says, "I did not earn my stripes on the battlefield of change and therefore I do not feel betrayed." Brink's generation is less apprehensive about exploring older aspects of the tradition because they do not have the same oppressive resonances, and in turn, Osiek's generation perceives their younger sisters as being conservative.[23]

In the meantime, the vast majority of Catholics who are not clergy or religious are swept up in their own negotiations of these generational differences. Some wonder if the reforms of Vatican II went too far and want to reemphasize those things that make Catholics different from Protestants. These are the Catholics who want the tabernacle returned to the sanctuary, and who attend Tridentine Masses whenever they are offered.[24] Others have little patience for old practices and feel the reforms of Vatican II have not yet been fully realized. Many others find themselves somewhere in between, feeling nostalgia for a real or imagined Catholic past but also living solidly in the Catholic present.[25] It becomes difficult to characterize any particular generation in any one way. In fact, younger

Catholics seem to come in all stripes. Some appear conservative and seek a certain amount of orthodoxy, but many disagree with some aspect of church teaching and seek creative ways of plugging into the received tradition. Tom Beaudoin, a scholar whose work focuses on "generation X" Catholics (born in the 1960s and 1970s) believes the American Catholic identity of the future will be a deeper mixture of historically Catholic and Protestant understandings of the church. In characterizing the movement toward a more Protestant sensibility, Beaudoin says young Catholics see the church as "ultimately something to be set aside if it interrupts one's relationship to God."[26] I think the operative principle affecting Catholics of all ages today is the idea of choice. Catholics find themselves in a larger culture of choice and now also choose how to be Catholic. The confluence of Vatican II and modern American culture has produced a range of available Catholic identities.

The multiplication of Catholic identities in the late twentieth century indicates many Catholics still share a feature which distinguishes them from Protestants: they do not easily leave to start or join another church. Thus, we have cradle, practicing, lapsed, cafeteria, Tridentine, Conciliar, feminist, orthodox, and a host of other "Catholics" who still claim a Catholic identity. Underlying these divisions is the unfortunate, and in many ways deceptive, dichotomy between liberal and conservative Catholics. This dichotomy, along with the host of other categorical markers dividing Catholics, may be an indication that the insider/outsider dialectic has now moved inside the boundaries of Catholicism. Catholics seem to compete more and more with each other over what constitutes Catholic identity. If Moore is right that outsiderhood is part of the construction of American identity, then perhaps perceiving oneself as a sort of "outsider" within the church is now a part of assembling an American Catholic identity. Indeed, it is striking that all of the autobiographers in my study sense having an outsider status imposed on them because of their gay identity; yet even among those who have "left" the church, the vast majority have not joined another church. Instead, they assert revised Catholic identities, such as "former" or "recovering." The Catholic factor in their lives is deep and formative.

All of the "pro-change" Catholics discussed in Michele Dillon's study (see above) could be said to exist in a sort of "outsider-within" status, yet they remain entrenched in the pool of symbolic resources provided by the Catholic tradition. Her Dignity respondents assert their Catholicity with statements like, "Catholicism is inescapably part of my life," or "Catholicism is an encompassing identity for me."[27] Even their arguments for doctrinal change are built upon other aspects of Catholic doctrine. The point of contestation between these Catholics and others is centered around the question of which teachings allow for a range of interpretation and the possibility of change, and which do not. Dillon's "pro-change"

Catholics are characterized as such because they seek changes in doctrine related to gender and sexuality. Other Catholics who are publicly unyielding on these issues might favor changes or allow for gray areas in doctrine related to war, unions, or capital punishment. Yet all of these Catholics feel at home in the same symbolic universe. One of the most useful aspects of Dillon's study is her comparison of these "pro-change" Catholics with members of the doctrinally conservative Catholic League for Religious and Civil Rights. Dillon finds both groups share a deep attachment to both the sacramental and universal dimensions of Catholicism. Additionally, both sets of Catholics value the idea of a communal identity and the unifying symbolism of the papacy.[28] The commonalities she uncovers speak volumes about the persistence and cohesion of Catholic identity, even in this era of seeming fragmentation.

Dillon's findings are further supported by a number of broader studies. The most recent of these is a 1999 survey of Catholics conducted by the Gallup Organization and supervised by noted sociologists Dean Hoge, William D'Antonio, James Davidson, and Katherine Meyer.[29] They found substantial agreement across a wide range of Catholics, including those who consider themselves marginal or "dormant," regarding what is most central about *being* Catholic (deliberately posed as an identity question). Topping the list is the sacraments, followed closely by a sense of spirituality, concern for the poor, and the spirit of community. Two other studies from 1997 and 1998 similarly found a set of elements or beliefs almost all respondents considered essential to being Catholic.[30] In his summary of the 1997 study, Davidson envisions these factors in a set of three concentric circles in which the core elements are considered the most central. In the inner circle lie the beliefs most widely held across the board to be the essence of Catholicism, such as the Trinity, the Incarnation, the Real Presence, and Mary as Mother of God. The second circle holds the church's social teachings and responsibility to the poor. The third circle contains rituals, such as attending Mass and receiving Holy Communion, the things represented by the phrase "practicing Catholic."[31] Davidson's model is useful in showing how Catholic identity hinges more on sacramental than juridical definitions of the church, and involves more than either holding certain beliefs or the fulfillment of ritual obligations.

Various writers and scholars have tried to address the dimension of Catholic identity that goes beyond the religious externals of creed and cult, the aspect that inheres in a person regardless of their adult faith commitments.[32] Lawrence S. Cunningham, for example, proposes that being Catholic is being part of a "community of memory," involving space, time, silence, prayer, sacraments, story, persons, catholicity, and community.[33] This relates to the sense of history so many Catholics consider a hallmark of Catholicism. But being formed in Catholicism also seems to affect the way one sees the world and negotiates reality. According to Andrew Greeley, the material culture of Catholicism (as found in things like statues, holy water, stained glass, votive candles, saint relics, religious medals, rosary beads, and holy cards) produces and represents an enchanted world and pervasive religious sensibility "which inclines Catholics to see the Holy lurking in creation."[34] In the "Catholic imagination," as Greeley calls it, grace permeates the natural world. "It sees created reality as a 'sacrament,' that is, a revelation of the presence of God."[35] In this paradigm, the world becomes revelatory rather than fallen, and creation takes on a metaphorical quality: "The objects, events, and persons of ordinary existence hint at the nature of God and indeed make God in some fashion present to us."[36] Catholic lives, even gay Catholic lives, then become instances of God's revelation, and autobiographical narratives provide windows into God's imagination and the fullness of ultimate reality.

Rosemary Haughton talks about the Catholic "thing," a "something else" deeper than the visible church and the external representation of Catholicism, which can only be articulated through the lives of individual Catholics.[37] This is the heart of Catholic identity, and autobiography is an ideal interpretive tool for trying to understand it. I want to reimagine Davidson's model of concentric circles to represent how I perceive this Catholic "thing" operating in the lives of these gay men. I envision an axis of Catholic identity grounded in each of their life stories. As their lives orbit this axis, some stay close to the Catholic core; its pull is inescapable, and they experience it as foundational in their lives. Because of its centrality, they struggle with its contradictions and find ways of remaining consciously committed to it. Others struggle with it and decide on a slightly wider orbit because the gravity has worn on them. Still others are in the widest orbit of all: For them, Catholicism plays a role in their life stories, but it is not so "visible" in their narratives. Their lives revolve at a greater distance from this core and other axes are more prominent. In any case, being Catholic is an inescapable and formative component in these gay lives no matter how tight or wide they maintain their orbits.

The Catholic Ethos: Sensual Memories

> I wished her a happy Easter, said nothing about her gloves, or perfume, or colored eggs, and hung up. As I sat there in my silent room I saw these memories would be with me forever, that wherever they were, I was: some part of me. But the life I must begin was my own —
> a separate person's.   —Andrew Holleran, *Nights in Aruba*

As I mentioned in the previous chapter, religious identity and sexual identity are only artificially separated from each other because both resonate in the core of selfhood and are directly concerned with human fulfillment. As such, these autobiographies provide a glimpse of Catholic identity as filtered and interpreted through the lens of gay self-understanding. This is a portrait of *gay* Catholic identity, yet many Catholics would certainly identify with the way they narrate their Catholic experience. Catholic identity begins in a world of sensory stimulation fueled by the materiality of Catholic culture, sometimes called the "smells and bells" of Catholicism. This is the world of sacraments, liturgy, rituals, and mystery that informs the Catholic imagination and teaches us on a subconscious level the answers to ultimate questions about who we are and who God is. It comes alive in Catholic homes, churches, and schools.[38] Brian McNaught compares having a Catholic background with having a Jewish background, "insofar as it involves growing up with rules, rituals and cultural idiosyncrasies which separate you from many of your friends and provide common bonds with others." He goes on to enumerate a few of these signifiers of American Catholic identity as he experienced it as a child:

> The Latin Mass, no meat on Fridays, the rosary, the May crownings, your new St. Joseph Missal, the nun's habits, being an Altar Boy and fainting from the incense, traditional rivalries with the athletic teams of the neighboring public schools, thoughts about entering the seminary or convent, holy cards, the "Decency Pledge" and a variety of other "typically Catholic" traditions are essential ingredients to my past which I share with other persons who grew up Catholic.[39]

David Kopay's childhood home in Chicago was marked as Catholic through and through, "with a Sacred Heart of Jesus over the door and religious figurines and objects in every room." Kopay remembers his parents kept a jar of holy water in the closet and would sprinkle drops of it around the house during storms. His family's life was centered around St. Christina's church, and they never missed going to Mass on Sundays and Holy Days. When he was in fourth grade, his family moved to California and immediately became a part of St. Patrick's church "without missing a mass."[40] Similarly, no matter where José Zuniga's military family lived, his mother walked him and his sister to church every Sunday and Holy Day without fail. Like Kopay's and most of the Catholic families profiled in these life texts, Zuniga's family never missed a Mass. The obligatory and rhythmic repetition of the ritual burned the imagery of Catholicism deep into their senses. It was awe-inspiring, terrifying, and comforting for the young Zuniga: "How portentous the epigrammatic words sounded to an impressionable ten-year-old: *Sin.* Benevolence. *Satan.* Saint Francis of Assisi. *Burn.* Resurrection. *Sinful.* Repentant. *Forever.* Amen."[41]

Fenton Johnson recalls the rhythmic cycle of the church calendar, re-peated year after year and ritually echoing the death and rebirth cycle of nature:

> Transmogrified cannibalism, mortification, exaltation — these were re-enacted according to a routine as dependable as sunrise and nearly (it seemed) as old. . . . The gritty rub of ashes on the forehead. Clouds of cloying myrrh ascending to the high-domed ceiling. Mind-numbing mantras mouthed in a tongue at once centuries dead and more evocative than our quotidian English, _ora pro nobis, ora pro nobis, miserere nobis._ Ours was a sensual church, the Opera of Faith, and we were its captive patrons.[42]

He realizes the lasting impression this sensual world left on him: "I ac-knowledge the shaping hand with gratefulness. Because of it I grasp in some way the incomprehensible magnitude of the mystery of being."[43] Johnson mourns the loss of this kind of spirituality for gays like him who feel alienated from the church. As an adult, he still feels drawn to ele-ments of it and takes comfort in some of the simpler rituals. For example, he stops to light a votive candle whenever he passes a church and has time to stop: "The habit is partly a remnant of Catholic grade school, partly a gift from a culture that valued remembering its past and the names of its dead."[44] Throughout _Geography of the Heart_, he lights the candles for his father and his many friends who had died of complications related to AIDS. Then, as his partner Larry's own disease worsens, the candles offer both of them a measure of comfort. Lighting the candles provided a structure for Johnson's interior prayer that Larry would die a speedy and painless death with him at his side.[45]

Catholic rituals and cosmology afford a sense of security and comfort during difficult moments in these lives. Brian Bouldrey recited the Prayer of St. Francis at night while his dying partner Jeff slept downstairs, too weak to make the trip up. When Jeff died, Bouldrey found solace in know-ing Jeff was now a saint in a heaven filled and alive with people like him. Bouldrey still finds himself praying to Jeff at times.[46] When John McNeill was taken captive as a prisoner of war in World War II, he and his captor passed a roadside shrine of the crucified Christ. He asked permission to stop and say a prayer. "I fell to my knees, made an act of contrition, and asked God to protect me and save me from death. . . . I surrendered my-self totally to God's mercy, and obviously God had other plans for me."[47] When Tony Laveccia was stabbed by a man he took home whose friends broke into the apartment after they got there, he prayed the Hail Mary over and over ("Pray for us sinners now and at the hour of our death") be-cause he thought he was going to die.[48] And when Scott Trepania learned he was HIV-positive in 1991, he immediately visited the Shrine of the Immaculate Conception in Washington. "I went into the crypt church, lay in front of the tabernacle and prayed the prayer that our Lord prayed in the garden." In light of his diagnosis, Trepania turned to the Mass, saying the rosary, and the stations of the cross to bolster his prayer life and his spirits.[49]

Catholicism provides these men tools and strategies not only for dealing with life's difficulties but also for relating to God in the process. When Dave Pallone's lover Scott died suddenly in a car accident, Pallone had not come out to anyone, and no one knew about their relationship. In his position as a "secret survivor," Pallone could only turn to God. At first, he was understandably angry. He went to his parents' graves and asked for their help in coming to terms with all of it: "Why would God . . . take away the only person in the world that I loved, the only stabilizing force in my life?"[50] Pallone later confided what had happened and the nature of his double life to a priest whom he considered his spiritual advisor. Fr. Piermarini told him to trust himself and to trust God, which gave Pallone the confidence to carry on with his life and be himself. He also found comfort in the idea that Scott was now part of the communion of saints: "Scott's up there saying, 'Life goes on, Dave. Be strong; keep fighting.'"[51]

For Rafael Campo, the Catholicism of his childhood was like a mother who cradled him in her accepting arms. The church provided restitution for all Campo lacked as a Cuban American living in suburban New Jersey, and he took comfort in the fact that the prayers he prayed in New Jersey were the same prayers being offered in far-off Cuba. "The bits of Latin uttered solemnly during mass were so much like Spanish that they implied that even my possibly shameful ethnic heritage was fit to be set to ethereal music."[52] Campo found a sublime and all-embracing poetry in the ordinary, tangible elements of his religious world:

> Poetry flowed in the supple warmth of votive candles lit by the trembling hands of supplicants, whose soft voices mixed with the tenuous light thrown across the highest rafters. Poetry blinded whole congregations in the gleam of the silver chalice raised for God's most precise inspection. The comforting word was present even in the worn and faded velvet lining of the offerings basket, which looked as if it might also serve as a cozy resting place for the neighborhood's stray cats that the priests took in. Any creature was welcome in my romanticized, hymn-drenched Catholic Church — even the most irretrievably lost of wanton souls.[53]

Campo's feelings of safety and acceptance were disrupted only when he grew up and realized the church did indeed consider some souls to be irretrievably lost and they were not necessarily welcome.

Patrick Horrigan also remembers the security being Catholic provided him as a child. He felt it let him in on secrets and truths that non-Catholics would never understand or appreciate. He enjoyed making people who weren't practicing Catholics feel like they were missing out on something.[54] He grew up in a very Catholic world in which the parish priest would sometimes say Masses in his family's home, and the sacraments marked some of life's most important moments. Horrigan recalls the emphasis his mother put on the ritual of First Holy Communion, as important to her as the day she got married and the times she gave birth to Horrigan and his siblings.[55] When he was a little boy, he imagined a movie being made of his life but ending just before the "big First Holy Communion scene." The audience would be devastated to miss it and would cry in vain until the big sequel was made.[56] While reflective of childlike egocentrism, the whole idea of his young life, down to the smallest diurnal details, being compelling material for a movie is indicative of his Catholic sense that whatever one does in this world matters.

Like Horrigan, Richard Rodriguez experienced his childhood Catholicism as something pervasive that marked him distinctively from others: "At home, there were holy pictures on a wall of nearly every room, and a crucifix hung over my bed. My first twelve years as a student were spent in Catholic schools where I could look up to the front of the room and see a crucifix hanging over the clock."[57] Catholicism shaped his whole day, every day, and framed the hours and the seasons. Rodriguez recalls an enchanted quality in his world, punctuated by Catholic rituals and celebrations:

> I felt the air was different, somehow still and more silent on Sundays and high feastdays. I felt lightened, transparent as sky, after confessing my sins to a priest. Schooldays were routinely divided by prayers said with classmates. I would not have forgotten to say grace before eating. And I would not have turned off the light next to my bed or fallen asleep without praying to God.[58]

For Rodriguez, being Catholic gave him tools to navigate a world filled with both good and evil. A prayer to his guardian angel and a sign of the cross aimed in the direction of his window would keep Satan from getting in his bedroom. The seasons of the church year accompanied his journey through time and the sacraments marked his coming of age. Rodriguez sensed how this world and its material sensuality set him apart from others and gave his life substance: "Catholics were mysteriously lucky, 'chosen' by God to be nurtured in a special way." Non-Catholics may have gone to church too, but "there was no incense, no sacred body and blood, and no confessional box. . . . For non-Catholics, it seemed, there was all white and no yolk."[59]

Andrew Sullivan writes at some length about this "yolk" of Catholicism. When he says Catholicism was always sacramental for him, he refers to the way God literally touches and is touched by this world. "By this, I mean that it was not about abstraction but about reality, not about words but about actions, not about the unreachable but about the physicality of the divine." He remembers the carnality of incense, bread, wine, vestments, pews, candle wax, and kneelers, all pointing to the reality and centrality of the Incarnation. "When sexuality burst in upon this boyhood scene, I was not so uninformed as to be guileless, but I was also primed to embrace it as yet another manifestation of a sensualized spirituality. It came easily to me. And not despite my Catholicism, but *because* of it."[60] Rodriguez was similarly affected by the sensual trappings of his Catholic world, noting how the church seemed to "excite more sexual wonderment than it repressed." The irony of it all was not lost on him, especially as he was coming of age in Catholic school: "When we were in eighth grade the priest told us how dangerous it was to look at our naked bodies, even while taking a bath — and I noticed that he made the remark directly under a near-naked figure of Christ on the cross." Rodriguez recalls the carnality of a nun's "wedding ring," pictures of martyrs in physical pain and virgins fallen in death, and the perfume of Easter lilies. His words echo Sullivan's: "At such moments, the church touched alive some very private sexual excitement; it pronounced my sexuality important."[61]

The liturgy, with its attendant ceremony and imagery, provides a host of sensual memories for these autobiographers. Fenton Johnson felt drawn into "a fantastical world — the world, in fact, of theater, where everything stood for something else and everything was or had the potential to be sacred."[62] There is much about the performative and decorative aspects of the Mass that resonates with the aesthetic interests of gay men. Gay men who are attuned to the artistic world can "plug into" the ritual world of liturgical celebration. Patrick Horrigan remembers when he was editor-in-chief of his high school yearbook, he had grand ideas for the special "yearbook mass." In the midst of planning, his faculty advisor warned him, "Patrick! We'll have none of your Cecil B. DeMille productions!"[63] I can relate to Horrigan's desire to choreograph a special liturgy. By the eighth grade, I was helping plan the music for our school Masses, and I have spent all of my adult life working as a liturgist and music director. I have always experienced the liturgy as an important point of connection with the church. Many of these writers who are active in Dignity comment on the importance of the liturgy and take special pride in the fact that their Dignity chapters concentrate on good ritual planning. It affords them an outlet for creativity and artistic expression within the arms of the church.

A number of the autobiographers, however, express some dissatisfaction with the new liturgy. In one respect, this is surprising because one

would expect most of them to support the reforms of Vatican II, especially in light of the way these reforms have empowered the people of the
church to take ownership and more openly challenge teachings they find
problematic. It is not surprising, however, in that the new liturgy is focused more on the immanence of God in the gathered assembly than on
the God who transcends this troubled world. As such, the new liturgy can
feel less aesthetically refined than the old liturgy for someone wishing to
be transported beyond the ordinary. Rob Nixon recalls how "very limp and
graceless" the new liturgy seemed when he first encountered it.[64] Richard
Rodriguez despised the new liturgy from the start:

> In college chapels I would listen to folk singing and see plain altars
> draped with bright applique banners: Joy! God is Love . . . one Sunday
> there would be a rock mass; one Sunday the priest encouraged us to
> spend several minutes before the Offertory introducing ourselves,
> while a small bad jazzy combo punched out a cocktail mix. I longed
> for the Latin mass. Incense. Music of Bach. Ceremonies of candles
> and acolytes.[65]

No doubt part of the "problem" in Nixon's and Rodriguez's experiences
with the new liturgy was bad execution of the new ritual. In their zeal to
update and "inculturate" the liturgy, many parishes turned it over to the
people without any particular training. The result was a pastiche of ritual
activity that reflected American culture of the 1960s and 1970s, more
so than any systematic liturgical theology. For gay boys and men who
were already feeling marginalized from mainstream culture, this liturgical
environment was not necessarily welcoming. It did not feel safe. Many of
them felt "robbed" of some of the otherworldliness of Catholicism that
afforded a space in which the unfairnesses of this world did not seem so
important. When they fondly remember the old liturgy, they reimagine
a bulwark of security and solidarity, where one's potentially threatening
personal uniqueness would not be noticed. Still, the Catholic world did
not disappear; it was merely altered.[66] James Morrison nicely sums up
this transformation when he discusses what the new liturgy would now
have to be about: "Where formerly I had been susceptible to a kind of
effortless transport from the modes of everyday life in church, now I was
surrounded by them, and what church would have to be about was the
nexus between the ordinary and the extraordinary."[67]

The Catholic world also communicates a host of particular values and
ways of interpreting reality, all encircling the idea that what you do in this
life, in this world, really matters. Fenton Johnson calls this Catholic world
view superstitious fatalism. When his lover Larry was still alive, the two
of them would read aloud every night, and Johnson was grateful to read a
long book: "So long as we were in the middle of a book, he wouldn't die.

The longer the book, the better."[68] In the Catholic imagination, one has the potential of controlling reality if one "behaves" the right way; yet one also knows the inevitability that something eventually will go wrong. In fact, Toby Johnson says he still experiences the feeling that the way God loves him is to foul up his plans.[69]

Richard Rodriguez constructs this Catholic fatalism on a compass of tragedy: "If I respond to the metaphor of spring, I nevertheless learned, years ago, from my Mexican father, from my Irish nuns, to count on winter."[70] This is why, according to Rodriguez, Catholics need the constancy and mediation of the church in their lives — an ongoing sense of the religious that is not about quick conversion but rather about God's sacramental intervention over time. As he says, "The Catholic part of me — ancient, cynical, feminine — is appalled by the nakedness, the humorlessness, the sweetness of evangelical conversion narratives."[71] Achieving salvation is about finding one's wholeness, and this is a lifetime process. There is something about being Catholic that takes the long view and recognizes the redemptive value of suffering. This piece of Catholic identity is particularly resonant for gay Catholics who feel alienated, and struggle for years to come to terms with their sexuality.

This sense of the long view — of history and memory — is part of what gives Catholic identity its persistent quality. Jim Bussen likens it to an ethnic identity and notes how disaffected Catholics usually just stop going to church rather than becoming something else.[72] Tom Kaun and Kevin Calegari say the same thing in the opposite way: "We are going to be Catholic no matter where we go, even if we join the Lutherans or Episcopalians."[73] Joe McGuire and Father Paul both echo the feelings among many of these gay Catholics that Catholicism is an integral part of their selves, as integral as their sexuality.[74] The rich material culture of Catholicism — the signs and symbols, smells and bells, rituals and sacraments — implanted something deep in their senses and memories.

"I Wanted to Be a Priest"

If I had to pick one phrase or sentence which popped up more frequently than any other in the course of reading these gay Catholic autobiographies, it would have to be, "I wanted to be a priest." Though it could not be said for all of them, enough of them felt this desire at some point in their lives that it deserves discussion. I can also think of no better illustration of the way gay and Catholic identities are fused in these life narratives. The isolation they feel around their sexual identity growing up makes them feel singled out by God. Gay Catholic boys sensing their sexual difference and being baffled by it see in the priesthood an opportunity to be respected while both inhabiting a mysterious world and not being married to a woman. In many ways it seems to answer a dilemma they are not quite able to articulate as boys. It also plugs into so many of the aspects of being gay I discussed in the previous chapter. James Heckman, for example, thought about joining the priesthood from third or fourth grade through high school, in part because priests were not supposed to have girlfriends. There was something intriguing and sexual about it: "I would sometimes have dreams about being with a bunch of guys in a monastery and not having any undergarments on underneath my cassock."[75] While some heterosexual Catholic boys want to be priests too, I do not think this theme would appear as regularly in their life stories, nor would all the reasons for their attraction be the same.[76] In any case, there is clearly something about the priesthood that resonates in a special way with emerging gay Catholic identity.

For a boy, being a priest means being in charge of a magical and important world. Patrick Horrigan remembers being fascinated by a large free-standing gold-papered wall that stood behind the altar of his hometown church, Sacred Heart, where he would eventually become an altar boy. It concealed the entrance to the sacristy and, in a telling bit of symbolism, Horrigan was always curious about "what went on behind that wall."[77] The first thing he wanted to be when he grew up was a priest. It may have been partially about curiosity; but as Horrigan narrates it, his desire to be a priest was wrapped up in ideas about "eternity, uphill struggles, self-sacrifice, and strong leadership."[78] José Zuniga became an altar boy at age eight, which made him feel closer to God. He enjoyed playing a role in the mystical and ancient traditions that were all so ominous to him. He too decided he wanted to be priest, but his military father scoffed at the idea: "He bought me my first pistol the day after I announced my intention."[79] Brian McNaught did not simply want to be a priest; he wanted to be a saint so he could be God's best friend:

> Believing a saint to be a "perfect person," I prayed daily, was obedient to my parents and teachers, never said "damn" or "hell," guarded the refrigerator between noon and 3 p.m. on Good Friday so no one would eat, built elaborate May altars for the Blessed Mother and said home "Masses" by tying a towel around my neck and passing out Necco wafers to my little sister and brother.[80]

I too wanted to be a priest when I was young — in the second grade to be exact. Like McNaught, I said home Masses on Sundays, but I wore a sheet around me and used Ritz crackers for communion. At these young ages, it is the enchantment of the Catholic world that draws boys in. For gay boys who are feeling different, but not yet sexual, the otherworldliness of the church is appealing. It is an alternative space where men wear "dresses" and are "queer" in comparison to other adult men. It is also a space in which being a good boy is not only perceived as normal, but is also expected.

In adolescence, the desire to be a priest becomes much more complicated as boys begin to feel sexual and to understand what the celibacy requirement means. For gay boys, it is even more confusing because they realize their emerging sexual identity is at odds with what the church says is normal. This is enough for some gay young men to abandon any thoughts of becoming a priest. For others, the celibacy requirement provides a potential excuse to avoid confronting their sexuality altogether. Of course, who actually becomes a priest depends upon a host of other practical concerns, and needs to be charted by generations. In the decades before Vatican II, it was almost a given that at least one child in every Catholic family would become a priest or join a religious order. Often, the fact that a sibling or aunt or uncle was a priest or nun was enough to inspire other young Catholics to pursue religious life. Being a priest (or monk or nun) was a noble calling — something of which to be proud — and it was also the path to a higher education at a time when Catholic families could not generally afford it. After Vatican II, the situation changed quickly as massive numbers of men left the priesthood in order to marry. In the following decades, fewer and fewer men went to seminary as becoming a priest came to be seen as more of an anomaly. With regard to the autobiographers who went to seminary in my study, some joined before Vatican II, some in the midst of it, and some at least a decade later. Even though they narrate a similar thread of feelings about the connections between their sexual identity and their call to be priests, it is important to keep in mind how different the connotations of joining the priesthood today are from fifty years ago.[81]

One obvious result of these shifts is a drop in the number of heterosexual priests — the ones who left to get married. That means a higher proportion of gay priests. Father Donald Cozzens, a former seminary rector, has discussed the disproportionately high percentage of gay men in the priesthood and especially among those presently studying in seminaries.[82] It is inherently difficult to pinpoint exact numbers of gay priests, either many decades ago or today, because of the difficulty in obtaining honest responses about priest sexual orientation. Closeted priests are unlikely to be counted because either they do not self-identify as gay or they fear the consequences if they are discovered. Surveys about the presence of gays in seminaries also reflect the particular perspectives of those being interviewed. For example, according to one recent survey of gay priests, those ordained before 1960 remember their seminary as having been 51 percent gay. Those ordained after 1981 put the number at 70 percent. These numbers may be inflated because they are likely including fellow priests whom they perceive as being gay, but who may not ever identify as such.[83] Even so, the most conservative estimates indicate the priesthood is at least 20 percent gay, and the percentage rises among younger priests. Regardless of the exact numbers, it is clear a sort of de facto gay subculture has existed across generations in the priesthood and now thrives even more intensely.[84] For Cozzens, this is one factor in a long list of "problems" the church must address with respect to the changing face of the priesthood. It is not that homosexual orientation is a problem in and of itself but rather that seminaries are not preparing priests well enough to deal with their sexuality in open and healthy ways. Cozzens also fears, rightly I think, that the expanding gay subculture within the ranks will alienate prospective heterosexual candidates.

In any case, the ever-increasing proportion of gay men in the priesthood is a reality deserving widespread discussion. Gay priests do have special gifts to offer the church that are developed largely through the experience of growing up gay. Jesuit Father James Martin considers some of these unique gifts, in response to Cozzens's findings, as a way of spiritualizing the phenomenon by acknowledging that God must be calling gay men to the priesthood for a reason. Martin highlights three particularly relevant aspects of gay experience, all of which I discussed in some way in the previous chapter: First, gay people know what it is like to suffer ridicule and rejection and may then be more sensitive to others who feel marginalized; second, gay people are often drawn inward and may develop a level of self-understanding that allows for a deeper spirituality; and third, the aesthetic and creative interests of gay men can be utilized in service to the liturgy and consequently enhance the liturgical reformation ignited with Vatican II.[85] Even though there is something very stereotypical about these "gay gifts," they are echoed in these autobiographies by gay priests themselves as they ponder the interplay of their gay and clerical identities. While the issue needs further thought and analysis, Martin deserves credit for asserting that gay priests have something positive to contribute to the church.

Given these positive contributions and the number of gay priests populating the clerical ranks, the intransigence of church leaders in refusing to reconsider the church's condemnation of gay relationships is disturbing. And the willingness of gay priests to tow the party line, upholding a system of teachings on sexuality they know does not adequately address the totality of gay experience, is indicative of a pervasive pathology. In rare and extreme cases, this pathology can lead to abuse, as it did for Kevin Killian. When Killian was sexually abused by members of a religious order, he observed a church hierarchy that preached self-denial even as its members indulged their desires: "Within the Church's apparently ascetic structure, the pursuit of pleasure has been more or less internalized. By and large, the pursuit (of violence, danger, beauty) is the structure."[86] For a while, Killian considered becoming a priest. He envied their privilege and entitlement. He saw a haven for queers, in which their love lives were forever shielded by the hierarchy that protected them: "I continue to see the Church as the house of Eros, a place of pleasure and fun, and I continue to regard men in religious costume as possible sex partners, yearning to break free. Such was my training, my ritual life."[87]

Let me be clear that most gay priests do not engage in sexual abuse. In fact, less than 2 percent of all American priests have been implicated in the recent revelations of clergy sexual abuse.[88] I am merely pointing out that gay priests directly participate in a structure and system of teachings that is not liberating for most gay people. I have already mentioned Mark Jordan's exceptional work about the homosexuality endemic to the clerical culture of the Catholic Church, and it is worth reiterating some of his points here. According to Jordan, the present power structure of the church provides a space for gay priests to engage in a culture of same-sex desire and affiliation, without the risks of identifying as gay, while also rewarding their silence with power. Church teachings in turn support this structure, resulting in the startling irony whereby any revision of doctrine that would make gay Catholic identification more visible and morally acceptable would rob gay priests of their hiding place. In other words, clerical culture relies on gay *in*visibility. This is why advocating for change in the realm of moral theology will only get us so far. As for numbers of gay priests, the exact percentage is beside the point:

> It doesn't much matter whether it is 5 percent or 25 percent or 50 percent. The construction and enforcement of rules of silence will operate at any of those levels, because the closet is a collaborative construction of gay and straight. . . . The recent increase in the perceived number of gay clergy has opened some closet doors, but it has locked others more securely.[89]

Jordan's analysis relies largely on his astute observations of Catholic clerical culture in general, and the parallels with gay culture he finds there. He exposes the "campiness" of the culture — the theatricality of liturgies, fanciful vestments, style wars, lifestyle excesses — all of which are stereotypically perceived as feminine when reflected in gay culture, but are "excused" when associated with priests. A wonderful example of this phenomenon, though not tied as directly to church imagery, is found in Fenton Johnson's autobiography. When he was growing up near the Trappist monastery of Our Lady of Gethsemane, in rural Kentucky, his family's lives became intertwined with those of the monks. The monks were fond of spending evenings at the Johnson home, having dinner, drinking, smoking, and talking late into the night. Brother A. was obviously the "performer" in the bunch:

Brother A. was fond of a fake grass skirt someone had sent my mother from Hawaii. When the moon was right and the whiskey flowing, he donned the skirt and some hot-pink plastic leis, then hoisted my mother to the tabletop and climbed up after. There she sang "Hard-hearted Hannah" ("the vamp of Savannah, G-A!"), while Brother A. swayed his hips and waved his hands in mock hula. Later he launched into Broadway tunes, warbling in falsetto with his arms thrown around one or more of his brethren.[90]

In most situations, Brother A.'s behavior would signify gay campiness in the extreme. Whether Brother A. was actually gay or not is irrelevant. Almost any other man engaging in such a drag performance would have been suspect. His membership in the clerical caste, however, "excused" his conduct and no insinuations were made about him. If it were today's world, with our heightened awareness of gay identity, Johnson's family might have been more "suspicious," but Jordan's point is that within the church, a certain campiness pervades the functions and roles fulfilled by priests. The priesthood provides a space where gay and Catholic identities can be performed simultaneously without being explicitly recognized.

This clerical climate simultaneously evokes and suppresses homosexuality; so it is not surprising young gay Catholic men might be drawn to it, especially if they feel conflicted about their sexuality. This theory is supported by the autobiographies in my study, in which a clear majority of these gay men wanted to become priests at some point in their lives. Some followed through and many went as far as seminary, but most of them at least toyed with the idea as boys and young men. Jordan, borrowing from John Shekleton, offers some insightful reasons why this is so:

Because they are promised an exchange of their anguished identity as outsiders for a respected and powerful identity as an insider. Because they want to remain in the beautiful, queer space of the liturgy. Because they are drawn to public celebration of suffering that redeems. Because they want to live in as gay a world as the Catholic church offers.[91]

Jordan's reasons represent the kind of allure to the priesthood that simmers at an almost subconscious level. The autobiographers articulate different kinds of reasons for wanting to be priests, usually more in line with James Martin's thoughts on the special gifts gay men have to offer. They consciously experience the desire as a "calling" to serve and help people in some way, which also gives them a sense of purpose. On some level, however, and more in line with Jordan, they are also drawn to find a space where their feelings of difference will not matter so much.

John McNeill dates his vocation to the priesthood from his time as a prisoner of war, when a slave laborer risked his own life to toss the starving young McNeill a potato. He saw the laborer make the sign of the cross, and McNeill interpreted it as a sign to be courageous and work against evil in the world.[92] Though this was a pivotal event in his discernment, he soon realized his vocation was also wrapped up in his gay identity:

> I was still ambivalent about my vocation, which was still based primarily in my fear that as a gay man the only way I could get to heaven was by denying and suppressing my sexuality and my desire for human love and my belief that the only way to accomplish that denial was to enter a religious order, which would provide the environment and the support for a life of celibacy that was possible and meaningful.[93]

In spite of his misgivings, he was ordained in the Jesuits in 1959, when he was thirty-four. Afterward, he felt depression instead of joy because he felt he was still going through the motions of religious life out of a fear of punishment. After some years of travel and his experience of a gay relationship, he ultimately realized complete sexual abstinence was for him "morally evil and psychologically destructive. Discernment of my own experience led me to the conclusion, after many years of struggle, that God was calling me to a ministry to gay and lesbian people but was not calling me to a life of celibacy."[94] McNeill soon met his life partner and tried to remain a Jesuit, but was finally dismissed for his strong and public challenges of church teaching on homosexuality.

McNeill wanted to remain a Jesuit because it was a core identity for him. Not surprisingly, this idea of priesthood as a central identity appears over and over again in the life texts of gay men who are still priests. These are the ones who are also most likely to have "known" they would be priests since they were very young, and who now consider their gay identity as a fundamental aspect of their priesthood. William Hart McNichols, another Jesuit, knew he would be a priest when he was five years old. He constructs his priesthood as something inseparable from his sense of self. It is a seal on his soul that cannot be shed, and being gay is an integral component of it.[95] Matthew Kelty states, "I wanted to be a priest and a monk since the time I knew what the words meant."[96] Kelty found the church and his religious training profoundly inadequate in terms of helping him come to terms with his gayness, so he did so on his own and now agrees with the church that gay men are called in a special way to celibacy. Richard John Cardarelli also knew from a young age that he wanted to be a priest and that he was different from other boys. He joined a conservative community so he could hide his gay identity, but he eventually found it suffocating and left. Becoming involved with Dignity "cured" him of his self-hatred, and he later returned to his religious order.[97] Brother Jonathan was marked early by his teacher nuns as the one in his grade school class who would have a vocation. Though he sensed his attraction to men at age five, he was long reluctant to come out, and remained closeted even when a close friend in his community came out to him. He later came to feel this blocking of his sexuality was blocking his entire emotional life. When he finally "owned" his sexuality, he felt his life and his ministry become whole:

> Sexuality enhanced my religious life, my personal spiritual journey, and also my work for the poor and oppressed. It made me sensitive to others' suffering in my community, to women's issues in church and society, and to the cry of all oppressed and marginalized people.[98]

This theme of gayness enhancing one's ministry recurs over and over again in the narratives of gay priests. Fr. T. Thompson feels being gay is almost revelatory: "Being gay in this culture and church can enable us to experience compassion. Being gay can be the threshold of the reign of God."[99] Father Aelred felt very naive when he entered the seminary and did not begin serious exploration of his sexuality until he was in his thirties. Though his first homogenital experience was with a fellow priest, he still felt like "the only homosexual clergyman in the world." One evening in a gay bar, he spied another priest with whom he had been secretly in love, and the two of them began talking. Before he knew it, and in a moment that confirms Jordan's thesis, he found himself in the company of several gay priests who were in the bar and joined in their conversation. Father Aelred soon found a lover and, with the support of Dignity, decided to remain a priest rather than choose between his priestly and sexual identities. He too feels his experience as a gay man enhances his sensitivity to the suffering of others and enriches his priestly vocation: "I have come to view my own sexual orientation as the source of many important vital traits that are making my ministry more sensitive and increasingly effective."[100]

Robert Arpin wanted to be priest from the time of his earliest memories, and by age five he too was playing priest and saying home Masses using Necco wafers. He associates his desire to be a priest with a need for respect and recognition.[101] Arpin never felt guilty about being both gay and priest because he experienced both as core identities and figured he could not cut himself in two. But it did make him wonder where he fit in terms of community: "So here I am in the middle, too gay for the Church and too Catholic for the gays."[102] When he learned he was HIV-positive, he also had to integrate that into the way he understood himself and his ministry. At the time, he was not certain how it would all fit together, "But I do

believe that God is calling me to use my sickness and my sexual orientation in some ministry to those who feel unwanted."[103] Arpin soon found
himself needed not only at Dignity but also in various care centers for
people with AIDS. One of the most poignant stories he narrates is about
his celebrating Mass with men in the hospital participating in drug trials.
When he spoke the words, "This is my body" and "This is my blood," the
power of those words in the context of what these men were undergoing
for the sake of people like him was overwhelming. For Arpin, it made him
realize the significance of his own vocation to the priesthood. He remembered the first time he celebrated Mass after his ordination when he felt
momentarily frozen: "I was gripped with fear because I realized for the
first time what being a priest meant. It was *my* body and *my* blood on the
line!"[104]

Arpin's words say a lot about the depth of priestly identity. His experience and that of the other gay priests I have profiled here indicate how
embedded are the components of being gay and being a Catholic priest in
the way they understand themselves. Their stories reveal how difficult it
is to unravel the complex clerical system, illuminated by Jordan, in which
these men are both protected and "hidden." The clerical culture provides
particular ways for them to be gay within the confines of the priesthood,
but it does so at the cost of maintaining a system of teachings that are
repressive for gay Catholics in general. Catholic scholars like me would
like to see gay priests band together and leave their active ministry, thus
depleting the ranks and forcing the church to reevaluate how it envisions
the priesthood; but I know this is a fantasy at this point in time. It ignores
some important things the life texts of gay priests reveal. Yes, they do reap
the dividends of priestly power by participating in the priestly caste of the
church, and I would challenge them to seriously examine the ethics and
hypocrisy of that aspect of the priesthood; but being a priest is also a core
identity for them. It is not just a job from which they can easily walk away,
even when their sexual identity is in conflict with their vocation. To make
matters worse, the church does not always deal fairly with those who do
resign.[105] Perhaps lay Catholics need to take the lead and find ways of
helping these men exercise their priesthood outside the official structure
of the church.

"Obscene Acts, Alone or with Others"

The hole I had dug in the sand—the sand itself having run through
the hourglass of several years—was not as dark as the confessional's
velvet gloom. If I felt at home there, it was because I was both reluctant believer and artful dodger. That is to say, I didn't want to "sin,"

but only to enjoy myself. A great part of the enjoyment was confessing the forbidden pleasures, because a great part of the pleasure lay
in the subsequent fall from grace.   —J. D. McClatchy, "My Fountain Pen"

Many of the autobiographers in my study are conscious of the way being
Catholic has given them a sense of the sacramental nature of the created
world.[106] They see a holy world in which God is revealed in bodies and
matter, even if church teachings on sexuality seem to mitigate against
this. David Plante writes about how being Catholic taught him an appreciation of the interconnectedness of body and soul, "and that we are in
the wholeness of our personalities what we are because we are both body
and soul."[107] For Plante, the body finds its fullest sensuality in the soul;
and the soul finds its fulfillment in the body, especially in the resurrected,
glorified, and entirely beautiful body we acquire at the end of the world.
Sexual desire then becomes part of this equation, especially in the context
of the basic Catholic teaching that sex is an expression of love for another
human being. Because of this, Plante trusts his body and his desire:

> If my sexual love for another was not sanctified by marriage, much
> less by heterosexuality, I never doubted, not for a second, that it was
> love, and even if I spent only one night with someone, what that
> person and I had exchanged over the night, in the wholeness of our
> love-making, was love. . . . I have always felt that in making love with
> a body in its wholeness, I was also making love with a soul. This idea
> fills me with the longing to make love, and this idea comes directly
> from my religion.[108]

For all Catholicism teaches about the dangers of the flesh, Plante and other
gay Catholics learned to listen for God in the created reality of the natural
world, which ultimately includes their bodies. This is why so many of
these writers have come to feel the natural law tradition is incomplete if
it does not take seriously the experience of gay people.

Sometimes it is participation in the very ordinariness of the world that
makes it redemptive. As a boy, James Morrison was so enamored with
his friend Craig that he went with him to his Baptist church and even
raised his hand when converts were being called forth, much to Craig's
excitement. After a nervous interview with the minister, however, Morrison knew he would never be a Baptist. He considered how much Craig
seemed sort of like a saint: "He was *in* the world, necessarily, but not *of*
it."[109] For himself, Morrison could not detach from the world. He realized
how comfortable he felt with his other friends who were not so concerned
about being "saved." The Catholic in him sensed that he needed to be a
part of this world in all its earthiness and vulgarity:

It had begun to seem to me that, in any case, the closer I came to exaltation, the further I was from God. Shooting the breeze with Kevin or Ronny, I felt I had come back to them after a long time away. There was something reassuring about their commitment to the known world....[110]

Part of this Catholic commitment to the known world involves the idea that one's actions in this world matter, that salvation is not just about *believing* but also about *doing*. As Morrison says to Craig a few days after the night of his "conversion" (and echoing Rodriguez's discomfort with instant salvation), "I don't think it happens that way, being saved. Like, you walk into a church and then all of a sudden you're suddenly saved.... Going to heaven depends on what you do. It depends on how you act."[111]

This focus on one's actions can be inspiring in terms of social justice and giving meaning to one's daily life, but it also encourages a greater consciousness of the ways one falls short. Many of these writers experience Catholic identity as an awareness of personal sinfulness — an awareness that, when taken to its extreme, can overwhelm any appreciation of one's self as good. This is especially true for young boys with emerging erotic desires. David Kopay remembers the intimidating feelings he had when he had to go to confession during puberty and confess that he had touched himself in "an impure way." One was supposed to be firmly resolved to change the sinful behavior in order to be forgiven, which made it all the more terrifying for the young Kopay. "I would say the words but I also knew I would do it again."[112] He then had to perform the penance prescribed by the priest. Doing the Stations of the Cross was the worst because he had to stare at Jesus suffering, all because he had touched himself "in an impure way." On one occasion of confessing this particular sin, the priest yelled at him through the confessional screen and ordered him to stay silent in his room for the rest of the night. Though the Kopays had friends for dinner that night, the young David stayed in his room and could not even explain to their guests why he had to do so. "In fact I was honestly frightened that I would be struck dead if I broke the penance, and convinced that I would suffer eternal damnation in hell as the priest had said I would." Of course, this all did nothing to curb Kopay's desire to masturbate; it just made him feel bad for it. "I learned a lot about fear and guilt through the church, and very little about compassion and love."[113]

During Fenton Johnson's single hour of sex education in the seventh grade, one of his classmates asked if jacking off was a mortal sin. Father Gettelfinger's uncomfortable nod confirmed Johnson's suspicion that "anything that felt this good must be really, really bad." Unlike Kopay, however, he could not imagine going to confession and admitting he masturbated. Not only had he "done the deed," but he had done it often, and he was constantly devising ways of prolonging and intensifying it. The thought of telling Fr. Gettelfinger in the confessional was for Johnson "as impossible as giving it up."[114] He simply resigned himself to the fact that he would have to live with this mortal sin on his soul. But he didn't feel bad about it as much as he felt angry and betrayed by the mixed messages of his religion. As with Plante, Catholicism had infused Johnson with the sense that God was revealed in the natural world — including the flesh — so the fear and shame around all things sexual felt like a discrepancy:

> This was a contradiction I could not sustain, between the frank sensuality of this most voluptuous of Western Christian traditions and its niggardly attitudes toward the body's rich and varied landscapes. Instinctively I knew that something was seriously amiss in this separation of body from soul, flesh from spirit, though I was unable to express this duality in words. I never went to confession again.[115]

Just as Johnson could not, as an adolescent, articulate the inconsistency and hypocrisy he intuitively sensed, most of the boys in these stores were unable to frame their feelings of shame and confusion as anything but their own problem. Feelings of guilt and personal sinfulness would then compound into the feeling that one is never good enough. Larry Ebmeier knew his same-sex desire did not match what the church said he should feel. When he fell in love with another young man, he was in constant turmoil about sinning. In his words, "I would go from masturbation to confession to masturbation to confession."[116] José Zuniga claims to have written his life story at least partially out of a sense of Catholic guilt and regret. Though he came out publicly as a decorated soldier in the army, and ultimately was discharged for doing so, he writes to talk about his mistakes along the way, and also because he fears "I may still not have done enough in this battle."[117] During one of his earliest sexual experiences with another man, he found himself plagued with thoughts of hell and damnation because of the Catholic prohibitions on sex.[118] When he was younger, he decided to masturbate and sin by himself, rather than risk the greater transgression of desecrating another person's body.[119] Tommi Avicolli Mecca also tried to resist those "near occasions of sin" he was supposed to avoid and which would lead to even worse sins. He writes, "My Catholic upbringing was always in direct conflict with my natural sexual urges." Even so, nature would sometimes win, and then confessing the sin only made him feel lonelier.[120]

Philip Gambone carried his "uptight interpretation of Catholicism" into his adulthood. Even with his first adult boyfriend, he was preoccupied with sorting sins into categories of mortal and venial, as all Catholics learned in the Baltimore Catechism.[121] The worst part of sinning was the feeling that one was disappointing God, and it seems even the youngest boy could upset God by "misusing his body." When Joseph Kramer was a very little boy (he says age three), he already liked the feeling of putting his hands in his underwear and rubbing; but his mother quickly pointed out the gravity of this kind of behavior: "You shouldn't be doing that. God doesn't like when you touch yourself."[122] Thus, a good Catholic boy already struggling with the sinfulness of masturbation also had to struggle with the thought that his behavior was alienating God. For a gay Catholic boy, the feeling of alienation would be magnified; his "abnormal" desires would make his behavior even more disappointing for God. When Richard John Cardarelli first admitted to himself he was probably gay, he felt he had let God down. This in itself made him feel completely unlovable. He felt terrible and internalized the shame: "I hate myself, and if anyone ever finds out, they will hate me, too. *O God, forgive me!*"[123]

Andrew Holleran struggles with his own sinful perception of himself throughout his life writings. For Holleran, growing up Catholic "meant refining what may have been an already intrinsic sense of sin":

> Faced with the list of sins in my missal, as I examined my conscience before Confession, I became a connoisseur of the evil that lurks behind our every act, of the duplicity, the obfuscation with which we hide our true natures. . . . Growing up Catholic meant being intoxicated with the sense of one's own evil.[124]

As has already been indicated, the "cure" for one's sinfulness was the sacrament of Confession. Holleran writes of his satisfaction with this sacrament as a child. Sitting next to the votive candles in the church and going through the list of sins in the "examination of conscience" in his missalette was a way of peeling away the layers of his soul. It made him feel special, devoted, and clean. I remember my own similar encounters with this sacrament when I was growing up. Our parish pastor was far too intimidating, so I would always go to the associate, Fr. Tevington. He made me feel I had made a perfect act of contrition, and I always left with the feeling that my soul was again a clean slate. I shared Holleran's trepidation in that moment: we both left almost afraid to venture into the world again. The commission of new sins was inevitable.

The onset of puberty changed the dynamics of Confession for Holleran. Unlike David Plante, Holleran always felt ashamed of his body, especially his sexual organs, and this shame was magnified when his sexuality was awakened. As for all Catholics, puberty also presented more occasions for sin. Holleran learned to think of his sins as a betrayal of Christ and the reason He had to be crucified:

> This sense of betrayal, of Sin, meant that when puberty arrived in the life of a Catholic idealist and the body asserted itself in a way that

nothing in Catholicism had prepared you for, that single phrase on the pages of the missalette — "obscene acts, alone or with others" — was literally breath-taking, heart-constricting, to the child who heard the screen slide open and knew he was about to say these words to a priest. "Alone" meant you had jerked off in the bathroom. "With others" meant you'd compared penises with the boy next door (the son of a Protestant minister, in my case). Either one was terrifying; a new order of guilt — so great one started to postpone, and fear, a sacrament which till then had been eagerly sought.[125]

Slowly but surely, Holleran just stopped going to Confession and his religious fervor dissipated as he became an adult and really explored his sexual identity. By the time he finally went to bed with another man at the age of twenty-six, the lateness of which he attributes to his Catholic upbringing, he thought he had left his Catholic identity behind him; but as with most of these writers, he found it was not so simple. He found himself "unwilling to cease the internal dialogue between my Catholic self and daily life":[126] "It was one thing to say, reasonably, that religion was only superstition: it was another to extinguish the self that had spent so many warm, happy hours in church preparing for Confession."[127]

I have already recounted Holleran's story of the first time he spent the night with another man and subsequently found himself in the shower washing his mouth out with soap the next morning. As told in his coming out narrative, it was about the dynamic of acceptance and resistance involved in coming to terms with gay identity. In his essay on Catholic identity, however, the same story has a slightly different resonance. He refers to his washing action as a "soapy purification of the Temple of the Holy Ghost," which was also his "first glimpse of the fact that we never really leave Catholicism behind."[128] The story thus becomes emblematic of the push and pull of Catholic identity, and a striking representation of the way sexual and religious identities are fused. After his mouth-washing, Holleran tried celibacy for about a year; but an unbearable loneliness pushed him to question the church's recommendation for gay people. This marked the beginning of a transformation in the way he experienced his Catholic identity:

> If God is Love, and sex is love, then sex between two people of the same gender can only be looked upon benignly by God. The real sin would be to live...without ever having this contact with another human being, and the relief from isolation it provides. I took my mantra from St. Augustine — "Love, and do as you will" — and distinguished between a human and a divine church; made my own list of sins; and became in the process what is known as a cafeteria Catholic.[129]

With this passage, Holleran ends up in a similar place as Plante in find-ing a core link between sex and God. Whereas Holleran ultimately remains ambivalent about the church and even the existence of God, Plante finally becomes an atheist; yet both maintain a Catholic identity and fill their fiction with Catholic imagery. Holleran, for example, still takes the sacra-mental system so seriously that he expresses reluctance to receive Holy Communion without being in a confessed state of grace.[130] And although Plante describes himself as an atheist, he still calls himself a Catholic writer. Being a Catholic inculcated in him a longing to be with God in eternity. "But," he says, "I think this longing is greater than my believ-ing or not."[131] Plante also says his book *The Annunciation* represents "a deepening of my devotion to my native religion," and even though his book *The Catholic* has the "longest sex scene in literature," he says it is really about being Catholic.[132] As for so many of these autobiographers, the gay and Catholic identities are so entangled, it is difficult to separate the two. Perhaps Plante's conflicted position is best understood in relation to something Dan, the protagonist in *The Catholic*, hears from a voice in his head: "It doesn't matter now if you believe or not, your beliefs are with you whether you want them or not."[133]

Shifting Orbits:
Deconversion and the Revision of Catholic Identity

> It was only when I had finally begun to sin in ways I couldn't think how to disguise that I lost my faith in both religion and language.
> Of course, language had been my religion all along, and my faith in its powers of salvation was only temporarily shaken. In the end, it was merely the heavy burden of the Church's authority that I had once and for all to shrug off.   —J. D. McClatchy, "My Fountain Pen"

Holleran and Plante seem to affirm the "Once a Catholic, always a Catho-lic" adage, yet their stories demonstrate this is not a static effect. Although Catholic identity remains persistent in their self-definitions, their rela-tionship to Catholicism is dynamic. When a gay Catholic comes to terms with his sexual identity, he inevitably comes to a new set of terms with his religious identity. His relationship to Catholicism and his construction of Catholic identity are tested and reassembled. John Barbour calls this process "deconversion." Barbour recognizes that the standard trajectory for traditional autobiography is the conversion narrative in the pattern of St. Augustine and so many autobiographies that have followed. But every conversion is a result of some kind of deconversion, or loss of faith in something prior. This is especially true for religious identity when a given religious system fails to adequately address the questions arising in the life that is narrated. Often, issues related to gender and sexuality provide the impetus for the deconversion. Barbour focuses primarily on women's life writings in his analysis of gender and deconversion,[134] but he acknowledges that men's life stories can also reflect these concerns. Augustine himself is a case in point: his dissatisfaction with Manicheism and other philosophies "was based partly on their failure to help him understand his anxieties about his sexual life."[135]

The gay Catholic autobiographies I study are prime examples of Barbour's deconversion theory. While Barbour sees his women autobiographers as "revisionists or reformers of traditional Christian assumptions about women," I view my autobiographers in a similar manner. All of these gay Catholics, in their own ways, are reformers of traditional Catholic assumptions about gay men. "In each [of their narratives], an experience of the loss of faith is central to the autobiographer's portrayal of [his] spiritual journey and demonstrates the inadequacy of some traditional Christian attitude, belief, or interpretation of a symbol."[136] For most, the "loss of faith" is not wholesale; rather, it is wrapped up in a complicated dialectic of embrace and abandonment in which repressive aspects of the institutional church are deconstructed. This has already been demonstrated in the texts by Holleran and Plante. The deconversion process is further complicated by the interplay of the doctrinal/ideological aspects of Catholicism with the cultural/"passed on" dimension. It is not simply a matter of remaining Catholic in an ethnic sense and discarding troublesome teachings. As I have been claiming throughout this chapter, Catholic identity involves a complex mixture of doctrines, practices, perspectives, and traditions, all of which are both "taught" in a direct way and "learned" more subtly. As these autobiographers come to terms with the meaning of their sexual identity through life experience and rational discernment, their religious self-understanding inevitably readjusts. They shift the position of their orbit on the Catholic axis. Their autobiographies recount and play out this readjustment, but it is never a finished story.

Rafael Campo uses part of his autobiography to discuss his own "fall from grace," as the church would view his relationship with Catholicism. Campo frames it as a sort of conflicted mutual abandonment. After feeling so comforted and accepted by the church in his childhood, he soon realized his gay identity seemingly placed him outside the community of the redeemed: "I was an abomination to the same God they said had created me, and whose forgiveness at the same time was the only hope for my salvation."[137] This was especially painful and confusing for Campo because he felt condemned for something he never chose, for the part of himself the church called "sin." "Of course, I remembered learning about other so-called sins as a child in Sunday school; they seemed carefully choreographed and intentionally committed, in contrast to the way my heart spontaneously quickened and lurched with a music my teachers said was abhorrent and unnatural."[138] What the church labeled a sin was an instinctive and joyous feeling within Campo, a feeling that would define his loving relationships with others: an identity. Campo was angry at the ironic situation created by church teachings in which sexual acts of any kind could be confessed and forgiven, but if he chose to live in a committed relationship with another man, he would remain separated from the very God who was supposed to be a God of love: "Clearly this horrible benefaction from my creator was to be my test in this life, my sexy crown of sharp thorns to wear."[139]

Gradually, Campo drifted away, and the church did nothing to stop him from straying. He was aware of the pronouncements coming from Rome that seemed designed to push gay people like him farther away. He saw no other recourse but to acquiesce to his exclusion, but this meant giving up another integral piece of himself, his Catholic identity:

> As I gradually relinquished what had been one of the greatest comforts in my life, one of the first things I forfeited was my capacity for believing in miracles. I was just sixteen years old. One day, with hardly a hesitation, I gave to my sister the shiny gold crucifix I had always worn faithfully around my neck. It felt like giving away a part of my body, like a heart valve or an eyelid or a small muscle in my hand.[140]

As so many of these autobiographers discover, shedding the Catholic identity from their selves is not so easy. There is always a part of Campo that clings to the Catholic, the part of him that gets angry when someone assumes he is a Catholic and defensive when someone speaks of Catholics with derision in their voice. When he was still calling himself a Catholic, Campo felt the ambivalence in the wholeness of himself, body and soul: "A queer still desiring and perhaps even needing some form of a relationship with God, I bitterly embodied as deep a schism as any in the Catholic Church's long divisive and blood-soaked history."[141] He would ultimately claim a space for himself "somewhere between what might be called atheism and secular humanism," formalizing in language his loss of faith in the church; yet in his text, he still associates aspects of himself with being Catholic, such as feelings of guilt and his respect for the mysterious workings of the human body and its ability to heal itself.

Philip Gambone writes of his long journey to find and claim a spiritual space that would fit his sense of self, all the while feeling the pull of his Catholic identity. He grew up with a typical letter-of-the-law Catholicism, in which his family always fulfilled the Sunday obligation. As is also typical for these autobiographers, Gambone felt an inner dissonance when he reached puberty. By the time he was twelve, he had added "impure thoughts and actions" to his list of weekly sins in the confessional. In college in the 1960s, he tried to live by the rules and even spent time with students who were affiliated with the ultraconservative Catholic group Opus Dei. Gambone realizes, in retrospect, his attraction to Opus Dei "had as much to do with the physical attractiveness of several of its members . . . as it did their theology." It was not helping him be a better Catholic: "By the time of Bobby Kennedy's assassination, I had driven myself crazy with ascetic practices — praying the rosary with the Opus Dei boys, going to mass, refraining from masturbation — yet none of these things had put a stop to the sexual urges that kept churning within me."[142] When he finally had a fulfilling sexual experience with another man after his second year at Harvard, his journey "away" from Catholicism began.

For a time, in the 1970s, Gambone tried the Episcopal Church because his boyfriend was Episcopalian. "I did not think of myself as leaving the Church but only of entering into a different (only *slightly* different, I reminded myself) 'communion' — the Anglican communion."[143] When he moved and became involved with his second lover, he began to attend a liturgically conservative Anglo-Catholic parish in Boston with a large gay population. His eventual drifting away from that church along with his drifting away from that lover led him to try a series of Catholic parishes, including Dignity; but by the end of the 1980s, he was fed up with the internal struggles and debates of Catholicism and drifted away once again. He tried a Unitarian-Universalist meeting house in Provincetown for a time, but now considers himself "free-floating." Even so, he still feels the push and pull of Catholicism within him:

> I want to be rigorously unsentimental about this. I want to say that my nostalgia for a sacramental religion is just that, a piece of nostalgia that I must get big enough to overcome. I want to say that the Church as I know it today — the Church of papal encyclicals against homosexuality, the Church of an all-male celibate clergy, the Church in whose name all manner of oppression and intolerance continues to be practiced — that that Church is an irrelevancy in my life. I want to say that I wish it a swift death.
>   And yet . . .[144]

Gambone is wrestling here with the dialectic of embrace and resistance that is so much a part of the gay-and-Catholic identities of these autobiographers. His "And yet . . ." is his acknowledgment that his journey of deconversion is not clear cut. There is something in him — that Catholic thing — that stays with him in spite of his intellectual objections. As he comments after his sojourn with the Unitarians, he is drawn by the "mystery" of Catholicism: "Yes, I missed that sense of mystery — that sense of the universe as a place that cannot be taken at face value — which seems to be at the heart of what is best in Catholicism."[145]

Like Gambone, Fenton Johnson explored other religions in his spiritual search for a place to fit. He considered atheism, but soon realized he had been "fated" for faith. Though he was attracted to the "easy alliance between democracy and theology" he found in the Protestant churches he visited, he left those Protestant services dissatisfied with their lack of primal mystery: "These services bore the imprints of hands of remembered generations, whereas the services of my childhood church had been shaped by hands outside of memory, embracing and incorporating the ancient rites along with their gods and goddesses of mountains and plains, skies and seas."[146] Johnson knew he belonged in the world of Catholicism, where the liturgies conveyed a connection to an enduring community that seemed to transcend time. "Those collective celebrations of faith were a powerful and binding magic: to have known them in the flesh means never to leave them entirely behind."[147] What he felt in his body, however, was not affirmed by the proverbial "keepers" of the tradition. Though he carried his Catholic identity in his flesh, he did not feel at home in the institution: " ... I'm a gay man and the Catholic Church has made it clear it has no place for me."[148] Feeling alienated from the church for being gay, yet valuing the Catholic tradition, he spent years feeling angry — so much so that he lost his impulse toward spiritual expression.

Johnson devotes his most recent life text to finding his way through this anger and back to faith — a narration of deconversion and reconversion. The boy who had once imagined the Virgin Mary might appear to him in the Kentucky hills[149] became an adult whose heart pounded with rage when he expected to make the sign of the cross. He still felt fated for faith, but it had been blocked by the institution and it seemed to elude him: "Why don't I have it, and is it possible, this late in the game, that I might acquire some?"[150] In his search, he gives himself over to the disciplines of monastic life by visiting and studying at both a Zen Buddhist monastery and the Trappist monastery near his childhood home. "What would be required of me to form an identity from some place other than my wounds? This was the scary, liberating question arising from zazen."[151] He learns to look inside himself and embrace the faith lessons already learned from his marginalization as a gay man:

My journey among the monks...was bringing me to understand that for me the wellspring of faith resides in the source of my otherness, my homosexuality — the condition that led me, or rather *forced* me, to seize my destiny and determine my own values, even as it taught me to respect the given, those aspects of life over which I had little or no control.[152]

Framing his journey in this way allows Johnson to shift his focus away from the death-dealing institutional church and to examine the inner "demons" that had maintained their white-knuckled grip on his wounds. By the end of his time at the monastery, he came to understand the sign of the cross as a gesture of community in suffering. He writes about that pivotal moment with the same kind of ambivalence expressed by Gambone: "On this my last evening of this stay among the monks, I signed myself a Christian. (*How hard it is for me even now, years later, to write those words.*)"[153] Like Gambone's deconversion, Johnson's "reconversion" is inevitably conflicted.

Richard Rodriguez understands the push and pull of Catholicism, but he remains devoutly Catholic because he senses something at the heart of Catholicism that resonates with his experience of being gay. Though he says he was born a Catholic and embraced it in his childhood without question, he later chose to be Catholic: "I do not wish to live beyond a crucifix. The crucifix does not represent guilt to me, but love."[154] He empathizes with those who "wish to be quit of the church," especially in light of bishops who seemingly hope to "rescue" gay people. Yet he feels a familial bond with these same bishops, rooted in his gay identity: "That which is homosexual in me most trusts the durability of this nonblood lineage. *Trees and their gracious silence.* Though I scorn them sometimes too and I ask forgiveness for my scorn. For none of us has made flesh."[155] Even so, Rodriguez experiences the dialectic of embrace and resistance that holds gay Catholic identity together. When he awakens in the middle of the night with his lover breathing at his side, he knows this breath is what sustains him. He feels angry the church would have him doubt that this is love:

> I turn the pillow to its cool side. Then rage fills me, against the cubist necessity of having to arrange myself comically against orthodoxy, against having to wonder if I will offend, against theology that devises that my feeling for him, more than for myself, is a vanity.[156]

In spite of his anger, Rodriguez lives at the crux of this tension. He calls it his "brown paradox," which he configures in the spirit of Walt Whitman as being brown in a deceptively black-and-white world: "*Of every hue and caste am I.*"[157] His gay Catholic identity, like his ethnic identity, is constructed upon the "impurity" that results when conflicting positions collide. Even though the church tells him his love is wrong and asks that he segment himself like a cubist drawing, it is also the church that taught him how to love in the first place. Ironically, it is the Catholic within him that enables him to trust the love he feels lying next to his lover in bed.

This irony is part of what propelled Peter Krask to enter a monastery just six weeks after spending his first night with a man. He went there for a three-month quest to figure himself out and to explore his vocation. True to the pattern of so many good gay Catholic boys, it did not surprise anyone in his family that he would go and that he might someday join a religious order. Of course, he had not planned on falling in love just before going, but this would also be the catalyst for his own deconversion. One morning, while watching the monks chanting in prayer, with his mind on the man he had left behind, Krask realized he believed so little of what they were singing. He even began to look at some of the monks sexually and developed a crush on one of them. When he finally got up the nerve to tell one of the monks he was gay, the monk did not judge him for it. Krask was able to vent the frustration he had been holding for so long about being gay and trying to be a good Catholic: "Being gay is this sick cosmic joke. How could God be so cruel? That's what makes me the angriest. How unbelievably cruel. Bolt a starving person in a chair and place a plate in front of him. Just out of reach."[158] A few days later, alone in the chapel and feeling the weight of his inner conflict, he stopped fighting himself: "And then the word came from my mouth. Alone, on my knees and terrified, I said yes. Yes to everything. To all of it."[159] All at once, Krask felt weightless. Although accepting his gay identity would mean not living up to his image as the perfect Catholic boy, he would finally be embracing that part of himself he had resisted for so long.

After David Kopay spent eighteen months in the seminary trying to live by the rules, he decided, "I'd had enough of the life." This was only the beginning of his complete break with church. As much as he tried to change it or deny it, he believed he was naturally attracted to other men and that sexual love was a good thing, not a sin. For Kopay, it was a rational and seemingly uncomplicated decision: "The Church couldn't accept me in my natural state so I could no longer accept the church."[160] The church had also caused a rift between Kopay and his parents, who accepted the teachings on homosexuality without question. Kopay felt like Isaac, whose father Abraham was willing to kill him in order to obey God's commands.[161] The church came to represent a God who would create him as a gay man and then sacrifice him for it.

For Kevin Killian, who had been sexually abused in his Catholic boys' high school,[162] his decision to break with the church was also rather uncomplicated. He says it was because of its policies on abortion, women's rights, and gay rights; but he had also been used by the church and found he could neither fight nor hide in its monolithic structure: "I tried to talk to It, but It just sat there, a big unresponsive sack of white sugar. So good-bye." At the same time, something inside him longs for and still pursues the bridging of human and divine that is at the heart of Catholicism: "And yet I suppose I'm a far better Catholic now than then. I dream of this God who took on clothes of man and then stepped forward to strip them off at the moment of humiliation."[163] Killian knows first hand what it is like to suffer degradation from his experience being sexually abused. Like Jesus, he was stripped both literally and figuratively of his pride. His identification with the suffering God-made-human resonates in the core of his Catholic identity. But it is not enough. Clearly wounded by his experience with his Franciscan teachers, Killian has lost faith not only in the institutional church but also in the goodness of human love. "I try to get closer to Christ through work. I tried love for a long time, but it only lengthened the distance between Him and me."[164]

Brian McNaught almost heroically resisted his deconversion. His life writings are part of what was once his larger life project of being a gay Catholic activist. He even spent twenty-four days fasting as a way of calling attention to the church's problematic teachings on homosexuality. He first talks about the old Brian, who spent "many, many years in the confessional feeling guilty about being a homosexual."[165] Later, he came to accept that part of himself as God-given and committed himself to helping gay Catholics recognize their self-worth. His life texts, however, reveal the emotional toll this took on him and his relationship to the church. In April 1979, he was unabashedly proclaiming his devotion to the church in spite of its hurtful teachings: "Lest anyone be confused, I love the Church."[166] Within a year, his writing reflects an overwhelming frustration and anger, due to the church's insistence on forbidding him to be himself, like a parent who secretly beats her child: "Today my pain is stronger than my devotion. Today I can't find the strength to defend [the Church] against the curses of the neighbors and relatives who know. Today I fear I will stand rigid and scream 'I hate the Church! I hate it! I hate it!'"[167] McNaught never again proclaims his love of the church; but he does settle into a revised relationship with the church, somewhere between love and hate, in which he rewards himself for his years of struggle and constancy. This is most tellingly revealed in a letter he wrote a year later designed to be read after his death by his partner Ray:

> If the Church should decide to begin canonization proceedings, don't discourage them! When they start looking for miracles, tell them I grew to my full potential. There is no greater miracle for a gay person today. Tell them, too, that I kept the Faith, which is also no small task. Finally (because they always look for three), tell them how we loved each other selflessly.[168]

McNaught demonstrates how "keeping the faith" for a gay Catholic necessarily involves a parallel loss of faith in the institutional church. The Catholic world may remain an enchanted place in which to dwell, but the enchantment is stripped of illusion. The deconversion is focused primarily on the "keepers" of that world, whose rigid rules and unidimensional view

of sexuality do not make sense in the lives of gay Catholics. For Fenton
Johnson, the task involves a reclamation of the spiritual legacy by those
who have been marginalized by it:

> I have been unable to use traditional language to describe my experi-
> ences of the sublime because I associated that language with a world
> that had failed me. But the fault lies not in the words but in the
> institutions that abused them. My task — the task of all seekers —
> is to find a way to reclaim the language of the spiritual life.[169]

For several of these autobiographers, Dignity empowers them to reclaim
the language of spiritual life. Dignity represents the kind of revision of
Catholic identity that provides a path for gay Catholics to both "keep the
faith" and be true to themselves. It could be argued that in the post–
Vatican II church, Dignity has made a fully gay and Catholic identity
possible. I have already mentioned the role Dignity played in the lives of
some gay priests. For other gay Catholics, Dignity is the space in which the
deconversion narrative is transformed into a narrative of recommitment,
after their relationship to the church hierarchy is revised.

The only way this kind of recommitment is possible is through an acceptance of the fact that the church hierarchy is composed of men who
are capable of making errors. In this model, these men get so caught up in
wanting the church to appear free of error that they seem to forget they are
dealing with a living and growing church. Tony Laveccia says, "My gripe
with the institutional church is that they are not interested in gay people
as people, but more concerned in upholding rules and regulations."[170] For
Gerald Allen, the problem is that church leaders are out of touch with
the realities of the people they are supposed to be serving: "Those who
are making these decisions are old men who are not married. They do
not have families or pay mortgages. There seems to be a real gulf between
them and where the people are."[171] Sometimes, seeing the hierarchy for
what it is creates too much cognitive dissonance so that any real recommitment to the church is impossible. William G. Storey spent years in
close association with church leaders during his long tenure as a professor
of liturgy and church history at the University of Notre Dame. He calls the
Roman system "false and pernicious" and "the antithesis of the Gospel."
He refuses to be associated with it any longer.[172]

The autobiographers who remain committed to the church in their life
texts find a way of separating the church from its institutional hierarchy.
Even Richard Rodriguez, who finds a certain amount of comfort and stability in the historical lineage of the institutional church, knows the dangers
posed by men who "presume to divine, to enforce, to protectively wear
the will of God."[173] After reflecting upon his own ambivalent relationship

with church leaders, Rodriguez turns to consider the perpetrators of September 11, 2001. He characterizes them as men of "certainty," who were waging a war against "impurity" — men who saw things in black-and-white, rather than brown — in the name of God.[174] Though Rodriguez does not directly draw the analogy, the same could be said of church leaders who maintain a rigid and singular position on homosexuality. They want pure boundaries for sexuality. They resist the "brown." They fear the "impurity" represented by gay Catholics. Yet many gay Catholics continue to keep the faith, and the Catholic tradition goes on despite the human beings who are its administrators. Jim Revak puts it this way:

> My basic feeling is that I am part of the Catholic tradition, and I have just as much right to call myself Catholic as a Pope, a Cardinal, or a Bishop does. . . . I live with the fact that there is a hierarchy that doesn't particularly like me as a gay person.[175]

Dignity was the first group to offer a space for being the kind of gay Catholic described above. By providing liturgies and sacraments — the material culture of Catholicism — in an environment that is openly affirming of gay identity, Dignity salvages the Catholic identity of many of these autobiographers. Tony Laveccia says Dignity has been his salvation.[176] Dignity provided Masses and prayer vigils for Tom McLaughlin when his lover was dying of complications related to AIDS.[177]

Of course, Dignity cannot accommodate all gay Catholics because not all of them want to worship in a separate space; nor is that the answer to the problem of the church's inadequate teachings with regard to homosexuality. Quite simply, the church needs to listen to the life experiences of gay Catholics and develop teachings on sexuality that make sense to them and respect their subjectivity. Their life texts reveal deeply ingrained and formative Catholic identities. Though Catholic identity is culturally constructed and informed, it feels for many of these autobiographers just as natural and essential as their (also constructed) sexuality feels.[178] Their revised versions of what it means to be Catholic also demonstrate the multiplicity and possibilities of Catholic identity, yet I am writing this book at a time when church leaders are increasingly concerned with tightening and policing what defines a Catholic. To pick up on the metaphor I was using at the end of the previous chapter, the church and gay Catholics seem to be seeking different landscapes. As American Catholics move increasingly from cities to suburbs, gay Catholics are seeking spaces for themselves in cities. Is this a literal representation of the reality that gay Catholics and the church seem to be moving in opposite directions?

Being gay and being Catholic are both deeply embedded identities in the lives of these autobiographers. It is a tragedy when gay Catholics are made to feel they have to choose between these two core identities. Jon

Soucy expresses this dilemma succinctly when he remembers his days as a conservative "defender of the faith" while a student at Georgetown University: "I just wish I'd spent less time saving Georgetown's Catholic identity and more time trying to come to terms with my own identity as a gay man."[179] When Catholic identity is displaced, revised, or rejected, it speaks volumes about the deficiency of church teachings on sexuality. Given the strength of the Catholic "thing" in these lives, consider how many of them would be committed and practicing Catholics today if church teaching took their subjectivity seriously. Their involvement and allegiance could only be a boon. Instead, the church insists on bifurcating their personhood by maintaining impossible dualisms. Church teaching falsely maintains a clean separation between sexual orientation and sexual behavior. In the realms of sexual and religious identity, however, it is not so easy to untangle being from doing, act from actor. At face value, this may seem possible; but gay Catholic autobiographies demonstrate how illusory such a separation really is.

Chapter 4

"Homosexual Acts"

> The main source of my fear was this: Each time we made love I took from him a little more of his self, and gave in return a little more of my self, binding us together a little more closely. We were becoming married, in fact if not before the law; we were becoming one instead of two.... Each time we made love I gave more of myself to him and took more in return and so enlarged my heart, made it bigger and stronger (like any muscle, the heart grows with exercise). But as we grew more a part of each other, I grew more terrified that when he died, he would take some large part of me with him and that I would fall into the hole he left behind, whose bottom (if it existed) I could not yet begin to fathom. —Fenton Johnson, *Geography of the Heart*

The dialectic of embrace and renunciation that is so much a part of gay Catholic identity as revealed in the previous two chapters is mirrored in the official teachings of the church. The same church telling gay people they are to be accepted with sensitivity, compassion, and respect, simultaneously tells them their sexual orientation is objectively disordered. True, official teaching distinguishes between the person and their sexual expression, but this distinction does not make sense in light of the way the gay men I profile here narrate their sexuality. As my analysis of their life texts reveals, sexuality is such an integral part of their human personhood, it becomes a piece of identity. While this is enhanced by the current historical context in which sexual identities are especially available and viable, this does not make their experience of gay identity any less valid. All identities, including Catholic identity, are culturally conditioned and socially and historically contingent. Indeed, in many ways it is easier to define and discuss gay identity today than it is to pin down Catholic identity, as my analysis also reveals. In any case, gay identity is much too complicated, multivalent, and wrapped up in other identity pieces for it to be summarily dismissed as disordered. Saying it is *objectively* disordered compounds the problem because it presumes sexuality can be evaluated outside of the particular context of persons and their relationships. On some level, of course, church leaders realize this and try to have it both ways. The result is the present bifurcation of church teachings into moral and pastoral rhetorics which attempt to both respect and condemn gay identity.

One troubling ramification of this bifurcation problem is the separation of persons from their acts. In a narrow sense, such a separation is understandable. When a person performs a particular action, it does not necessarily alter who he/she is. A person is not the same as his/her actions. The church rightly recognizes this with respect to human sins, which are construed as aberrations in the course of who we are and what we are supposed to do. This clean separation, however, becomes quite messy when applied to sexuality and sexual identity, which encompasses both being and doing. When these autobiographers discuss being gay, they relate it to a range of feelings, perspectives, *and* behaviors that are deeply interconnected. The same can even be said for the way they talk about Catholic identity. It too is related in these narratives to a host of interwoven perceptions, attitudes, and activities that are separable only on the most simplistic and deceivingly obvious levels. These sexual and religious identities do not inhere in a vacuum, apart from one's actions and relationships.

The church says gay people should be treated with friendship and justice, even as it says homosexual acts are intrinsically evil — love the "sinner"; hate the "sin." In other words, you can be a homosexual as long as you do not act like one. But what does it mean to perform a homosexual act? What *is* a homosexual act? Church officials may think the terminology is obvious, but one must wonder if they are all on the same page in their definitions. Are they thinking only of genital activity or any kind of intimate, physical contact between two people of the same gender? The term can be nebulous. My point, however, is not to urge the church to codify what constitutes a homosexual act (though I have no doubt there are scholars in the Vatican ready and eager to do so) but rather to demand contextualization of the concept. Homosexual acts, like all sexual acts, are always performed in the context of other life experiences and relationships. They cannot be fully evaluated in isolation, as if these acts are free-floating and disconnected from their actors and their complex lives. This is not a foreign idea in Catholic moral theology for actions the church finds problematic in some way. "Just war theory" was developed in order to contextualize the "problem" of war and killing in Christian ethics, and a range of opinion on the subject has been expressed throughout Christian history. Acts must be appraised in relation to actors and their life situations.[1]

One might object that it is impossible to achieve ethical clarity without focusing on acts; that juridical discussions and decisions must be centered on acts in order to achieve a sense of fairness and impartiality; that even personal meanings, motives, and decisions always relate to and result in actions. Of course, acts matter in the realm of sexual ethics, but they are only one piece of the equation, and the church errs when the focus on acts shrouds other mitigating factors. One might contend the church does consider both act and actor when it considers the genders of those involved in a sexual act, but this is not really the case. When the church condemns same-gender sexual acts, it does not care about the persons who inhabit the bodies involved. It is only interested in the way these bodies are anatomically sexed as male or female. It is not even accurate to say the church considers "gender" because that word implies a social meaning layered on the body. In the church's assessment of homosexual acts, homosexual persons are effectively obliterated, no matter how much the pastoral rhetoric tries to gloss it over. At least for heterosexual persons, the church makes some space for the acceptability of their sexual acts by contextualizing them in personal situations. Here too, however, church leaders fail to take seriously the full range of heterosexual lived experience.[2]

Part of the problem which prevents the church from seeing alternative ways of developing sexual ethics is the persistence of procreationism in Catholic moral theology. Procreationism is the assumption that sex is naturally oriented toward creation of human life. Christine Gudorf spells out some of the ways this assumption is manifested in our society. The first is the common view that penile-vaginal intercourse is *the* sexual act. Heterosexual coitus is "real sex" because it is procreative; all other sexual acts are either perversions to be avoided or foreplay. This attitude then leads to the denigration of sexual relationships in which coitus is not possible: "real sex" requires a penetrating and impregnating penis. This works against gay men in fostering the assumption that the primary gay sexual activity is anal intercourse, thus delegitimating other sexual practices like mutual masturbation. It also belittles the sexuality of anyone who is or is perceived to be incapable of coitus. Finally, procreationism too easily supports an understanding of children as the "cost" of sex, which ironically fosters the attitude that sexual activity without contraception is somehow more "moral" than sex with contraception, even when conception is not desirable or advisable.[3] These attitudes, so endemic in the history of Christian moral theology, work against viewing the purposes of sex in new ways.

Twentieth-century and subsequent moral theology has begun to witness the reinterpretation of procreation as a norm for sexual ethics, even among conservative ethicists. Kathy Rudy elucidates a few of the factors contributing to this shift in consciousness. First, there is a recognition that contemporary life does not always allow families to adequately provide for a large number of children. Second, the good of unitivity between sexual partners sometimes conflicts with the end of procreativity, prompting some couples to forego the good of sexual relations in order to limit family size. Third, we now recognize that good parenting is not simply a biological function; the ability to make new life is not as important as the ability to nurture that life. Lastly, and I think most importantly, new reproductive technologies have made reproduction possible without physical, sexual contact.[4] Gays and lesbians have seized upon these last two factors — through methods like adoption, foster care, and artificial insemination — to be procreative in their own way, without necessarily ever having personally experienced penile-vaginal intercourse. If reproduction no longer requires heterosexual coitus, then it is no longer necessary to assume that sex is naturally oriented only toward the creation of human life. We can also then put aside the mind-set that delegitimates sexual acts outside of heterosexual intercourse. Once we have abandoned the necessity of procreativity as a norm for sexual ethics, we can begin to reimagine a Catholic moral theology which includes homosexual acts as legitimate and morally sound expressions of intimacy.

Of course, we also need to overcome the heteronormativity that has similarly constricted the imagination of the Catholic moral tradition. The "heterosexual grid," as it is currently constructed, is based on the same faulty binary economy which is at the root of the church's bifurcated teachings on homosexuality. It posits one sexuality as the norm — the "real" sexuality — and all others as deviant. Mary McClintock Fulkerson suggests that the importance placed on absolutized notions of sexuality which support heterosexism represents a form of idolatry for Christians. It relies on a cultural code to restrict membership in the Christian community, much like some early followers of Jesus sought to do with their insistence that one had to first be circumcised (become a Jew) in order to become Christian. As the early Christians decided after some debate, such a restriction goes against the grain of the Gospel. For Fulkerson, the refusal to accept the heterosexual grid is like the refusal to accept the circumcision requirement.[5] Given that sexual identities are culturally and historically contingent, it is unwise for Catholic moral theology to rely on heterosexual identity as normative. Heterosexual identification is as much a socially constructed phenomenon as gay identification. In fact, heterosexual identity is currently available largely because of gay identity, on which it relies for its definition. Without the constraints of procreationism and heteronormativity, each of which increasingly look like a theological straw man, there is little left to sustain the church's position that all homosexual acts are morally unacceptable.

The blanket condemnation of homosexual acts, whatever that means, results in an ethical vacuum about the "doing" of being gay. Andrew Sullivan calls this an "unethic," which he explains as "a statement that some

people are effectively beneath even the project of an ethical teaching."[6]
This contributes to the deafening silence so many of these autobiographers
experienced growing up gay. Rather than consider the possibility that some
homosexual acts might be ethically permissible or even morally sound,
the church leadership instead backs out of the conversation entirely. Fortunately, the discussion takes place in spite of them. There is a prevailing
awareness among Catholic moral theologians of the inadequacy of the deontological, confession- and act-centered approach to sexual ethics that
has traditionally been employed. The newer model situates sexuality in a
broad social context by shifting the discussion from an emphasis on acts
to an emphasis on the meaning of acts and relationships, forming ethical
ideals independent of the genders involved. In this paradigm, new values emerge as the basis for developing sexual norms, such as mutuality,
hospitality, maturity, and responsibility.

Margaret Farley is an example of a Catholic moral theologian whose
work reshapes the conventional approach to sexual ethics and thus provides a way of rethinking how we understand human acts and desire.
Farley builds her sexual ethics on the foundations of justice, commitment,
and respect, suggesting all relationships and acts within those relationships need to be assessed according to these kinds of standards. Most
useful for my purposes is her discussion of what it means to really respect persons, as the church instructs Catholics to do with regard to gay
people. Respect for persons recognizes them in their wholeness and in their
context: "We are who we are within social, cultural, linguistic contexts,
formed in our understandings and our desires. We do not produce our own
meaning out of nothing, nor are our actions wholly our own."[7] As we interact with the world, we become ourselves, and this interaction gives rise
to our own actions: "Every action that we choose is for the sake of some
love, whether for ourselves or for another, whether for persons or things.
When we choose our actions, we ratify, identify with, some of our loves
(deferring, or refusing to ratify, other loves that are thereby not expressed
in action)."[8] For Farley, true respect of persons affirms their freedom to act
on behalf of the loves and desires that arise from their interaction with
others.

The same idea about the origin and meaning of our actions is articulated differently and applied directly to homosexual acts by Andre
Guindon. Guindon posits that because human sexual activity expresses
and communicates emotions and meanings, it should be understood as
language. Building on the insights of contemporary linguists like S. I.
Hayakawa, he describes language as the way one thinks about and expresses oneself. The meanings of the words one uses to express oneself
are always modified by the particular context in which they are deployed,
such that no word ever has the same meaning twice. Guindon extends this

to the concept of "homosexual acts," which are part of the self-expressive language of gay identity. He criticizes church leaders for assuming "there are specific instances of 'physical behavior' or 'material performances' which, independently of any user's meaning-making operation, have an evil meaning."[9] Gay persons will employ a variety of words and actions, including the language of physical, sexual activity, to express their sexuality and the feelings that go along with it. This shifts the discourse from "homosexual acts" to "gay speech." For Guindon, "Each modulation of self-expression and communication [between gay persons] is a 'homosexual act.' "[10] To say such actions are forbidden is to deny gay persons the capacity to make meaning out of their own language. In effect, it denies gay persons their ability to speak.

We need not look to Catholic theologians, however, for a way out of the ethical conundrum left in the wake of inadequate church teachings on sexual identity; we can look to gay lives themselves as represented in life narratives. Here, the discernment of right and wrong is played out in concrete ways, with real-life consequences. These autobiographies stand as testaments to the untenability of bifurcated church teachings which presume to separate the being and the doing of gay identity. If we are to take seriously gay men's subjectivity as narrators of their own lives, we must also take seriously the conclusions they provide with regard to "homosexual acts." First, homosexual acts are not exclusively physical. What gay people do as a consequence of being gay involves a variety of actions and interactions with themselves and others. Second, these actions represent an integration of gay identity within the whole of themselves and so should be viewed as outgrowths of their personhood, not of some free-floating sexual desire. Third, these are the actions of gay men who are themselves moral agents, who evidence a great deal of discernment and struggle as they decide how to act. This last point, especially, underscores the artificiality and uselessness of a phrase like "love the sinner; hate the sin." As Andrew Sullivan states:

> When you begin to see homosexuality not as some bizarre and willful attempt to practice a specific sex act, but as a deep and complex part of a human person, a person who needs as much love and as much divine love as any other person, then it becomes clear how it is, in fact, impossible to hate the "sin" and love the "sinner." Or how the very formulation is, in fact, a way of denigrating homosexual people, denying their humanity, erasing their integrity. It is as if we were to say that we loved Jews, so long as they never went to a synagogue; or that we welcomed immigrants, so long as they never tried to learn English. It is a rejection masquerading as an acceptance,

and it perpetuates, in the guise of alleviating, the very ethical conflict from which homosexuals are doggedly trying to escape.[11]

Sullivan's words indict church teachings that effectively denigrate and deny the moral agency of gay people even as the church professes to love and respect them. The ethical conflict to which he refers is rooted in the silence gay people face in trying to find any framework for understanding and assessing the choices that result from their gay identity.

Some gay activists might be wary of the implication that there *needs* to be an ethical framework around gay identity. In the earliest days of the gay pride movement after 1969 and through the 1970s, activists emphasized the need to question the values and institutions of mainstream society. As these pioneers saw it, the problem was not that gay people needed to be accepted by assimilating into hegemonic cultural and religious values but rather that these values need to be overthrown. Institutions like marriage and ethical mandates like monogamy simply do not fit the needs of all people. In fact, these societal "values" effectively control and oppress people. These activists viewed attempts to fit gay relationships into conventional norms with skepticism. Would this not serve to reinforce the very structures which had marginalized them in the first place? In the words of Audre Lorde, "The master's tools will never dismantle the master's house."[12] Instead, the value of freedom in desire and pleasure should be the norm for which gay people should strive. This would mean challenging anything designed to restrict sexual freedom in any way, calling into question the need for norms and ethics regarding sexuality.

Successive generations of gay activists have been exploring the viability of this strategy, especially in the face of dramatic shifts in gay visibility in the last three decades of the twentieth century. The AIDS pandemic intensified the dynamics of this debate.[13] Some of the first activist pioneers witnessed the deaths of numerous friends and worried that the emphasis on absolute freedom was killing the gay community. They began to insist on an ethic of *safe* sex, and advocated restrictions which would curtail the practice of risky and deadly behaviors. Some focused on behaviors only, while others went further and found "protection" in conventional norms like monogamy. Others maintained that any return to restrictive, traditional codes would only recreate the situation of marginalization that had initially prompted gay men to engage in covert and risky behaviors. By the late 1990s, gay activists were divided into conflicting positions in the debate, with the extremes identified as radical and neoconservative.[14] The most important thing this debate reveals is not the *need* for an ethical framework around gay identity, but the fact that there *is* always an ethical framework in place. The question is what kind of ethics and how these ethics are formulated and articulated.

The real-life ethical struggles represented in these kinds of debates are played out and applied on a practical level in gay lives. Choices are made and actions are performed against the backdrop of this larger socioethical context, and gay life narratives recount these choices and actions. By and large, the autobiographers in my study do not evidence an ethic based purely on freedom as the overriding norm in their life narratives.[15] These are not stories in which finding and having unencumbered access to sex is the most important theme. Quite the contrary, these are stories of men who grapple with the ramifications of their actions, for themselves and for others, in both their nonsexual and sexual relationships. Yes, they feel sexual desire for other men, and they want to affirm that desire as an integral part of themselves — as a sexual identity; but they also sort out its meanings and implications. I think this is a reflection of the way their Catholic identity informs their sexual identity. Rather than occupying the extremes of the debates I discussed above, these gay Catholic autobiographers reflect a both/and sensibility. As a whole, they make a case for sexual freedom *and* responsibility as norms. They challenge the church's apparent belief that there can or should not be any discussion at all about the ethics of "homosexual acts."[16]

The fact that these life narratives already provide an ethical framework for understanding and assessing the choices that inhere with gay identity is what enables us to recognize these autobiographers as moral agents themselves. The idea of agency, however, has been called into question by postmodern theorists who have deconstructed the notion of the "subject." According to the theory, the subject is not the originator of subjectivity but rather the effect of social and symbolic processes. This would seem to foreclose any possibility of personal moral reflection that does not simply replicate prevailing conventions. Marilyn Gottschall uses Judith Butler's deconstruction of gender to deontologize the subject and then reimagine a moral agency that is consistent with postmodern subjectivity. Following Butler, Gottschall sees agency as being embedded in power and discourse: "The potential to act emerges within the interface between the subject and discursive/cultural injunctions and practices. . . . It is in performativity, the reworking of the discursive processes, that the process of change is opened up."[17] For Gottschall, agency is not found in the world of free will facing infinite possibilities, but paradoxically, within our constraints. It is agency limited by the interaction of the subject and its formation. Once agency is reconstituted in this way, ethical analysis can move beyond the determination of rights and wrongs, toward an inquiry into "the multiple levels of contingency and complexity that accompany the desire to act."[18]

Autobiography seems to be the perfect vehicle for the conveyance of this kind of ethical reflection. It represents in narrative form the interface between the subject and the context of its formation, which Gottschall posits as the site of agency; and it is a window into the "multiple levels of contingency and complexity that accompany the desire to act." Autobiographers are moral agents in their own right and their autobiographies are moral performances of a kind. Diane Bjorklund points out how the construction of the self in autobiography is inextricably linked with moral values:

> Autobiographers offer a public explanation of how they have led their lives. To tell their life stories, they must speak of their beliefs, actions, intentions, choices, and goals. Because they pursued such goals and actions in a social context where others may be harmed or helped, their actions and intentions become moral topics.[19]

When autobiographers account for their choices and actions in their life texts, they are doing so, "not just in terms of personal goals achieved or personal problems solved but also in response to prevailing moral values."[20] The life writer ponders questions about personal responsibility; self-control; the relative importance of will, reason, and emotion in decision making; and the meaning of freedom in terms of human conduct. The resulting life narrative will ultimately help to articulate, sustain, or challenge prevailing ethical norms. According to Bjorklund, an autobiographer whose life narrative challenges conventional norms will also guide the reader to agree with their choices or at least not judge them harshly for it. In this sense, autobiographies are moral performances in which ethical issues are worked out and justified in the context of concrete lives.[21] The autobiographies I analyze are no exception. They challenge the church's narrow meaning of "homosexual acts" and guide us to reconsider traditional assumptions that simplistically sever the connection between doing and being gay. If we are truly to respect these autobiographers as persons, as the church enjoins us to do, then we must take seriously their moral agency as subjects of their actions and relationships as they reconstruct them in their life texts.

"Acts of Faith"

" . . . and homosexual acts saved my life."
— Mr. Friel, in Andrew Holleran's *Nights in Aruba*

Daniel Curzon's largely autobiographical novel begins with his own real-life memories as portrayed through his protagonist Benjy.[22] He then projects, in the progressively older characters of Ben and Benjamin, what his life would have been like had he lived out the heterosexual expectations of the church. In an imaginary scene in a church confessional, Ben (Curzon) is able to take a personal stand against his priest-confessor, who presumes to know what is best for Ben's life based on the teachings of the church:

"Don't raise your voice; this is a confessional!"

"I know what it is, Father. All my life I've known. It's a place where everything's a *sin!* Everything's a *sin* unless it's done exactly the way somebody else tells me to do it! And now I'm supposed to get up off my knees and walk out of here and go back to my wife and kids and stick with my job selling ads in a magazine and never go to a park again, never play basketball with men again, never think what I really *do* think again!"

"You're committing sins right *here* in the confessional!" Father Agler said severely.

Ben stood up, although his heart was failing, although he felt stunted with fear and anger at what he was saying to the priest. "That's exactly what I mean, Father. To the Church, questioning, living — *everything* — is a *sin!*"[23]

Curzon overturns the oppressive process he felt during confession as a child and seizes his own power and moral agency to determine how he does and does not sin. He is empowered in his narrative to resist the church's deontological, confession- and act-centered moral theology, which so conveniently polices his sexual identity and forbids all "homosexual acts." He is then able to articulate how gay acts are inextricable from gay selfhood. Each of these autobiographers are similarly empowered in their narratives.

My goal in this chapter is to lift up pieces of these life stories that resonate very directly with the concerns I have outlined above. There are particular aspects of these life texts which represent the kinds of choices and struggles that form the nexus of being and doing gay Catholic identity. These moments, especially in the context of valuing oneself and one's relationships, complicate what it means to engage in a "gay act." I want to use these life texts to subvert the church's simplistic usage of the word "acts" with regard to sexuality by extending its meaning.[24] My reading of these life texts in this way can be understood as "queering" the ethics of homosexual acts. I want to further extend this idea by queering the aspect of Catholic prayer life that is also called "acts." When Catholics recite certain formulaic prayers, they engage in acts of a certain kind, according to the title of the prayer and the context in which it is spoken. Wrestling with the ethics of gay identity in the construction of one's life text is another kind of act, a sort of queer prayer of discernment. The acts these autobiographers narrate and the act of narrating them bring alive an ethical world in which the being-and-doing of gay-and-Catholic are deeply entangled. When a gay Catholic comes to terms with the implications of his unique identity, he performs an "act of faith."

Coming to terms with gay identity requires a readjustment of one's self-image. The act of letting go of an old and often destructive image of the self and embracing a new one involves a courageous leap of faith. Fr. Roberts recounts feeling this shift within himself literally exploding in his body. After years of being a successful parish priest and keeping his sexuality suppressed beneath his clean-cut image, he finally reached a point where he could no longer stand the pressure. In the wee hours of the morning, he wandered outside the rectory and began to cry. In anger, he shook his fist toward the sky and at God, feeling like a dirty joke had been played on him. "My whole body convulsed, my head became dizzy, my legs gave way, and I crumpled to the ground in the middle of the church parking lot."[25] In addition to the powerful symbolism of having a nervous breakdown close to, but still outside, the church building, Roberts's episode represents a moment of hitting bottom. He believes "it was a birthing experience, a new awareness of myself, of my sexual identity and sexual desires, my skin hunger and craving for intimate relationship....It was time for an integration of mind and heart. It was time to deal with my sexuality and my true self."[26] In that moment of physical and emotional agony, Roberts decided it was time to open the door to his gay identity. From then on, his actions would be defined by self-exploration rather than self-denial.

Rafael Campo also felt the destruction of his own self-denial in his body. By the time he went to college and was experiencing the first glimmers of his sexual desire, he had decided to deny himself love and pleasure rather than give in to what his Catholic upbringing had told him was evil. The more he desired anything, or anyone, the less he ate. As his health deteriorated, he became increasingly isolated and fearful of what his desire meant for him: "I fantasized about suicide as the only way out of humiliating my parents...I was fulfilling all their prophecies for homosexuals, and I had not even had homosexual sex. I was unsuccessful even in the expression of my own hideous vice."[27] Eventually, Campo wound up in the hospital with an intense pain in his upper abdomen. He realized as he lay on the examination table that he had reached the threshold between life and death:

> I had located an intersection between my own mortality and the world around me, which was named desire. I wanted to live and to be loved, and at the same time I yearned to erase myself from the face of the earth. I wanted the morgue-like steel and chill of the doctor's office, and the warm hands of another upon my body telling me by their touch that I would endure.[28]

From that moment, Campo took action to cross that threshold "from bodily illness to mental health, from repressed misanthrope to unabashed queer." He made love shortly thereafter with his best friend, the man who would ultimately become his life partner. His decision to embrace his sexual identity literally saved his life. Though he could not articulate this at the time, it was clear to him in retrospect: "I can report now, however, the healing I felt in each kiss, each touch, each murmured word. My body belonged to me again, as soon as I had owned its desire."[29]

Learning to own one's sexual desire is a struggle with ethical ramifications for gay men. To deny one's desire is to deny the wholeness of oneself, which can lead to the kinds of physical and emotional problems recounted above. Wholeness is linked to both body and soul; cutting one off from the other is tragic. As Brian McNaught says, "It is a sad thought to know that you have hated your body."[30] It also leads to a lack of integrity in dealing with others. McNaught confesses to having cooperated in the purging of his college fraternity pledgemaster who was accused of being "queer." He configures this failing in the context of the unresolved anguish he felt about his emerging sexual identity during his college days. When he looks back, he is confronted by memories of a Brian he hardly recognizes, the one who hid behind the "good boy" facade. He would like the people in his past to understand what he was going through, so they could understand why he was so moody; why he did not maintain his heterosexual relationships; why he avoided other men who were perceived as gay. He regrets what that other Brian did back then, but he also understands it was all part of who he has become: "There is the Brian who met others' expectations and the Brian who struggles with his own. I don't understand why I had to go through those painful experiences, but I don't hate the other Brian any more than the butterfly hates the caterpillar."[31] This kind of language is not surprising given the way coming into gay identity often reads like a conversion narrative.

Each of these gay men senses he is somehow not the same person he was before he self-identified as gay. In becoming who he is now, he may have acted in ways he now regrets, but these choices and losses were part of a larger identity project. Writing about this provides a structure for articulating and conceiving this process of self-definition. As Richard Rodriguez introduces his first autobiography, "I turn to consider the boy I once was in order, finally, to describe the man I am now. I remember what was so grievously lost to define what was necessarily gained."[32] Rodriguez knows that the regret that comes with personal growth is wrapped up in loss. José Zuniga also explicitly understands how the gains of "finding oneself" are always beset with losses. He notes the most important lesson he learned about coming out was "that there has to be a certain degree of destruction of familiar structures in order for a person to build at last the very individual structure of his or her own life."[33] In his life text, Zuniga is able to mourn the destruction of the familiar as he navigates his way through the unfamiliar geography of his emerging gay identity.

Though people with heterosexual desires can also struggle with their body image and their emerging sexuality, they are not told their desires are unnatural or disordered as gay people are told in church teachings. Gay Catholics must make an active choice to own their desire, which is an act of faith in oneself and in God. John McNeill calls this "taking a chance on God."[34] While doing so can be scary, as conscientious ethical decisions often are, it also opens the doorway to love. For Fenton Johnson, desire is intimately linked to both faith and love, as the life force that motivates people who seek God: "Desire is to love as belief is to faith: each is a means to an end; each is so easily mistaken for the end."[35] Desire leads to love through faith. Owning one's desire as something given by God in spite of societal messages to the contrary — an act of faith — leads to love. "Desire coupled with reason is what brings us to God, who is love."[36] Passing through the struggle to accept and embrace his desire earned him the "right" to passionately love and to be loved in return. After that, there was no healthy way of going back: "I have, in fact, arrived at the heterosexual take on passionate love, which is to say that I have integrated that love so wholly and completely into who I am that to deny it would be to deny my whole being."[37]

Denying one's self as created by God is certainly a sin according to Catholic moral theology. This is part of the anguish gay Catholics feel whenever they deny or conceal their sexual identity. It may be a strategic decision and it may even protect their safety in dangerous situations, but it does not feel like the honest thing to do. Andrew Holleran compares this self-denial to Peter's denial of Jesus in the Passion. In *Nights in Aruba*, Paul's mother asks him one evening if he is homosexual:

I jumped up from the sofa, said, "No! Of course not!" in a voice as sharp as my father's when he was angry, and left the room. My heart hammered as I stood in the kitchen, however, thinking of the scene in the Gospels in which Peter denies knowing Christ when the woman asks him if she has not seen him with the Galilean. The comparison was disproportionate but in a sense exact: for if the Gospels told us one would have to leave one's family to follow Christ, the curious thing was that loving men had the same effect.[38]

Gay Catholics are seemingly put in an ethical double bind. Both the denial and the owning of one's sexual identity have potentially devastating consequences. Holleran's narrative highlights how owning one's desire risks the loss of one's family, a potential fate also shared by those who choose to follow Christ.

José Zuniga discusses the risk of losing one's reputation and credibility. When he came out after being named soldier of the year in 1993, he did so to call attention to the problematic policy banning gays and lesbians from serving in the military.[39] When asked if he had ever had sex with another man, he decided to lie rather than risk a court-martial. Subsequent personality features focused on his virginity even more than on the army policy. When a reporter learned of a man named Russell in Zuniga's past, with whom Zuniga had, in fact, had his first gay relationship, she asked Zuniga point blank if he had been his lover. Like Holleran, Zuniga's heart skipped a beat when he was asked, but he did his best to evade answering honestly while still acknowledging his friendship with Russell. When he recounts this in his autobiography, Zuniga also compares his denial with that of Simon Peter; but he turns it around to justify his evasion of the truth:

> The apostle Simon's threefold denial of Jesus, who had been arrested in the courtyard of the Sanhedrin, had been a central doctrine drilled into the pliable minds of Catholic children on the Sunday mornings dedicated to theological study. As far a stretch as it might seem, my conscience had applied this doctrine to my quandary with Russell. Just as Sister Marie Jésus interpreted the Scripture to say Simon's denial had been a morally neutral and prudent act, so too I came to consider my denial.[40]

Even so, Zuniga still wrestled with his ethical dilemma, and the fact that he could not be totally honest caused him great anguish: "The guilt of betrayal flooded my heart. I had come out to stand for honor and integrity, my soul screamed out."[41] Though his decision was strategic and self-protective, the fact that his public image did not reflect the wholeness of his sexual desire and experience felt self-effacing.

As a teenager, Patrick Horrigan created a fantasy wherein he exploded the myth of his public image as a way of coming into his own. Horrigan imagined himself costarring in a movie with Al Pacino and being romantically involved with him both in the movie and in real life. He further imagined a late night TV interview of the two of them with Dick Cavett, in which Horrigan would talk candidly about his role and his love life. Whenever he thought about the interview, he always envisioned them wearing tuxedos:

> Somehow the tuxedos heightened for me the shattering discrepancy between my public image (nice, clean cut, obedient, from a good Catholic family) and what I was doing privately (having sex with men on screen, talking openly about it on TV), between my ostensible identity as an "artist" and the homosexual content of my art. But the tuxedos also domesticated and legitimated, in my mind, the frightful power of my sexuality, of my character's homosexuality.[42]

For Horrigan, the idea of owning his same-sex desire in such a public way was also a way of owning his personhood. It was his way of becoming an adult, taking ownership of himself, and doing what he felt was best for him. He knew it would shock people. He wanted others to feel "disappointment and moral outrage" about him: "I wanted people to think, Patrick's not the boy I used to know."[43] It was his way of dramatically visualizing what it would be like to unleash and simultaneously "tame" that part of him that his good-boy image denied.

Several of these autobiographers explore the ethics of hiding their sexual identity behind the facade of an "acceptable" public image. Sometimes it is directly related to the kinds of careers they have chosen, as with Fr. Roberts (the clergy) and José Zuniga (the military) above. Not surprisingly, this is also a central concern in the life text of Dave Pallone, a professional baseball umpire. As his narrative progresses, his "double life" becomes his biggest problem, and he constantly fears being exposed. Whenever he was out with his lover Scott, Pallone constantly feared being seen by someone who knew him. When Scott traveled out of town for games with Pallone, the two devised strategies to avoid any suspicion they might be more than friends. These included things such as not going to the hotel room at the same time, not sitting together on airplanes, and not meeting each other at the ballpark gate after the game.[44] Later, when Scott died, Pallone could not even share the depth of his loss with any of his colleagues. It all came to a head for him when he was set up and falsely accused of engaging in sex with some teenage boys. He was betrayed by "friends" who knew his secret, and he eventually found himself coming out publicly in the worst possible circumstances. Pallone reflects on the problem of having a "hidden life" and the fact that his "mask" could be yanked off at any time: "The real problem wasn't *being* gay; it was the fear of people *finding out* I was gay."[45] Clearly, if he had to do it all over again, he would not have kept his sexual identity hidden. He thought he was protecting the most important thing in his life — his career as an umpire. In the end, he lost his career anyway, and at the cost of denying his wholeness: "If you live a lie, you're a completely lost soul."[46]

One might raise the objection that everyone keeps parts of their private lives hidden in various contexts and life situations. Some might say it is important to keep private matters out of the public workplace, for example, so hiding one's sexual orientation and preferences in a situation like that is appropriate anyway. But it is clearly not that simple when we are talking about sexual *identity*. Consider the fact that in the current American system, the extent of employee health insurance benefits is usually tied to marriage and family, which are legally, as of this writing, facts of heterosexual identity.[47] Just as the line between doing and being gay is not so well-defined, the clean separation between what is public and private is illusory with regard to one's sexual identity. When things like career, reputation, livelihood, and health coverage are at stake, the message is that sexual identity does matter, whether it should or not. Many advocates of gay rights have built the case for the decriminalization of same-sex acts based on the "right to privacy." As Mark Blasius, asserts, "The 'privacy strategy' for lesbian and gay rights is necessary but has its limits." Ironically, such a strategy actually supports a very flimsy "tolerance" of gay people: "What is least tolerated about homosexuality is not the sex acts themselves (since they are rarely engaged in 'in public view' anyway), but the *appearance,* the social visibility of lesbians and gay people and their affectional relations with each other throughout the fabric of social life."[48] In other words, acceptance is predicated on gay invisibility — and gay identity matters all the more.

Most of these autobiographers know sexual identity matters because they grew up in a societal context in which they were told it does. They write in a societal context that still tells them it matters. Each act they make toward acknowledging their sexual identity is a leap of faith. Andrew Sullivan likens his own faith journey to his coming to terms with his sexuality:

> Like faith, one's sexuality is not simply a choice, it informs a whole way of being; but like faith, it involves choices — the choice to affirm or deny the central part of one's being, the choice to live a life that does not deny but confronts reality, the choice to persist in the adventure of one's own existential journey, despite its destination's being uncertain and its hazards unknown.[49]

The idea that choosing to affirm one's sexuality is an act of faith suggests gay men make this choice knowing some of the potential ramifications of their decision, without fully comprehending where this affirmation will take them. Their life texts reveal not only the difficulties of coming into gay identity but also the hazards of keeping it hidden in the name of abiding by church teachings. As Sullivan recounts it, echoing the warnings of Pallone, Zuniga, Holleran, and Campo, trying to follow the church's teachings on homosexuality "led not to virtue but to pathology"; rather than requiring trust and faith, it required "the first lie in a human life, which would lead to an entire battery of others."[50]

This is an extremely important point with regard to church teaching. The intention is to promote lives of virtue for gay people, but the effect of trying to live according to church teaching on homosexuality is usually the opposite. For example, the church insists upon life-long celibacy for gay people, even though they may not possess the charism necessary for such a commitment. Without the charism, the requirement is no longer life-enhancing but rather death-dealing. It relies on an artificial separation of doing and being gay, and transforms into a bare-bones order of abstinence — a suffering to be offered up, a cross to bear. As Sullivan says, "Abstinence forever; abstinence always; abstinence not for the sake of something else, but for its own sake; abstinence not just from sex, but from love and love's hope and the touch of a lover's embrace. Abstinence even from recognition, acknowledgment, family."[51] This last statement underscores how the pathology spreads beyond just the individual gay person. Families can also cling to unrealistic images of their gay relatives and fail to fully recognize and acknowledge them. Derrick Tynan-Connolly notes how his parents who are normally "the most hospitable, generous and kind people in the world," treat his life partner Jimmy as if he doesn't exist. His parents perceive as evil and sinful a relationship that is based on trust, faithfulness, and commitment, and they condemn what is clearly a central component of their son's identity. They think they can love their son and hate his "sin," but they are clinging to an illusion: "I keep telling them when they say they love me that they don't love me but rather an image in their mind [of] who I should be. I told them that person doesn't exist."[52] Love premised on a false image is a lie.

The imperative to seek wholeness and honesty and to embrace a gay identity with integrity assumes a greater urgency for some of these writers in light of the scourge of AIDS in gay communities in the last two decades. In his San Francisco circle of friends, Richard Rodriguez was always the cautious one, the skeptic who would not fully indulge in the aesthetically rich world they had created for themselves. He watched as each of his friends was diagnosed with AIDS and was especially saddened when his dear friend César was found to be infected too. As César lay on his deathbed, he said Rodriguez would be the only one of his friends who was spared. "You are too circumspect," César told him. Though the sad situation confirmed his cautious reluctance to indulge himself in the material world of his gay community, Rodriguez felt remorse when his wise and loving friend issued his accusation: "It was then I saw that the greater sin against heaven was my unwillingness to embrace life."[53] James Morrison recalls an experience with a friend who was dying of AIDS that powerfully underscores the illusory nature of loving and hating when bodily integrity is at stake. Morrison remembers telling his sick friend Owen how much he hated AIDS, but he was quickly corrected: " 'You *can't*,' Owen said, his clear eyes shining with anger. 'It's *in* me. If you hate it, you hate me.' "[54] Owning our bodies and our desires means owning everything that comes with them. The fullness of gay identity involves body and soul, desires and actions.

With AIDS in the background, the performance of homosexual acts becomes even more significant, especially in the context of physical intimacy. Rafael Campo discusses this resonance in terms of his own identity construction: "I have in the past resisted the simplistic notion that what I do in bed primarily defines my overall identity as a person."[55] He especially resented the many assumptions foisted upon him by homophobic society — that he was not manly enough to be a physician, that he could not maintain a long-term relationship, that he would probably die of AIDS someday — because he was gay. Campo deliberately bucked these assumptions and forged a successful path for himself despite messages that gay men were fated for a certain amount of misery. He decided his "homosexual acts" did not really matter. "So the specific experience of having another man's cock inside my mouth, or having mine inside another man's rectum, had to be trivial, totally irrelevant."[56]

When he began to treat more and more AIDS patients, however, he came to see things differently. He realized how unfairly AIDS attacked those who were already marginalized, even as religious conservatives used AIDS as a symbol of the demise of traditional family values: "How convenient, I thought, that the same terrible disease could be used to decimate minority cultures and simultaneously to destroy the values of the much stronger mainstream."[57] In the minds of those self-appointed protectors of morality, gay people are guilty of crossing hallowed ethical boundaries, just as "illegal aliens" violate the geographical borders of an exalted nation. For Campo, AIDS makes the situation even more palpable and accents the need for gay men to claim the fullness of their sexual identities. Now he perceives the meaning of his homosexual acts differently: "In the face of the AIDS crisis, however, such physical expressions of love have become revolutionary indeed, as revolutionary and as physical for me as the act of writing poetry."[58] Just as writing poetry is embedded in his personhood, so too are homosexual acts intimately linked to gay identity. Campo finally realized:

> that our sexual acts are among the few scraps of identity that we do own, that we must own. The kiss that locates us on a map of the known world, the interlocking legs that are the sextant pointing the way home, the renewing embrace that does not transmit HIV — even if they do not make up our identities entirely, we must give them to ourselves freely and without remorse or encumbrances.[59]

Campo writes this in the name of saving lives. He recognizes that safe-sex admonitions with a focus on "dangerous" acts only serves to perpetuate the negativity that drives such acts in the first place. Focusing on acts in the context of relationships and connections to others validates the personhood and identity of the individual in question. Similarly, the church's focus on acts without context fails to affirm the wholeness of gay individuals. Each of these autobiographers writes his story to save lives — his own and those of other gay Catholics who have tried to bifurcate themselves in order to mirror church teachings, only to find themselves spiritually emaciated. Some of these writers are explicit about the deadly risks of this bifurcation: if a gay man is valued only when he is less than whole, he may feel his own life is worthless. José Zuniga draws a link between the negative attitude toward gay identity and suicide. He mentions the 1989 Department of Health and Human Services report which demonstrated that "lesbian and gay youth are two to six times more likely to attempt suicide than other youth, and they accounted for thirty percent of all completed suicides among teens."[60] Surely these are the kinds of acts we should all be working to eliminate.

James Heckman writes movingly of the circumstances which led to his making a suicide attempt as an adult. He got married when he was twenty-seven because a priest advised him he would grow into it and because "it was time to get married." Though they had children together and he thought of her as "a fine woman," he was clearly not sexually attracted to her. Sex with her eventually became impossible for him and he became visibly despondent: "I had decided to suppress my homosexual feelings, and that I would end my life if they ever came to light." Sure enough, he met a guy when he was about thirty-four and fell "head-over-heels in love." It was all more than he could bear, so he drove his car into the barn on his farm, intending to end his misery. "There was no reason why it failed, except maybe the grace of God. The vent came loose from the tailpipe. I kind of lost consciousness, rolled out of the car, and found myself on the ground when I came to." Heckman finally told his wife he was gay during his third stay in the hospital psych ward. She was hurt but relieved to know what was going on inside him. From that day forward, he was able to move on with his life — no longer burdened by the demands of living a lie.[61]

Richard John Cardarelli shares the story of his own suicide attempt during college, which ultimately led to his becoming a priest and then becoming active in Dignity: "My emotional scars disappeared as I dared to love without fear."[62] Brian McNaught shares the story of his suicide attempt, after which he "vowed never again to live [his] life based upon the expectations of others."[63] It also propelled him into a life of activism and speaking out so that gay and lesbian people would not feel isolated and thus not feel drawn to put themselves in dangerous situations.[64] David Kopay likewise has no regrets about speaking out and putting his career on the line whenever he hears stories of gay people who see no other way out but to kill themselves.[65] Fr. Raymond Calabrese writes about the suicide of a friend from seminary who could not handle the supposed contradiction of being both gay and priest. He shares his own story of being gay in part because he worries his silence contributed to his friend's despair.[66] When gay people acknowledge the fullness of their personhood and share their stories with others, these actions save lives. These are homosexual acts to be celebrated, acts that inspire survival, which can be very brave indeed. In the words of Stephen McCauley, "Let's say it's easiest to believe that you did the best you could at the time, and so did everyone else. It's a blessing even to be alive, an accomplishment, a privilege. Let's leave it at that."[67]

"Acts of Love"

My deciding to take care of Larry as he goes through this is in part a religious decision — a decision to thank the power, or powers, that have granted me life. And it's a humanistic decision — a storing up, I can hope, of grace; if I stand at someone's side during this hard portion of his journey, perhaps, I can hope, I will have someone to stand by me when my time arrives, be that one or five or fifty years away.   — Fenton Johnson, *Geography of the Heart*

The decisions to be in relationship with other human beings and to meet the demands of those associations lay the foundation for gay Catholics to perform acts of love. Whether it be in relationships with friends, parents, lovers, partners, or colleagues, these autobiographers spend their lives invested in ethical situations that require discernment and action (or inaction, which is a kind of action in itself). Homosexual acts are not only about self-care and personal wholeness; they also involve interacting with and potentially loving an other(s). When Richard Rodriguez considers love, he notes, "The way we are constructed constructs the violin. The violin constructs the music." Yet many different kinds of instruments make music, so he is certain music comes first. In turn, he asks if the way we are constructed constructs love? He is similarly assured of his answer: "Love comes first. The first principle comes first. God's love comes first and is not changed, cannot be diminished or turned away by the instrument."[68] Rodriguez knows love functions regardless of the particular bodies that transmit and receive it. We all understand the emotion expressed when Shakespeare says, *"Shall I compare thee to a summer's day? / Thou art more lovely and more temperate."*[69] Like all people, gays and lesbians are drawn to particular others, with whom they engage in loving and hopefully life-enhancing relationships. Their decisions to act within the context of these particular relationships are rooted in the many dimensions of the meaning of love. The men of these life texts manifest their love and caring for others in a variety of ways and, in these gay acts, provide new ways of understanding what love entails.

Fenton Johnson's life text focuses on his relationship with his lover Larry. As time went by in the course of their partnership, Johnson noticed how well-suited the two of them were for each other. At times, they seemed a model of the kind of unitivity espoused in Catholic moral theology as an essential component of a valid marriage.[70] They effortlessly complemented each other in numerous ways. As an example, Johnson notes, "Without my knowing it, our two ways of being engaged each other — my preoccupation with the future; his immersion in this day, this hour, this minute."[71] Johnson weaves his own life story with that of Larry's to represent their interconnection. He also notes the different ways they were engaged in their relationships with their parents. Johnson's parents "released" him and his siblings to make their own ways, as much out of financial necessity as any belief in letting go. Larry's parents, survivors of the Holocaust, clung to their only child who, for them, represented survival and the new life they forged in America. The first time the two men visited Larry's parents, Larry's mother was not comfortable with both of them spending the night there, so they were faced with a decision that would seemingly prioritize one relationship over another. Larry decided he needed to stay alone at his parents' house, so Johnson stayed at a nearby hotel. "Alone in that room, I considered the enormous burdens of love, its two-edged sword, how large and daunting the responsibility of knowing when to cling and when to let go."[72] Both men performed gay acts of love that night. Larry took care of his mother, even though he wanted to be with his lover; Johnson helped his lover out of his predicament by honoring Larry's relationship with his mother and letting him go for the evening.

The biggest issue the two of them had to confront was Larry's HIV-positive condition. Though Johnson felt that love had chosen him rather than the other way around,[73] he still asked himself again and again: "How could I fall in love with someone whom I knew to have a terminal, transmissible disease?" One evening, while they were lying in bed together, he was able to tell Larry his greatest fear — that Larry would die and leave him infected and alone. In the silent moments following, as they held each other, Johnson began to understand the completeness of his love, that he could "speak aloud the unspeakable, secure in the knowledge of the bedrock on which you rest."

> I was beginning to understand how I might love through pain and ugliness, for better or for worse, up to and beyond death. I was beginning to understand how love offers some kind of victory, the thing that enables us to become larger than ourselves, larger than death.[74]

Because their love felt so solid, Johnson knew he would have the courage to stay with and care for Larry, even through the ugliness of AIDS. He could rise to the occasion, an act not so much of courage as of love. It was this love that drove him to keep in touch with Larry's parents after Larry died. It started with weekly phone calls and grew into occasional visits to their home in Santa Monica. He still keeps in touch with Larry's mother, who has come to rely on Johnson even more since the death of her husband. Theirs is a story of how acts of love can build a family, but it also demonstrates how simplistic it is to reduce gay identity to merely sexual acts. Johnson's sexual acts, whatever they are, are embedded in an entire set of acts and choices made between people who came to know what it means to love each other.

Despite the intentions of church teachings, the church inadvertently encourages gay sex acts outside of the context of love and relationship. As John McNeill explains it, according to the pastoral practice of the church, a man could have gay sex one night and then be absolved for his "sin" in confession the next day. If, on the other hand, he fell in love and moved in with another man, he would be denied absolution unless he broke off the relationship. This is how he experienced his own coming to terms with homosexuality as a Catholic: "Ironically, the church fostered promiscuity and felt that the enemy was not gay sex but gay love."[75] Fortunately, McNeill disregarded these messages when he met Charlie, who would become his life partner. Like Johnson in his relationship with his partner, McNeill eventually found himself taking risks in the name of love. For McNeill, the risks were financial. Charlie had a series of heart attacks beginning in 1990 that forced him into early retirement and required serious long-term medical care. They had to sell their dream house at half its value just to pay off their debts. For McNeill, this meant having no savings of his own for retirement, since his dismissal from the Jesuits left him with virtually nothing. He knows now that if Charlie dies ahead of him, he will live in poverty because he will not be eligible for Charlie's pension or social security (yet another societal unfairness against gay couples). Despite this, McNeill performs his act of love without question; he is committed to Charlie for better or for worse.

In trying to live up to the expectations of the church and society, a few of these men made commitments "for better or for worse" to a woman within the framework of a heterosexual engagement or marriage. They usually do so in the hopes of somehow regulating or covering their gay identity, but this creates conflict when they realize they cannot turn off that part of themselves or the false image becomes too much to bear. We have already seen how a situation like this led James Heckman to attempt suicide. Fortunately, when he finally told his wife he was gay, she found a way to accept it and helped them both move forward. In fact, when Heckman later told his parents he was gay, his wife told them "that if they wanted their grandchildren to be a part of their lives, they would have to accept their son for who he was.[76] His honesty and her acceptance of his sexual identity in the name of his personal wholeness represent acts of love.

Dave Kopay told his girlfriend Mary Ann he was gay before they ever decided to marry. He felt it was important for her to know why he "couldn't do more for her in bed."[77] She said it did not matter to her as long as she was the only woman in his life. Kopay eventually decided it would be expedient to marry her, especially in light of his pro football career. It was only a short time, however, before he realized he had made a mistake. He felt that "no matter how much we could do for each other in some ways, I just wasn't capable of the deeper emotional commitment with her I felt I could have with another man."[78] The emotional fallout for Mary Ann was devastating. She was initially suicidal and felt she was a failure. On some level, she had hoped to change Kopay and believed they could "live happily ever after." Kopay, on the other hand, seemed to know their marriage was doomed from the beginning. He regretted the whole thing. He stayed with her a while until she was more stable and then continued to help her financially in the hopes of making amends: "I didn't know what else to do for her. I did know I could no longer go on trying to change into the husband she wanted and needed."[79] Kopay's attempt to "live a heterosexual life" put him in an ethical double-bind and created a tragic situation in which both he and Mary Ann suffered.

Dave Pallone dated a woman named Linda, to whom he was attracted in most every way except sexually. He felt very comfortable with her and liked the idea of having a girlfriend because he felt society's pressure was off as long as he was with a woman. He also thought she might be able to "change" his sexual desire: "I ignored reality and hoped against hope that I would eventually be physically attracted to her. It was the most terrible thing I could have done to anybody, including myself."[80] As time went on, he feared losing her if he did not make a firm commitment, so he proposed to her. While she "heard bells" and said yes, he heard alarm bells and immediately felt he may have made a mistake. Two months later, he finally summoned the courage to break it off with her, but he was not able to tell her the real reason why. He knew telling her he was gay would likely make it easier for her to understand, but he feared her reaction and had not yet come out to anyone else. After he broke up with her, he still called her now and then because he felt so bad about hurting her, but it only strung her along and made her angry. They parted with bitterness between them and Pallone felt ashamed and sorry: "I promised myself that I would never hurt anyone again like I'd just hurt Linda. To this day, I hate thinking about what I did to her. I consider it my ultimate sin against another human being."[81] In this confessional moment, Pallone comes to terms with the negative effects of trying to maintain a romantic relationship that went against the thrust of who he knew himself to be. His acts of love, however well-intentioned, became acts of harm.

Situations like that of Pallone and Kopay are not uncommon among gay Catholic men who try to bifurcate themselves in order to have a relationship sanctioned by the church. Church teachings that say in effect, "a heterosexual relationship or no relationship at all," prompt many gay Catholics to seek such connections. Many of these autobiographers also came of age at a time when they did not see many other options for themselves because gayness was not as visible as it is today. Some of them got married, had children, and tried for a long time to make things work out because they sincerely loved their wives and wanted to honor their commitments. Larry Sullivan threw himself into work to escape his feelings until he met a younger man and began a passionate affair with him. "I didn't know what to do about it. I loved my wife and my kids, but I felt more fulfilled this way."[82] He felt tremendously guilty for his dishonesty and finally told his wife everything, which led to their divorce and coming out to his kids. They handled it well enough, but he always wished things could have been different. He felt lonely, stressed, and absent in his marriage, but happy and present to himself once he acknowledged his gay identity. William Storey went through a similar experience, being married and having seven children before coming to terms with his sexual identity. Though he now enjoys a fulfilling, long-term relationship with another man, he too regrets how acts of love can be double-edged: "The only sadness I feel periodically is that I did not discover my sexual identity earlier in life and that I had to wound my wife and children in becoming who I am."[83]

Some of these autobiographers have tried, with varying degrees of success, to restructure the terms of their relationships in the hope of being gay and remaining married. James Abdo was in his mid-twenties and married several years when he had his first sexual experience with a man. He felt compelled to explore this part of himself but did not want to just break up his marriage: "It was clear that my marriage and my responsibility to that marriage came first. That was tremendously influenced by my Catholicism."[84] They tried opening their relationship so that both of them could have other sex partners, but this plan ultimately failed and they ended their marriage as adversaries. Abdo still weighs the decisions he made and is disappointed he was unable to balance his marriage and gay identity: "I certainly don't perceive that I could have denied my homosexuality and remained healthy, and particularly spiritually healthy. But it has cost me a lot."[85] Gerald Allen, on the other hand, provides an example of a gay man who, with the help of his wife, did manage to hold his marriage together. Allen is a lector in his parish and serves as vice-president of the parish council. As of the writing of his life text, he had been married to and in love with the same woman for twenty-five years. He did not act on his homosexual desires until he was thirty years old, and he kept his behavior a secret from his wife for at least a decade. Eventually he found the pressure of the dual life too much to endure, so he told his wife he was involved with another man. They both found support groups to help them through this and they stayed together. It seems to have worked out remarkably well for him: "My wife and my lover are good friends. The two of them have helped me solve some of my own problems."[86]

The above stories demonstrate there is no single, correct solution to the ethical problems of being gay and married. In all of these cases, however, the men were driven to act with honesty. Being honest was an act of self-love that relieved them of the burdens of a heavy secret, yet it also created a burden for their wives. While it might be fair enough to interpret their actions as selfish and harmful, these men were also motivated by a sense of respect for their wives. They knew their wives deserved honesty and the option to decide for themselves if they would rather be with a man who could be totally devoted to them, emotionally and physically. These men tested the boundaries of relationship and found the best possible resolution in their circumstances.

James Morrison feels being gay should be all about testing boundaries and forging new ways of structuring relationships. Since gay people are already marginalized for their intimate relationships and erotic desires, they are in the position to question all conventional norms. He feels gay people can lead us to explore new frameworks for understanding what constitutes an act of love. "Gay men will have accomplished nothing, I believe, if we do not create new kinds of relation — to one another, and to others, and to ourselves — different from the ones we have been given."[87] As an adult, Morrison found himself being abandoned by a man he loved because the man wanted a conventional relationship and he did not. He questioned if committing to an exclusive, monogamous pairing was really the best way to be in a loving relationship with another man.

Other autobiographers contemplate these kinds of issues too. Gerald Allen, above, found a way to balance two important relationships at the same time — with his wife and with his lover. José Zuniga tried for a time to maintain a three-way relationship with his friends Dave and Laurie, who were themselves romantically involved. He was always sexually and emotionally attracted to Dave; at the same time, he loved Laurie and their physical acts together were an outgrowth of their spiritual intimacy.[88] Then there are those who, like Morrison, wonder if monogamy is necessary for building a healthy relationship. Brian McNaught used to think monogamy was the only appropriate choice to legitimate a committed relationship. He learned, however, from gay friends of his in open relationships, that there are other forms of "monogamy" that matter just as much if not more. Physical, sexual monogamy does not guarantee emotional fidelity and intimacy. As McNaught says, "If having a consistent sex partner is all a relationship is about, it would be smarter to find a young whore."[89] Just as the church fixates on a narrow set of acts in order to condemn all gay relationships, it is a mistake to emphasize sexual monogamy as the primary glue for holding two people together. Obsessing over sexual acts misses the point:

> If, on the other hand, your ideal relationship is based on deep love; if your dream is to share yourself as a friend and companion with another; if your life course is to grow and discover, be sick and healthy, rich and poor in the company of a particular one whose devotion and whose growth prompt an internal peace, then seek out a person who shares your ideal, and don't settle for less. Sex will take its appropriate place.[90]

The point, of course, is to find an arrangement that honors the needs of all persons in relationship. McNaught and his partner Ray decided physical monogamy was the right thing for them. Fenton Johnson and his partner Larry argued over Johnson's sexual forays in other cities, which he sought whenever he traveled. Larry wanted Johnson to be monogamous; but Johnson wanted to keep other doors open, knowing Larry would die before him. They worked out an arrangement allowing Johnson to have sex with other men only when he traveled out of town, as long as he told Larry about it afterward. Johnson writes about this arrangement with a certain amount of ambivalence. He knows their relationship was founded on an emotional monogamy, but he also realizes how his position blocked a channel of intimacy:

> In refusing what he wanted, in denying us both this commitment, I kept some doors open, but at the expense of other, more sumptuous rooms. Monogamy, or the lack of it, would not break us up — we were too much in love, both of us, to break up. But after this conversation Larry held a part of himself in reserve, however small, a protected place where he did not allow me to go.[91]

In retrospect, Johnson would have handled things differently in order to be as close to Larry as possible. Since Larry died, he has the privilege of writing about his acts of love from the perspective of having lost the one he loved. He now knows the importance and value of honoring the needs of the other, which in turn pushes the self to grow: "To advance into our lives, to open new doors, we have to shut old doors behind us."[92]

The death of his lover also taught Johnson the urgency of love. James Morrison learned this lesson too late with a close friend in college. He knew he loved Nicholas and that Nicholas loved him, even though neither of them had yet come to terms with being gay. When Nicholas came out to him, hoping for a reciprocal utterance from his friend, Morrison could not say the words. He did not want to say he was gay and he did not want to say he loved him because that would imply his homosexuality. Instead, he put it off:

> I would tell him in the springtime, I thought, and meanwhile I would love him, in a language definite as speech, and hope that he knew. It was not so long a time, and the innocence before experience has experience in it too, just as the fullness before loss has loss in it, and the loss after, fullness.[93]

By the springtime, however, it was too late. Nicholas was gone, seemingly killed in an accident, though Morrison leaves the details unclear. The time before the end is what matters most. Indeed, acts of love are not as freely given after a relationship ends, yet Morrison realizes urgency is a luxury. Most of us who love are faced with making commitments which must last a very long time. Morrison knew from what he had observed in his life, "that vows of allegiance or resolution were always followed by obtuse breadths of time that made those vows hard to keep, and that this very phenomenon was what life was mainly about."[94] Even though Morrison advocates finding new ways of relating, he recognizes both the centrality and the difficulty of commitment, regardless of its specific content and form.

Within the context of important relationships, commitment is bolstered by love, which is reflected in actions. Whenever these autobiographers discern and act on their responsibilities to themselves and to their "significant others," they perform acts of love. Sometimes these "homosexual acts" are physical and sometimes they are not, but they are performed within the particular context of a loving and committed relationship. To ignore the context is to ignore the person, whose gay identity is a combination of being *and* doing. To deny gay people their acts is to deny them love; and if we believe God is love, as Catholics do, then to deny them love is to deny them God. Church teaching on homosexuality should then be considered not only inadequate or insufficient but also sinful and idolatrous. These gay Catholics have loved as deeply and intensely as anyone, and in that love have attained glimpses of the holy. When Philip Gambone was intimate with his first lover, it was about much more than sex: "I wanted to do everything for him, give him everything, surrender totally, the way the saints had surrendered to God."[95] William Storey cannot imagine a relationship more loving and fulfilling than the one he has with his life partner: "We enjoy a spousal relationship that is a true marriage of minds, hearts, and bodies in every way — except legally!"[96]

It is these kinds of connections and relationships — manifestations of divine love — that matter the most in human lives, especially in the face of death. Rafael Campo learned about the power of love and forgiveness in an encounter with a close friend who was dying of complications from AIDS. Gary was a fellow writer Campo had met through a teacher who had inspired them both. Campo writes about Gary as a man who was not afraid of his sensuality. In sharing their poetry with each other, Campo learned from Gary how to explore the dimensions of his sexuality he had previously held beneath his surface consciousness. When Gary's condition began to worsen, it was overwhelming for Campo. The link between desire and disease was too much to fathom, so he withdrew from the situation entirely. Campo did not return phone calls and he ignored the messages that Gary might be dying. When Gary was brought into the ICU where Campo was working, Campo still avoided contacting him. He did not know how to be both friend and doctor for this man who represented so much for him. One night, he finally visited Gary. Though Gary was angry at Campo for having kept his distance, he offered his forgiveness and understanding. In that moment of reconciliation — made possible by Gary's act of love — Campo felt the grace-filled touch of a man who not only had forgiven himself and his body but had also transcended the boundaries that limit and constrict:

> He forgave me my own needs, understanding at once my preoccu-
> pation and fascination with his death and my fear of it consuming
> me. In that tiny hospital room, on my own turf and surrounded
> by devices familiar to and workable only by me, fairy-godmotherly
> Gary orchestrated with the sweep of his pen my salvation. Capable
> of levitating above his bed, lashed down only by the chest tube that
> attached him to the mortal world I inhabited, he made me feel fab-
> ulously and unabashedly queer, made me want to sing the soothing
> Spanish lullabies whose words I knew but had never learned.[97]

In that grace-filled moment, Campo felt the touch of liberation to embrace the fullness of himself, the self he knew inside but had never learned to contact. His encounter with his friend Gary helped Campo to embrace his gayness on his own terms. Gary's act of love, expressed by granting forgiveness of his friend, was redemptive for both of them.

In old Catholic practice, we were encouraged to *seek* forgiveness when faced with our own deaths — to make an act of contrition. It represented the need for our souls to be pure when coming face to face with our eternal judgment. The focus was on our sins, our actions and inactions in which we failed to live according to God's will. While Catholics probably still hope for purity of soul at the time of death, as symbolized in

the sacrament of anointing of the sick, contrition is no longer the dominant theme. Love seems to take priority. Catholics have followed other
Americans in being less concerned about sin and judgment at the hour
of death, and more concerned about connecting with loved ones. Eugene
Kennedy notes how the fateful events of September 11, 2001, as recorded
in countless phone calls and voice messages, provide a portrait of what
people do when they believe they are going to die: "Hearing death's door
unlatch where preachers had warned them the ghosts of judgment waited
for them, they did not enter a plea of mercy to God but instead pledged
their love to their wives and children, their families, and their friends."[98]
Now, while it is true some of them may indeed have implored God's mercy
in their final moments, the point is they wanted to be sure others knew
they loved them. They wanted their final acts to be acts of love. They
knew that in love, they would find God.

Just as these people facing death sensed that acts of love would help ease
their passage from this life into the spiritual realm, these gay Catholic
autobiographers know love — of self and in intimate relationships with
others — is part of finding salvation. Fenton Johnson, whose relationship
with his lover Larry has played such a prominent role in this part of the
chapter, captures the connection between gay acts of love and the realm
of the holy:

> In caring for my lover I came to understand the tautological rela-
> tionship between God and love. My lover's love for me and mine
> for him made me into something better, braver, more noble than I
> had imagined myself capable of being. I was touched by the literal
> hand of God, for this is what love is, in a way as real as I expect to
> encounter in this life.[99]

In loving and nurturing his partner, Johnson achieved a new level of wholeness and holiness — a touch of salvation. The wholesale denigration of gay
acts of love by the church presumes to sever this important connection
to the divine, yet it is in these very acts that redemption is found. If gay
people are not allowed to love as deeply and intensely as everyone else,
then their acts will, of necessity or despair (the greatest sin of all), become
acts of harm:

> What is the cost of cutting love from the heart? I have spent a good
> deal of time considering that question, and this is part of what I have
> learned: The cost translates into acts that can be counted and tallied
> and for which we all finally pay. Violence against others, violence
> against oneself; bigotry, drug addictions, suicides, assaults, murders,
> or the simple, dull passing of a life given to self-pity, self-denial, and

bitterness; contempt for others, so as to reduce them to something like the contempt one feels for oneself.[100]

The church's refusal to view homosexual acts in the context of particular situations and relationships is death-dealing. Being gay and doing gay are inseparable, so our survival is linked both to who we are and what we do. The church needs to recognize that homosexual acts are inextricable from gay selves. If church leaders really grasped this, they could reshape the tradition and dialogue with gay Catholics to help us discern when our acts lead to good and when they lead to harm. Instead, the church has withdrawn from *any* conversation about the potential goodness of homosexual acts, so gay Catholics have begun to develop their own sexual ethics. This is most appropriately where the conversation should begin anyway, with the lived experience of those who have been marginalized for their sexual identity. As Johnson says, "We are in the earliest stages still of creating a community, which is to say a stable set of values against which we may measure and reward or correct our conduct."[101] These life texts provide the initial transcripts of the conversation. They are narrative portraits of gay-and-Catholic identity, written by persons whose authorship of their own lives is at the same time their claim to authority over those lives.[102]

And what of this question of authority? Critics inevitably make the charge that when gay people call for a revision in church teaching, they are trying to "conform the truth to fit their lives rather than conforming their lives to the truth." But this seemingly clever turn of phrase is nothing more than word play. It creates an artificial dichotomy in a relationship that is more realistically symbiotic. If "truth" is to be more than an abstraction, it can only be apprehended through real lives. It is wonderful when people find a truth that works for them and answers whatever is unresolved in their lives, but it is a problem when they decide this "truth" must work for everyone. Insomuch as "truth" is reflective of societal norms, it always represents and "fits" the lives of those considered normative, which by extension are those who have the power to set the definitions. Thus, to some degree, people always conform the truth to fit their lives, or at least to what they need or desire in their lives. To insist that the whole church in all its diversity must live by that partial "truth" is to conform the truth to people's lives. Instead, we need always to be seeking the fullness of truth. The "truths" we have received through church teachings about sexuality are not complete because they do not account for the experience of all sexual lives. Gay Catholic autobiographies reveal a different "truth." In these sacred texts, we observe men who try very hard to conform their lives to the heterosexual norm, but who eventually realize this is not their truth. It does not include their reality. If church teachings on sexuality are to be "truthful," they must encompass the moral universe found in these life narratives and reflect an understanding that the best authorities on sexuality are those who live sexual lives.

Gay Catholics are ready and willing to develop a gay moral theology in a dialogue of mutual accountability with the church, but only if the church takes gay lived experience seriously.[103] It would not be enough for the church to simply subsume gay people into the present system of sexual ethics, in which the wisdom of many sexually active Catholics is already discounted or ignored entirely. Taking lived experience seriously means listening to more than just those people for whom the traditional rules work. Gay people have long been shut out of the traditional system of sexual ethics, and we must not replicate the same disenfranchisement when we develop a gay moral theology. Laurel Schneider cautions us against "advocating 'good' homosexuals who incidentally look and act a great deal like good heterosexuals at the expense, perhaps, of many of the rest of us."[104] It may be true that many gay people want to assimilate and mimic heterosexual norms, or minimally desire the benefits of those norms, as the strength of the gay marriage movement might indicate. But such norms will still exclude those who structure their moral lives in other ways, a point queer theory has made abundantly clear. As I discussed earlier in this chapter, there is always an ethical framework in place, even among those whose life texts do not look traditional. The gay Catholic autobiographers at the heart of this book are both blessed and cursed by the church's exclusion of their lives: cursed because the church does not take their experience seriously, but blessed because their marginal position gives them the perspective to explore a range of ethical options. Their life texts can help us move toward the dismantling of the oppressive categories that cause exclusion in the first place. As Schneider says, "In the end, full inclusion may mean that neither homosexuality nor the heterosexual norm will be left intact."[105]

In one of his autobiographical essays, Andrew Holleran devotes much of his thoughts to a reconsideration of what constitutes sin in his life. He does so in light of the church's condemnation of all homosexual acts as sins. All gay Catholics ultimately face the same dilemma: we all must discern if our gay acts, which we experience as actions of love and faith, are truly the sins our church tells us they are. Holleran comes to the conclusion that homosexual acts are not among the sins that have characterized his life, but "[t]he way I've treated others because of the conflict between my religion, society, culture and those acts may well be, however."[106] Until the church overcomes its fear of "homosexual acts," gay Catholics will have to reshape the tradition themselves. We will continue to reappraise what constitutes sin in light of our experience of being gay.

These autobiographies, texts infused with gay subjectivity, show us gay identity manifested in acts with ethical ramifications — acts that are not "intrinsically evil" but rather integral to full personhood. As such, they provide a necessary foundation for a realistic discussion of gay sexual ethics and the revision of problematic church teachings on homosexuality. The church would do well to join in the conversation.

Chapter 5

Reconciliation

So when I came to be asked, later in life, how I could be gay and Catholic, I could answer only that I simply was. What to others appeared a complete contradiction was, in reality, the existence of these two inextricably connected, yet sometimes parallel, experiences of the world. It was not that my sexuality was involuntary and my faith chosen and that therefore my sexuality posed a problem for my faith; nor was it that my faith was involuntary and my sexuality chosen so that my faith posed a problem for my sexuality. It was that both were chosen and unchosen continuously throughout my life, as parts of the same search for something larger.

—Andrew Sullivan, "Virtually Normal"

My goal in the previous chapter was to profile some examples of the choices and relationships that inform the ethical world of these autobiographies and to place these in the context of my discussion of gay Catholic identity. Within that context, we find these gay men already engaging in the work of moral discernment and performing their actions accordingly. Respecting these autobiographers as persons requires that we respect their subjectivity as narrators of their own moral agency. While this material is already a kind of moral teaching that provides fertile soil for developing a gay sexual ethics, my book is not explicitly a work of moral theology. My intention, for example, has not been to analyze gay acts according to the technicalities of moral theology, with an eye toward evaluating whether these acts are good or evil.[1] My analysis does demonstrate the inadequacy of church teaching on homosexuality, particularly in the way its moral and pastoral bifurcation falsely separates the doing and being of gay Catholic identity. This makes a strong case for the reconsideration and revision of these teachings. But working through the field of moral theology will only provide limited success at this point in time. A great deal of ethical analysis has already been done by notable Catholic moral theologians, but we are still stuck with the same teachings and sometimes even retrenchments in this these teachings. I agree with Mark Jordan that moral and doctrinal analysis alone will not change toxic church teachings on homosexuality until the current structure and culture of the clerical caste is unraveled:

> Correcting Catholic teachings on homosexuality is not only or mainly a matter of proposing amendments to specific documents. The official doctrine is more deeply embedded than that. It is more intimately connected to old arrangements of institutional power. Changing the language without reforming institutional arrangements would be useless, even if it were possible. The most important relations between Catholicism and homosexuality are not embedded in official propositions about homosexuality, nor even in official regulations for homosexual behavior. The forces at work here are not only the forces of words.[2]

So where do we go from here? As I have been saying throughout this book, the church needs to listen to the experience and wisdom of its gay members. We need to move gay life texts to the center of the church's conversation about human sexuality. Gay Catholic autobiographies need to be primary sources in the tradition — sacred texts in their own right, revealing divine intention in the lives of people who have been marginalized for their sexual identity. This is the first step in overcoming the lack of gay subjectivity that is so problematic in the church's understanding of homosexuality. To accomplish this, we will need to engage the Catholic imagination and view these autobiographical acts as "sacramental" events: as grace-filled moments of self-expression and self-understanding, as representations of selves in search of wholeness, integrity, and meaning. Here, I am using the principle of sacramentality in its broadest sense: the notion that "all reality, both animate and inanimate, is potentially or in fact the bearer of God's presence and the instrument of God's saving activity on humanity's behalf."[3] Recall from my discussion in chapter 3, that sacramentality is considered a primary element of Catholic identity across the range of American Catholics, while moral teachings are widely disputed. It seems reasonable then that a more fruitful way forward and a more "convincing" approach to the problems I am addressing will bear this in mind. Reading gay Catholic autobiographies as instances of revelatory grace taps into this dimension.

Gay Catholic autobiographies reflect many qualities of sacramentality as it might be broadly interpreted. They are written in the context of a community that makes gay identification possible; and they aid in the creation of that community, which in turn empowers the life writer to speak his truth in the name of liberating the wholeness of his being. They recount and attest to encounters with the divine that are rooted in loving, interpersonal relationships and encounters. They are metaphorical

representations that facilitate self knowledge and allow gay Catholic reality "to be there" for the sake of the whole church. The experience they
narrate transcends binaries and bifurcations that separate the ambiguous
elements of being and doing gay and Catholic. The early church applied
the Greek word *mysteria* to early liturgical practices, such as the reenactment of the Lord's Supper, initiation of new members, the laying on of
hands, and practices of public repentance — practices which would later
be called sacramental.[4] The use of such a word as *mysteria*, which means
mysteries, or "secrets whispered by God," indicates how beyond definition
early Christians considered these actions. It is this sense of sacrament I
want to link with gay Catholic autobiographical acts. As Doris Donnelly
explains, sacraments "are the places where God's story and the human
story connect. Not only do we need to tell the human story; we need
to hear the human story *first.*"[5] When these life writers narrate their
gay Catholic identities through autobiography, they proclaim "from the
housetops" their own "secrets whispered by God."

In the written narrative, these autobiographers find a space to share
intimate, private information with us about how they experience their
sexuality. Such information needs a public hearing if church teaching is
to be reconciled with the reality of gay lives. Writing provides a kind of
"shield" between the autobiographer and the forces that would have him
policed and silenced, so that he can discuss his sexual desire:

> The act of writing functions as a buffer between private and pub-
> lic discourse. [Autobiographies] mediate intimacies. They transform
> inarticulate experiences into speech, body into voice. They are a safe
> way to acknowledge the woundedness which men may not other-
> wise admit. There is no immediate other to dispute the retrospective
> construction and interpretation of the male self.[6]

The "safety" of uncoerced writing lies in the absence of a policing con-
fessor who would attempt to edit previously unspoken desires of which
others may not approve. Such uncensored intimacies may make readers
uncomfortable. We see what these life writers hold within themselves, and
it forces us to reassess what we previously took for granted as ethically normative. We observe both their moral victories and their moral failures, yet
we must identify with their human struggle and quest for integrity. As
Stephen Spender notes, "Self-revelation of the inner life is perhaps a dirty
business. Nevertheless, even in its ugliest forms we cannot afford altogether to despise anyone who — for whatever reasons — is the humblest
and ugliest servant of truth."[7]

These gay Catholic autobiographers are indeed "servants of truth." In
writing their life narratives, they engage us in a sacramental encounter
with the reality of their identities. Their texts provide a tangible form

through which we can make contact with their lives. Ron Hansen explains how the art of writing is holy and reciprocal: "Writing not only gives form and meaning to our sometimes disorderly existence, but gives the author the chance for self-disclosure and communion with others, while giving readers a privileged share in another's inner life that, perhaps imperceptibly, questions and illuminates their own."[8] This is the foundation of *reconciliation*, which is one of the effects of sacramental grace. At this point, we are very much in need of reconciliation — between the church and its gay members, and for gay Catholics themselves, whose identities have been ruptured by teachings and attitudes that ignore their authentic voices and the fullness of their personhood. Because of this rupture, the journey to reconciliation is a struggle — one that can feel like a battle against internal and external demons. Fenton Johnson notes that writing is his battleground and "the prize in the struggle is nothing more or less than life, which is to say love, which is to say God."[9]

In the aesthetic process of writing their life texts, these gay Catholics reconcile their seemingly conflicting sexual and religious identities. Or at least they find a way of holding the two together. For Richard Rodriguez, it is a matter of accepting his inner plurality. When asked how he can call himself both gay and Catholic, he takes this as "a question about the authenticity of the soul": "When you slice an avocado, the pit has to go with one side or the other, doesn't it?" But Rodriguez is not either/or, or black/white; instead, he is both/and — what he calls *brown*. His is a mixed soul, which has to do "with the irreconcilability of questions and answers." Thus, he finds a better analogy in the image of a wishbone that is tugged on, but still held together in tension: "The tension I have come to depend upon. That is what I mean by brown. The answer is that I cannot reconcile. I was born a Catholic. . . . I was born gay."[10]

The reconciliation afforded for gay Catholics in the autobiographical process is not based on resolution but rather on a coming to terms that is founded on a deeper self-awareness. Their life texts represent a discovery and acknowledgment of divine intention in their lives. By the time they write their texts, their "conversion" or self-healing has already begun to occur. In a sense, the autobiography reenacts this process. It is a sort of "ritualizing" of the transformation that has already begun to transpire in a life. The autobiographical act gives birth to the constructed self of the text, a representation of who the autobiographer imagines himself to be. As the life writer moves through his "rebirth," he begins to tell his story differently. Part of healing is imagining how he wants his life to look. The past is rethought and reworked through memory in order to redeem the present and forge a new self-concept, a process that is intrinsically sacramental.

For true reconciliation to occur between gay Catholics and the church, both sides have important roles to play. Mark Jordan insists gay people must continue to be pioneers of identity and try to move beyond those terms altogether. We must not be satisfied with familiar categories and constructs of sexual identities, which, as generated by the church, have been "officially sin-identities, identities of condemnation." "The identity was conceived precisely as lacking human fullness, as a deficiency, as a permanent human poverty." Jordan suggests gay Catholics need to repent of having ever put on the identities made for them in the first place. "We should feel contrition for having pretended to have a sexual identity, when what we had were desires, memories, loves."[11] By shifting the terms of the debate, once again taking it out of the realm of moral theology, we begin to ask new questions. We begin with our own subjectivity — that sacramental encounter with God's design in our lives — rather than re-lying on preconceived notions. In the sacramental process, we touch the whole community. We queer the church. As Jordan states, "We want to queer Catholicism so that we can be queerer than 'homosexuals' were ever supposed to be."[12]

Gay Catholic autobiographers call attention to the inadequacy of the objective moral system itself. They help us revise what needs policing in the first place and name the kinds of sins that have kept us from realizing our human potential. The prophetic task for gay Catholics is to open the eyes of the church community to its own sinfulness, and thereby participate in a sort of institutional "examination of conscience." Their autobiographies represent an important way of carrying this out. The lives narrated in these texts are filled with examples of the way church teaching on homosexuality can be damaging. These life texts move us away from hypothetical theories about sexuality toward a deeper grasp of the real-ity of gay identity and experience. We observe in these autobiographies the impossibility of being a gay person "without acting like one." We ob-serve the church's denigration of loving relationships and commitments in the name of condemning a particular subset of acts that are integral to those same relationships. We observe gay men coming to terms with their own failure to live with integrity, even as we observe these same men overcoming debilitating teachings that would have them neglect and deny important dimensions of themselves. In taking these stories seri-ously, as true respect demands, we Catholics come face to face with our own failures as the people of God.

The gay men of these autobiographies may experience pockets of rec-onciliation in particular church communities that welcome them as full persons — Dignity chapters and "gay friendly" parishes, for example — but in general, their experience of the institutional church is one of alienation and rupture. Whenever the church excludes people from the eucharistic table, or communicates that there is a hierarchy among us in terms of gender, sexuality, vocation, lifestyle, etc., it runs the danger of participating in societal sins of injustice, the "sin of the world." When the church paints itself as the perfect society against the backdrop of a perceived "culture of death," it is failing to see the plank in its own eye and the lovable-ness of God's world. Kathleen Hughes brilliantly expresses how such an attitude works against reconciliation:

> The difficulty is this: there can be no reconciliation until there is recognition of need, of rupture, of alienation, of sin, of being drawn to conversion and a new life. If you are a member of the perfect society you have no need of conversion and little need for adequate rituals to express healing. Who needs healing if you aren't broken? . . . How difficult it is to stand in need of the mercy of God if some in the community think they are able to define it and mete it out. Reconciliation cannot happen in a community where the majority believe that they don't need it and that the minority don't deserve it.[13]

The way to overcome this obstacle to reconciliation is to maintain a stance of inclusivity. As much as exclusion is participation in the "sin of the world," inclusion, or the valuing of a high degree of diversity, reconnects us to community. The "sin of the world" prevents us from recognizing the other (those who are different or "queer") as gift. To be authentically Catholic, on the other hand, is to embrace pluralism (both/and rather than either/or), to unite without erasing differences.

This is the role the church community must play if reconciliation is to take place. Such a stance of inclusivity is an example of what Toinette Eugene calls "reconciliatory emancipation." Eugene draws on James Lopresti to discuss marginalized people who tell the truth of their stories and themselves over and against the sin of the community. Such people are the "prophetically alienated." Eugene argues that true reconciliatory emancipation must not just proclaim deliverance and forgiveness for individuals, but it must do so "through a redress of specific social and public expressions of oppression and repression in our era of church and world history, from which profound and prolific deliverance is needed."[14] "The two elements expressed in the term 'reconciliatory emancipation' work together to structure the salvific communal dynamic of sacramental realities toward an end of alienating and destructive responses to human difference and of oppressive forms of domination."[15] We have a model for the inclusive embrace of human difference in St. Paul's analogy of the Body of Christ with the human body:

> As it is, God has put all the separate parts into the body as he chose. If they were all the same part, how could it be a body? As it is, the

parts are many but the body is one. The eye cannot say to the hand, "I have no need of you," and nor can the head say to the feet, "I have no need of you."

What is more, it is precisely the parts of the body that seem to be the weakest which are the indispensable ones.... If one part is hurt, all the parts share its pain. And if one part is honoured, all the parts share its joy.[16] (1 Cor. 12:18–21, 26)

Reconciliatory emancipation is necessarily about communal liberation. Raymond-Jean Frontain points out that beleaguered cultures often survive oppression through storytelling. Autobiographical narratives assist in this task. According to Frontain, "Memory is driven by the will to survive. If narrative is both the product of and the stimulus to memory, then narrative, in its richest form, can enact the hope of redemption."[17] Similarly echoing Eugene's injunction, Walter Holland states, "Gay autobiography employs various strategies to validate homosexual identity, depathologize it, and move it toward a political construction of identity, community, and a liberationist ethic."[18] As gay autobiographies expose the political nature of the church's construction of "homosexual" identity, à la Jordan, the reality of gay existence in all its diversity and its full dimensions of being and doing can be revealed.

As members of the church encounter these narratives and take them seriously, the opportunity arises for reconciliation. Then, the long work of healing can begin. Narrating one's life story thus lays the foundation for conversion, or *metanoia*, not just within individuals but also in the church and in the world. As Georges Gusdorf points out in his discussion of the interface between memory and autobiography, "In becoming conscious of the past, one alters the present."[19] When the church community reads these life texts and identifies with their common humanity, we can begin the work of putting aside those long-held attitudes and beliefs that effectively dehumanize particular members of the church. Perhaps then we can move forward to heal the ruptures in gay Catholic lives and create a space within the church for gay Catholics to realize their fully human and embodied potential.

One of the central themes in the stories of gay Catholic identity is regret for the times we failed to be ourselves by trying to live up to others' expectations and images of who we should be, rather than existing as we are with our own unique thoughts, feelings, memories, and desires. Mark Jordan suggests the first step, not only in coming to terms with this failure but also in redefining the terms of self-identification altogether, should be repentance by gay Catholics: "The 'invisibility' of our sexual orientation, the possibility of keeping it as an open secret, has tempted us with silent collaboration for centuries."[20] This silent collaboration only serves to perpetuate damaging church teachings which are designed to erase, or at least hide, gay existence. James Morrison is explicit about why he wrote his autobiography: "I wrote this book to know myself better, and maybe to help certain children, or the grown-ups who tend them, or the adults they grow into, to understand that they exist."[21]

Fenton Johnson notes the irony of the church's reluctance to affirm gay existence in light of its past errors in validating reality. It makes gay people a kind of modern Galileo, whom the church only recently "forgave" for his assertion that the earth was not the center of the universe. "Yet here we are, living, omnipresent evidence of a fact of life far more obvious than the heliocentric planetary system . . . but apparently just as difficult for Christianity to accept."[22] Perhaps these grand gestures of reconciliation begin on the smallest level, when those who read these autobiographies realize, one by one, their common humanity with these gay Catholics. Then we can begin to imagine the rejection and abandonment of church teachings that effectively turn fellow Catholic Christians into alien "others." Then we can heal a rupture in the mystical Body of Christ. As Rafael Campo says so well:

> I want to be mistaken for your brother, or your son; I want to remind you of your daughter, your mother, your sister. I want to give you something, not a disease, but perhaps a cure. I want you to look into the liquid mirror of my eyes, and see someone you recognize. Someone you have always known, someone you might even love.
> Yourself.[23]

Acts of Contrition?

> Every time I pass a crucifix I wonder, what if it had been me up there instead, could I have said, *Father, forgive them, for they know not what they do?* I don't think I'm so special, not any more. At the church here in San Francisco, I bow down and make the sign of the cross, the logo of the Church, an imprint deep within forces me to replicate this logo. Up, down, left, right, the hand that seeks, then pulls away frustrated. The hand tightens, becomes a fist, the fist is raised to the sky, on the desert's edge, angry and queer.
> —Kevin Killian, "Chain of Fools"

Recent events have created a stormy context for the appearance of a book dealing with Catholicism and homosexuality. While I was working on the final chapters of this project, the Catholic Church in America was being rocked by numerous revelations of sexual abuse by clergy over the past several decades, causing even more ruptures in the church community and within individuals. Kevin Killian's anger stems from his own experience of being abused by members of a religious order. Such abuse leaves the deepest of scars. When those who are supposedly God's representatives violate the trust of their position and perpetrate acts like this, it is yet another blow to Catholicism's institutional integrity and credibility. It calls the moral authority of church leaders into question. As Fenton Johnson remarks with due frustration, "A reasonable observer might comfortably characterize the history of the institutionalized church as a series of greater and lesser blunders, and yet its priests and ministers and bishops still claim the authority to judge the realities of our lives."[24] The need for church leaders to listen to the experience and acknowledge the authority of the laity—people who live sexual lives—is apparently more urgent than ever.

Almost equally upsetting as the fact that sexual abuse by priests occurred at all is the way such cases typically were handled by the bishops in charge. In a flood of reports touched off by the criminal trial of priest serial abuser John Geoghan in Boston, the mainstream media uncovered case after case in which the priests in question were reassigned to parish work and then continued their abusive patterns.[25] Staggering sums of money were spent in dioceses across the country to settle these cases without notification of civil authorities and to keep the victims isolated and quiet. The concern with protecting the status and reputation of the clerical caste seems to have taken precedence over the well-being of the faithful. No longer able to control the information related to these cases, the bishops have been forced to confront this issue and deal with the reality of their collective moral failure.[26] In their first official response to this situation, the bishops not only acknowledged their mistakes and apologized for "too often failing victims and our people in the past" but also affirmed their concern with regard to "issues related to effective consultation of the laity and the participation of God's people in decision making that affects their well-being."[27] While it remains to be seen how such a general statement of concern will actually be realized, it is an ideal and standard to which they must be held for the good of the people of God.

The bishops' actions in most of these cases are reflective of an organizational structure in which the top is severed from the bottom. In such a paradigm, the leaders are not answerable to those whom they are "leading." Acting as if they have been granted a sort of "divine right" to rule, the bishops of the church have long operated out of this medieval model. The current crisis illustrates the disastrous results of this kind of unchecked power. Catholic historian R. Scott Appleby notes this scandal "has never been just about the incidence of sexual abuse. It's been about a culture of secrecy, clericalism, a lack of trust and confidence in the laity, a lack of transparency and accountability in the church, and an arrogance that is used to dominate and not to serve."[28] Overcoming these problems will require an "opening up" of the hierarchical structure. In light of the current situation, Catholics on the right and left seem united in recognizing the need for lay Catholics — especially those who live and work with children — to be more involved in church governance.[29] The bishops need to be accountable to us, the laity of the church. It is our children and families who have been put in harm's way and it is our financial contributions they used to "settle" so many of these cases.

The sexual abuse crisis is not only one of unchecked authority and misuse of power with regard to church administration, however; it also illustrates the bishops' inability to fully appreciate and address matters related to sex and sexuality. To put it more bluntly, their understanding of human sexuality needs a "reality check." This crisis is a result of priests dealing with their sexual desire in inappropriate ways, and the bishops have obviously been confounded by the problem. Within their insular system, the bishops have not adequately understood reality as lay, noncelibate people see it. They need to listen to Catholics who are raising families and are responsible for the healthy formation of children and teenagers. They need to listen to Catholics who are actively engaged in sexual relationships, people who can help them understand a dimension of human life in which we can assume the clergy are not the most experienced.[30] The bishops also need to hear the voices of gay and lesbian Catholics, who know the difference between sexual identity and sexual abuse. As Andrew Sullivan states, "We have attempted to explain the moral lessons we have learned in the real world of family and sex and work and conflict. But so many church leaders — from the Pope on down — do not seem to hear or even care."[31]

At various points throughout the unraveling of this crisis, there has been an unfortunate and dangerous tendency on the part of some Catholic leaders to conflate homosexual orientation and pedophilia, in spite of the fact that psychologists mark the former as a natural variation in human sexuality and the latter as a function of arrested sexual development. Some church leaders voiced their opinion that gay priests were *the* problem. In the Vatican's first public comments on the current crisis, papal spokesman Joaquin Navarro-Valls said men who are homosexually inclined "just cannot be ordained," and he even suggested annulling the existing ordinations of gay men.[32] Archbishop Tarcisio Bertone, secretary of the Vatican's doctrinal congregation said that "persons with a homosexual inclination should not be admitted to the seminary."[33] Philadelphia's Cardinal Anthony Bevilacqua remarked, "We feel a person who is homosexual-orientated is not a suitable candidate for the priesthood, even if he has never committed any homosexual act."[34] Even celibacy is not enough to make a gay man worthy in Bevilacqua's eyes — never mind current church teaching to the contrary.

Why would men who would ordinarily claim absolute fidelity to church teaching make remarks which so clearly deviate from it? And why the quick connection to homosexuality in the first place? Let me start with the second question. Given the sexual nature of these crimes, I think it is fair to take the sexuality of these priests into account, but only as one piece in the larger puzzle of this problem.[35] While pedophilia in the strictest sense does not correlate with the sexuality of the perpetrator, not all of these cases are about pedophilia. According to the information currently available, a large percentage of these cases involved teenagers, which experts agree is more accurately called ephebophilia. Adults who find adolescents sexually attractive usually experience this desire according to their sexual orientation, especially when the teenager is clearly maturing into a young adult.[36] In our overly sexualized culture, we are bombarded with images of teens portrayed as sexual objects, particularly in movies and marketing. Indeed, it is almost normative in hegemonic heterosexual masculinity to "want" teenage girls, as long as they are "legal."[37] Inasmuch as this kind of sexual attraction tends toward a "disorder," particularly when it is manifested in an obsessive, multiple, or compulsive manner, it is certainly not what we think of as pedophilia, which turns prepubescent children into sexual objects regardless of gender. The fact, then, that the majority of the teenagers abused by priests were male makes gay priests seem especially culpable, even though ephebophilia is not just a gay issue.[38] Experts also observe more women slowly coming forward to reveal their past abuse by priests, so we do not yet have all the facts we need to accurately assess the problem (if we ever will).[39]

In April 2003, eight internationally recognized psychiatric and medical experts were invited to a symposium at the Vatican to discuss the sexual abuse problem. These experts told church officials that "banning homosexuals from the priesthood would not solve the problem." One of the experts said there is no evidence "that a homosexual orientation, specifically sexual attraction to another adult man, increases the risk of sexual molestation or repeated sexual offenses." Another expert reminded church leaders that "most male homosexuals do not molest children or adolescents," so the presumption of any one-to-one correlation between homosexual identity and abuse is unfounded. They indicated homosexuality is only one of many "risk factors," but that is far different than a "cause" of abusive behavior. More salient risk factors for abuse include access to children, intimacy deficits in adulthood, antisociality, and an exaggerated sense of self-worth. According to one expert, a more central issue in Catholic seminaries is "whether or not students have a mature understanding of their own sexuality."[40]

All of this leads me back to the first question. The reason some church leaders would stray from church teaching that insists on the "worthiness" of celibate gay priests is that it is easier to lay the blame on gay priests than to seriously examine the underlying factors contributing to this situation. As I discussed in chapter 3, the Catholic priesthood contains a disproportionate number of gay men. By now, this is relatively common knowledge in church circles. To suggest there are none in a particular diocese or seminary is naive at best; and to propose the nullification of their ordinations (if one could actually identify which priests really are gay) is outrageous, if only for the impact in terms of numbers. Church leaders who blame gay priests do not want to examine the obvious connections between an all-male, celibate clergy, on the one hand, and church teaching that "requires" celibacy of gay men, on the other.

Let me briefly articulate some of these connections. Gay Catholics are expected to completely sever the *being* from the *doing* of sexuality, a separation most of them find untenable on a permanent basis, as these autobiographers attest. Some gay men (and even some heterosexual men) turn to the celibate priesthood in the hopes of escaping the integration of orientation and acts that would enable a healthy sexual identity. In their striving to be faithful to church teaching, they avoid a healthy sexual formation and an open embrace of their sexuality. In the priesthood, they find an all-male atmosphere, which ironically promotes a culture of homosexuality. These same men traditionally have had unfettered access to young people, young men in particular, who were effectively at the same level of sexual development and experience as the priests themselves. Given this kind of access and their level of sexual immaturity, it is not surprising some of these men might seek carnal experiences with other "boys," sadly violating their position of trust and authority.[41]

Church leaders must share the blame for what has happened — not just for the way they handled the cases, but for maintaining teachings and a structure which implicitly supported occurrences of this kind of abuse. Some conservative commentators are using this crisis to assert the necessity of reinforcing current church teaching on human sexuality.[42] They feel ideals of chastity, abstinence, and celibacy have become diluted and even lost in the midst of a promiscuous popular culture. While it is reasonable enough to frame the issue in this way, I do not agree it captures the real problem: current church doctrine does not reflect the full range of sexual reality and ethical possibilities. Rigid, one-size-fits-all teachings on sexuality inevitably lead to the duplicity we now see with regard to sexuality and the priesthood. Yes, there are many priests, including gay priests, who live celibate lives, but many do not.[43] Strategies for being celibate and still embracing one's sexual self, which seminaries are supposedly emphasizing, simply do not work for everyone. Thus, we have cases of sexual abuse, priests having affairs, and an active homosexual culture in the priesthood.

Minimally, the bishops need to understand that healthy sexuality formation must integrate both *being* and *doing* — orientation *and* acts. Celibacy works only if it too is both orientation and act: an interior charism and a choice freely sought and embraced for as long as it nourishes the soul. In other words, celibacy and priesthood are distinct vocations.[44] When celibacy is forced, it becomes a preoccupation with avoiding all things sexual, which in turn makes it a greater risk factor in terms of sexual abuse.[45] Dropping the celibacy *requirement* and letting women be ordained will not eliminate cases of clerical sexual abuse, but changes like this could go a long way toward solving the problem. It is time for church leaders to abandon old ideas about gender and sexuality and learn from lay people whose experience communicates a different reality. It is not enough to frame this crisis exclusively as an administrative problem, in which bishops are called to accountability in the way they deal with personnel. They also must be accountable in terms of their moral and pastoral teaching. Especially with regard to sexuality, lay people simply have more experience than the celibate clergy has.[46] And no one has more to teach about gay identity than gay people themselves. That is why heeding the lessons of these autobiographies is so important.

Behind the scapegoating of gay priests in this crisis lies an antigay agenda. Catholic lay people need to check not only the bishops' power and lack of expertise but also the bishops' biases and homophobia. It is an animus against gay people which prompts men like Cardinal Bevilacqua and papal spokesman Navarro-Valls to issue a wholesale condemnation of gay men — even to the extent of making remarks that do not accurately reflect church teaching or the reality of the priesthood. The depth of societal enmity toward being gay makes these autobiographies even more consequential. I hope my analysis of these "sacred texts" will enlighten the church to the reality of gay lives and lay bare the inadequacy and injustice of current church teaching on homosexuality. These life texts offer a corrective to simplistic constructions of what it means to be gay and to act gay. The "homosexual lifestyle," as naysayers like to call it, is no more or less complex, rich, and varied than the "heterosexual lifestyle." These autobiographies represent the lives of real people making sense of the various identities with which they have been dubbed in the present social and religious context, a challenge we all share in different ways.

Conclusion: An Act of Hope

> So, we are obliged to live out the telling of our individual stories, and
> then we are obliged to attempt to tell the church secrets that begin
> to appear through them.   — Mark Jordan, *Telling Truths in Church*

I write this book as an act of hope: I hope my work will be a contribution to
the ongoing and worthy effort to destigmatize being gay in the church. As it
is now, even though the church teaches respect and justice for gay people,
the bifurcated and confusing teaching interferes with the realization of
that goal. Consider the case of celibate gay priests. According to church
teaching, they should be able to share the truth of their sexual identity
with their parishioners; but we know this is rarely the case. Ignorance and
misconceptions about being gay work against an honesty that would no
doubt be life-saving for some of their congregants. The same can be said of
gay teachers in Catholic schools. One risks one's job if one comes out; yet,
consider how meaningful it would be for a student with an emerging gay
identity to have a positive Catholic role model. One gay Catholic man who
attended a high school seminary recalls being counseled by his spiritual
director, a priest whom he later learned was gay: "[Being gay] was still
something I was trying to figure out, I was struggling with, and all he
could do was listen to me."[47] Just imagine the positive interaction which
might have occurred if the priest/director had been able to share his own
sexual identity with a student who likely felt alone. The church needs
visible gay role models, but fear on all sides buttresses the closet walls. I
hope my opening up of these gay life stories will help lower the fear factor
that functions to overdetermine the differences in our sexual identities.

My biggest hope lies with gay Catholic students. I hope work like this
will alert school administrators to the way their institutions reinforce
heteronormative assumptions that marginalize sexual minorities. Catholic schools should be places where the values of respect, friendship, and
justice for gay people are clearly communicated. This too is not generally
the case. In his recent book, *Being Gay and Lesbian in a Catholic High
School,* Michael Maher documents through personal interviews and two
survey studies the many ways lesbian and gay Catholic high school students still experience what he calls "dis-integration." The integration of
student, studies, family, community, and faith that is a mark of Catholic
education is not happening for students who are gay. Catholic educators
who attempt to rectify this situation by providing supportive experiences
for gay students often find themselves facing a storm of criticism from
parents and colleagues. Maher's conclusions about the double message of
church teaching on homosexuality mirror my own. Maher asks in his conclusion, "Can most people defend the rights of gay and lesbian people and
at the same time condemn the actions they take in expressing love?" He

answers, "In my 1995 survey study, I found that most adolescents cannot hold both of these views simultaneously."[48] The students who agreed with statements based on the church's moral rhetoric were less likely to agree with statements based on the pastoral rhetoric. The opposite was also true. It seems even teenage Catholics find the bifurcated church teaching on homosexuality sends a mixed and confusing message.

Mixed messages like this have serious repercussions within schools and in society at large. Although surveys disclose a majority of America's high school students tend to hold more liberal, "pro-gay" opinions than previous generations have held, high schools remain largely hostile environments for gay students. In a recent poll conducted by Zogby International, half of high school students surveyed admitted having witnessed gay students being called "faggot," "homo," or "dyke" to their faces, and an astounding 88 percent of those polled used the phrase, "That's so gay," to describe something they do not like.[49] Happily, Catholic students in the survey stand out as a group in having particularly liberal opinions with regard to gay civil rights and marriage issues, so something positive is getting across; but direct harassment of gay students persists. This paradoxical behavior reflects the contradictions inherent in bifurcated church teaching and presumptions that it is realistically possible to love a person but hate the actions that help define who they are in the first place. These schizophrenic attitudes contribute to the higher rate of gay teenage suicides. In April 1997, an eighteen-year-old football player named Marcus Wayman killed himself after a police officer stopped him and a male friend and threatened to out him.[50] I hope my work will help to enlighten more people to the full reality of gay experience so we can work to save the lives of young men like him.

American society is increasingly divided over the issue of homosexuality and lesbian and gay rights. Instances of harassment and violence toward gays and lesbians have been on the rise in recent years. The church is not entirely to blame for this volatile atmosphere, but it must own its share of responsibility for the ambiguous message and attitudes its teachings promote. It denounces violence against gay people even as it calls into question their relationships. I hope this book will help move the societal debate forward in a productive and nonviolent way by taking us beyond the constraining assumptions religious institutions have fostered about gay people. We need to see gay people not as a category about which simplistic generalizations are to be made, but as complex individuals dealing with multiple concerns in their lives. Gay people want the same social recognition as heterosexual people for their loving relationships and families.

On October 16, 2000, Robert Daniel was admitted to a Shock Trauma center in Baltimore for complications arising from AIDS. His partner Bill

Flanigan was not allowed to see Daniel or confer with Daniel's physicians, even though he had a Durable Power of Attorney for Health Care Decisions. It was only after Daniel's mother and sister arrived four hours later that Flanigan was allowed access or information. By that time, Daniel was unconscious with a breathing tube he would not have wanted. He died shortly thereafter without ever having been able to say goodbye to his partner.[51] I hope my work will highlight the validity of gay relationships and the importance of giving them the same protection and benefits as heterosexual partnerships. Then, men like Robert and Bill will not have to be separated from each other when they need each other the most.[52]

This kind of social change will require a conversion of heart on the most personal levels, so I return to my hope for reconciliation. It is a difficult task because it is not only a matter of memory, healing, and forgiveness, but also, as Robert Schreiter says, "about changing the structure in society that provoked, promoted and sustained violence."[53] Yet gay Catholics continue to seek reconciliation with the church. In these life texts, gay autobiographers engage in an exercise of self-examination which discloses not only their own personal struggles and shortcomings but also the ways the church has failed them. My analysis of these texts reveals that church teaching on homosexuality is not just inadequate but also injurious in the way it bifurcates human beings. On this level, these autobiographies are confessions of the "sinned against," stories of the way church teaching has victimized gay people. When gay Catholics tell their life stories, they stand as alienated prophets. James Lopresti links the term "prophetic alienation" with those

> who take a stance over against the community because of what they claim to be the community's own failure or sin. In its classic forms, such alienation resulted in schism, the separation of the churches. In contemporary forms, while schism may not be publicly acknowledged, that is the private experience of the prophetically alienated. In the past, doctrinal or juridical questions may have caused the separation. Today it is usually a matter of disagreement about moral principles, the acceptability of variant lifestyles, or disputes over the roles of church leadership.[54]

Church leaders need to take the steps to overcome this de facto schism. They need to listen to the life stories of gay people and take seriously their moral agency and life experience. They need to recognize that the pastoral rhetoric about respecting gay persons is meaningless when the associated moral rhetoric undercuts gay personhood. Consider the case of Bill Stein, who was fired from his job as Music Director at Holy Family Parish in Rockford, Illinois. Though Stein had worked at the parish for five years and had performed with the church choir for the pope in Italy, he was fired for refusing to end his relationship with his partner of ten years. According to news reports, Stein had never hidden nor flaunted his relationship; it only became an issue when parishioners learned he and his partner were planning to adopt a child.[55] Something is terribly amiss when a person who has competently served his community for several years is fired for loving another human being and wanting to care for a child in need of a home. Such an action on the part of the church in no way signifies the respect and justice that is supposed to be accorded gay people. Quite the contrary, the church is participating in a grave injustice when it imposes a penalty — the loss of one's livelihood — for remaining in a committed and loving relationship. In the collision of the moral and pastoral rhetoric, it seems the church is more than happy to take advantage of gay people and to use their talents as long as they do not act like full human beings.

Gay Catholic autobiographies reveal what it means for a gay person to be a full human being. In light of the complexity of gay lives, it is untenable to make sweeping condemnations of gay acts and relationships that are directly linked to gay identity. It is no longer admissible for church leaders to ignore the unitive and procreative aspects of so many gay relationships, and it is absolutely unacceptable for church leaders to blame gay people for problems like clergy sexual abuse. Just as listening to the stories of abuse victims prompted the bishops to take action and make changes in policy, listening to gay life stories should prompt a similar *metanoia* on their part.

In a recent apostolic letter, the pope stated, "It is clear that penitents living in a habitual state of serious sin and who do not intend to change their situation cannot validly receive absolution."[56] Whereas the pope was likely referring in part to gay people who reject the church's ban on homosexual acts, I would turn his statement back on church leaders who, despite overwhelming testimony by faithful Catholics, refuse to consider any modification of the church's teachings on homosexuality. We cannot absolve church leaders of their sin until they demonstrate a serious intention to change their situation. As Richard Rodriguez declares, "I predict the Vatican will one day apologize to homosexuals, just as Rome has needed to apologize to Jews, for centuries of moral cowardice."[57] I will not hold my breath for such an apology in the near future, but this book is a testament to my belief that things can and eventually must change.

Once I had finished the first draft of this book, my partner and I decided to paint one of the bedrooms in our house in anticipation of a visit from my mother. As we worked, I realized how much more difficult it was to paint inside the closet than in the rest of the room. It required all sorts of bending and a great deal of discomfort to make the inside of that closet as pretty as the rest of the room. Taping off corners in there was twice as difficult because the light was poor and the space was cramped. The irony of this image was not lost on me in light of having read and analyzed so many gay autobiographies. There is so much more room to move outside of the closet, but church teaching would have us remain still rather than moving as the Spirit might will us. I hope for a day when gay identity does not have to matter so much, when our whispers from the housetop become full-throated and joyous proclamations.

In order for gay identity to no longer matter, we as Catholics will have to recover a sense of what matters most in terms of Christian identity. We need to unravel the categories and assigned meanings that stand in the way of recognizing our common baptismal bond. To be baptized is to be a member of the mystical body of Christ. This is the communion we should experience whenever we participate in the Eucharist. It is the bond that gives meaning and purpose to our gathering for liturgy. It is the reason gay Catholics like Fenton Johnson continue to participate in the life of the church: "I receive [communion] in part because so few gestures remain that bind me to the stranger, that declare that our common fate, which is to be human, transcends distinctions of race or gender or sexuality or economic or social class."[58] This is *koinonia* — the vision of true reconciliation. Once again, the view of a Catholic youth is instructive and hopeful. As a recent graduate of a Catholic high school says about his experience being gay as a teenager:

> On the one hand, I was hiding it. But on the other hand, I knew it was not *the* most important thing at the time. That's what messes you up, because, rationally, you know, "This isn't the most important thing about me, necessarily." But then you get all this information and background that it's bad, so it just kind of blows it out of proportion. It should be an important part of you, but it shouldn't have to be inflated.[59]

From his mouth to God's ears! I hope for a day when coming out does not have to overshadow everything else. I hope someday research like mine will not be so vital — when being gay will simply be something to be celebrated along with so many other human traits.

Appendix

The Gramick and Nugent Investigation: A Test Case for Church Teaching

---

Sister Jeannine Gramick, SSND (now SL), and Father Robert Nugent, SDS, began their official ministry to gay and lesbian Catholics in 1977 with the founding of New Ways Ministry. Under pressure from the Holy See, they disassociated themselves from New Ways (which still operates with the same mission) but continued to minister to lesbian and gay Catholics. In 1988 an investigation was launched by the Vatican's Congregation for Religious and Secular Institutes, to evaluate the orthodoxy of their ministry. After some preliminary communications between the Congregation for Religious and Secular Institutes, Nugent and Gramick, and their superiors regarding who would be on the investigative commission and how it would proceed, there was no word from the commission again until January 1994. In fact, Gramick's and Nugent's religious communities believed the whole thing had been dissolved. Apparently, however, they had been conducting a "study phase" of Gramick and Nugent's ministry. It seems there was a great deal of pressure brought to bear on the Congregation for Religious and Secular Institutes (now called the Congregation for the Institutes of Consecrated Life and Apostolic Societies) by Cardinal James Hickey of Washington, D.C., who was Sister Jeannine's local bishop, to proceed as quickly as possible with the inquest. He had written them "many times concerning this matter" and had clearly already decided that she (and Nugent, by extension) was guilty of "ambiguity with regard to the wrongness of homosexual activity."[1]

After some discussions about the process, Gramick and Nugent were eventually sent a series of questions about their work and texts from their book *Building Bridges: Gay and Lesbian Reality and the Catholic Church*, which they earlier had acknowledged was most representative of their approach to this ministry. They mailed written responses to the questions on June 24, 1994, and discussed them in person with the commission on July 26, 1994. The Maida commission's questions and concerns reveal its attention to the moral rhetoric of the church's teaching on homosexuality, while Gramick and Nugent's responses illustrate their persistent emphasis on the pastoral rhetoric, which they characterize as portraying the full range of church teaching on the subject.

Nugent and Gramick begin by describing the basic purpose of their workshops and writings: "The basic purpose of our ministry is to serve as bridge builders between the church and its gay and lesbian members. We accomplish this as advocates for both groups to be reconciled."[2] With regard to the church, they state they are advocates by presenting

> the full range of teaching on homosexuality and homophobia [a word the Vatican does not use] to lesbian and gay persons. Although Catholics are knowledgeable about the teaching on the objective immorality of homogenital acts, they are largely unaware of the other teachings on homosexuality: the personhood and human dignity of gay and lesbian people, social justice and civil rights, the immorality of unjust discrimination and violence toward homosexual persons, and the mandate for authentic pastoral care.[3]

With regard to lesbian and gay persons, they are advocates by "listening to their experiences, by articulating their concerns, and by being present to them pastorally in their efforts to integrate their sexuality and their faith lives."[4] They state one of their goals is to provide "responsible, balanced, and contemporary information," which includes not only the official teachings of the Roman Catholic Church but also "positions and studies from other Christian denominations, and relevant data from the empirical and social sciences on human sexuality, sexual identity, and sexual orientation."[5] They further nuance this by saying they distinguish between doctrinal affirmations which require assent from Catholics and those which allow for differing judgments. This is a strategy often deployed by progressive Catholics to underscore the fact that very few church pronouncements carry the official distinction of being infallible. In fact, none of the church's teachings on homosexuality could be considered officially infallible. Members of the hierarchy will say these teachings are "definitive," but that in itself is a rhetorical tactic designed to muffle dissenting voices, and it is a category lacking solid canonical grounding. Needless to say, these discursive strategies feed on each other and lead to a combative tension that is difficult to reconcile.

When asked if their goal is to draw people to an acceptance and practice of the official teaching of the church on homosexuality, Nugent and Gramick respond affirmatively, with the caveat that this includes the "full range" of teachings as described above. They are admirably adamant about maintaining this emphasis on including the pastoral rhetoric over and against the commission's obvious preoccupation with the moral rhetoric. The commission notes that the two have been charged in the past with "ambiguity" regarding their treatment of the prohibition on homosexual relationships because they present other theological opinions (regarding the acceptability of homosexual acts) as viable. They do indeed present other views, but Nugent and Gramick claim these are not offered as viable alternatives to magisterial teaching.[6] As the investigation unfolded, the way they handled these "dissenting" opinions became a key sticking point between them and the commission. Interestingly, the commission admittedly had on record letters from five Roman Catholic bishops who had attended Gramick and Nugent's workshops and determined them to be orthodox.[7] This was still not sufficient to assuage the concerns of the commission.

The specific passages of Gramick and Nugent's book, *Building Bridges,* selected by the commission further illustrate the commission's fixation on the moral rhetoric of church teaching. Much fuss is made over the use of the word "natural," which Nugent and Gramick use to describe homosexual feelings and orientation. They use the term in accordance with church teaching that homosexual orientation is innate and unchosen, and to incorporate the position of most modern psychologists. The church also uses the term "disordered," in relation to the orientation, but Nugent and Gramick resist this term for pastoral reasons. They defend themselves by turning on itself the Vatican's argument that "ambiguity" on this subject confuses the faithful. Gramick and Nugent note:

> The layperson, even if well-educated, is not aware of the different technical uses which philosophers and theologians have made of the word "natural" and of the continuing debate about natural law. So, it is somewhat confusing to such a person to hear statements which appear to contradict contemporary scientific claims.... It would be less problematic for the ordinary faithful and for the *pastoral* minister if theologians and philosophers were more sensitive to the way words are generally understood in contemporary society.[8]

In the same document, Gramick and Nugent are asked to discuss their criticism of the 1986 "Letter to the Bishops of the Catholic Church on the Pastoral Care of Homosexual Persons," from the Congregation for the Doctrine of the Faith. One of their primary points relates directly to the bifurcation problem I have been delineating. They state, "Most of the document is concerned with explicating the *moral* evaluation of homogenital activity. As such, it would more adequately be characterized as *doctrinal,* rather then *pastoral.*"[9] The bifurcation problem is further implicated, albeit with different words, in one of the book passages the commission wants clarified: "We may have to choose between 'defending Church teaching' and proclaiming Jesus' message of love."[10] Yet another selected passage from *Building Bridges* reconfigures the bifurcation under the guise of American (pastoral) versus Roman (moral) concerns: "Attempting a delicate balancing act, the U.S. hierarchy is trying to demonstrate to lesbian and gay Catholics a sense of care and compassion while, at the same time, trying to maintain loyalty to Roman expectations."[11]

On October 4, 1994, the commission issued a lengthy report of its findings, and on January 12, 1995, Nugent and Gramick submitted an equally lengthy response analyzing the commission's report. Looking at the two documents together, I see the same fundamental sticking point solidifying: the commission is seeking unequivocal emphasis on the moral condemnation of homosexual acts and relationships; Nugent and Gramick continue to deemphasize the moral rhetoric because they feel that aspect of church teaching is already "well-known and clear."[12] The commission insists this moral teaching "is a crucial question for the moral choices that affect the human person, and, therefore, it cannot be considered incidental."[13] This is an essential and legitimate point, which undergirds my argument about the bifurcation of church teaching. Lesbian and gay persons cannot be separated from the actions and choices which flow directly from their sexual identity. The church recognizes this reality (at least narrowly) with heterosexual persons by enunciating a moral theology of what constitutes good sexual expression and relationships. For homosexual persons, however, all sexual expression is denied, in spite of the assertion that they are to be accorded the dignity and respect due all people, and despite the theological understanding of celibacy being a special charism not granted to everyone. The commission investigating Nugent and Gramick is right: the moral rhetoric cannot be incidental. Nugent and Gramick's ministry is problematic because, in the name of building a bridge, they gloss over the "well-known" moral rhetoric that denies full personhood to gays and lesbians. They know they cannot harmonize the moral and pastoral rhetorics. The commission, on the other hand, marginalizes the pastoral teaching to fully respect gays and lesbians by fixating on the moral condemnation of gay relationships. They too know they cannot harmonize the moral and pastoral rhetorics.

The commission is especially bothered by Gramick and Nugent's reluctance to clearly use the term "disordered" in relation to homosexual orientation. In a strange distortion of logic — an attempt to put a pastoral spin on the moral rhetoric — they insist that the use and precise explanation of the word "may conceivably lead those who are offended by the perceived meaning of the word to cease being offended."[14] It is as if the pastoral component of church teaching exists only to make us feel better about the moral rhetoric. Gramick and Nugent recognize that most gays and lesbians experience their sexuality as a factor of identity, and labeling a person's identity as disordered is pastorally problematic. Couching it in the language of moral theology in order to assuage offense is a ruse. The commission reads this resistance to using exact terms as a lack of loyalty to the church's teachings: "They merely *present* the Church's teaching, but give no evidence of personal advocacy of it."[15] Nugent and Gramick are quick to point out in their response that the question of personal assent came up at the hearing, but Archbishop Maida decided it was not a fair question to ask. Yet the commission undoubtedly wanted Gramick and Nugent to be personally invested in the moral rhetoric. This issue would eventually come back to bite them.

At this point in the investigation, Nugent and Gramick had now submitted supportive letters from fifteen Roman Catholic bishops. Despite this (!), the Vatican commission was still not satisfied and even seemed to ignore them. Gramick and Nugent were asked to respond to three additional questions from the Congregation for the Institutes of Consecrated Life and Societies of Apostolic Faith. In their response, dated February 22, 1996, they clarify that while church teaching considers homosexual orientation "natural," it also describes it as "a pathological constitution judged to be incurable" and as "an objective disorder . . . ordered toward an intrinsic moral evil."[16] Yet Gramick and Nugent still maintain, "On a pastoral level, it is important to help people understand that this assessment of the homosexual orientation does not imply moral failing or sin and that fundamental respect is due to gay and lesbian persons as bearers of the image of God."[17] Talk about an impossible gap to bridge! I respect Nugent and Gramick for their persistence in the face of the commission's interrogation and their insistence on reconciling the two incompatible rhetorics; but most gays and lesbians will hear language such as "pathological," "incurable," "disorder," and "intrinsic moral evil" as attacks on their very souls.

The Vatican's emphasis on the moral rhetoric was ultimately symbolized by the transfer of the case to the Congregation for the Doctrine of the Faith (CDF), headed by Cardinal Joseph Ratzinger, in late 1995.[18] Clearly, the focus of the investigation was now officially centered around moral, doctrinal concerns. The CDF issued a "Contestatio" entitled "Erroneous and Dangerous Propositions in the Publications *Building Bridges* and *Voices of Hope* by Sister Jeannine Gramick, SSND, and Father Robert Nugent, SDS,"[19] which was approved by Pope John Paul II on October 24, 1997. This document deserves special attention because it represents the priorities of the Vatican at this point in time in relation to lesbian and gay Catholics: the moral condemnation of homosexual behavior and relationships must be defended at all costs and dissent from this teaching must be actively restrained. As disturbing as I find this document in terms of its notion of pastoral care and its lack of genuine respect of gays and lesbians, it does adhere closely to the logic of the moral rhetoric in church teaching. After all, it is Ratzinger's job to be the guardian of this rhetoric, and from that perspective, his document accurately names problems in Gramick and Nugent's ministry.

The document begins with a bow to the pastoral rhetoric and some remarks about the intrinsic dignity of all people. That being said, however, it then discusses the importance of "truth" in leading homosexuals to goodness and freedom. This truth is found in the *entirety* of church teaching:

> Clearly, every form of pastoral care must be undertaken in accord with the full truth of the Church's teaching on this problem. When pastoral initiatives are at variance with doctrinal truth, their inherent nature is compromised and they no longer constitute a true help[20]

I agree with this statement at face value, but it is problematic with regard to the issue of homosexuality on at least two levels: First, the bifurcation of church teaching into antagonistic rhetorics makes it virtually impossible to realistically communicate one "full truth." Indeed, Gramick and Nugent are perceived by the CDF to be in error precisely because they strive to convey the "full truth" of the church's teaching. Second, the "full truth" of the church's teaching does not adequately reflect reality as all gays and lesbians experience it.[21] The document is largely concerned with these issues of truth and experience, so it will be helpful to flesh out what I mean here by focusing on examples from the text.

The CDF cites passages from Gramick and Nugent's publications to address their methodology. It is flawed, they say, by "an appeal to a form of moral reasoning in which the category of 'experience' becomes the criterion through which the objective norms of morality are judged and set aside."[22] Several contemporary Christian sexual ethicists have suggested moral theological reflection should draw on more than one source. In general, these sources have been scripture, tradition, reason, *and* experience.[23] To their credit, Nugent and Gramick do utilize all of these categories in their work. The CDF's problem seems not to be that Nugent and Gramick overemphasize lesbian and gay experience as a source, but that they use such experience at all. Both the Maida commission and the CDF selectively cite passages in which lesbian and gay experience is articulated, without acknowledging Gramick and Nugent's use of the other categories. The CDF then accuses them of using experience as the sole criterion. Ratzinger is leery of allowing experience as a criterion because of its link with conscience. He is reacting to the use of obeying one's conscience as a defense for dissent from church teaching, a strategy often deployed by reform-minded Catholics.

This is no small matter. The very authority of the church's teaching is at stake. The primacy of one's conscience is enshrined in the documents of Vatican II (see the introduction), and lesbian and gay Catholics have long used this teaching to justify their life choices. In the passages selected by the CDF, Nugent and Gramick affirm such personal conscience decisions when they are made after a process of deep, prayerful discernment. Ratzinger calls this faulty moral reasoning. In a footnote, he quotes from John Paul II's Encyclical Letter *Veritatis Splendor* (The Splendor of the Truth):

> To the affirmation that one has a duty to follow one's conscience is unduly added the affirmation that one's moral judgement is true merely by the fact that it has its origin in the conscience. But in this way, the inescapable claims of truth disappear, yielding their place to criterion [*sic*] of sincerity, authenticity, and 'being at peace with oneself,' so much so that some have come to adopt a radically subjectivistic conception of moral judgment.[24]

Pope John Paul makes a valid point here. If personal moral decisions are to be taken seriously, at least within the framework of Catholic moral theology, then they must be rooted in something more substantial than an appeal to "what feels good to me." It is also not enough to speak solely of "gay and lesbian experience," when engaging in moral theology because that experience is too diverse to be captured in any single formulation. But I do not think John Paul's critique applies in this case. Nugent and Gramick are thorough in their use of sources other than experience, and gay and lesbian Catholics rarely make decisions to act on their sexuality solely from a position of "it feels good." Our "lived experience" in its multiplicity encompasses all that is involved in being fully alive and engaging with other human beings and the world. Indeed, we are (in)formed by and struggle with the tradition, as many of the autobiographies I discuss attest.

On the other side of the coin, if church teachings and moral doctrines are to be taken seriously, then they too must be rooted in something more substantial than an appeal to an "objective truth," which does not reflect the lived experience of those to whom the teachings are directed. For example, many lesbian and gay Catholics have chosen to express their sexuality by engaging in homosexual relationships, yet church teaching does not recognize any of these. All forms of homosexual expression are denied. Inasmuch as I agree with John Paul about the inadequacy of "radically subjectivistic" conceptions of moral reasoning, I would say church teaching on homosexuality is "radically nonsubjective." There are literally droves of faithful lesbian and gay Catholics acting on their sexuality; ignoring their life choices without even considering the possibility of learning from their experience is short-sighted. There is enough critical mass by now that it seems inadequate to conceive of all homosexual relationships as dissent from "the truth."[25] Church teachers must find a way to take this reality seriously. That is, in fact, what Gramick and Nugent are trying to do in their pastoral work: they know no ministry to gay and lesbian Catholics can succeed if it does not listen to their experience.

The CDF also accuses Nugent and Gramick of tendentiously using church documents to promote a reformist agenda. It is true enough that Nugent and Gramick selectively edit the church documents they cite, especially in *Voices of Hope*; but again, it is not so much to promote a radical agenda as it is to balance the moral and pastoral rhetorics. They even say as much in their book: "A change in the Church's teaching on homogenital expression is not the goal of the positive statements and documents found in this book. . . . We need to interpret, understand, and apply the tradition of the Church in an authentically *pastoral* way."[26] It should be remembered these documents are for the most part written by bishops and bishops' conferences. The CDF fails to address why so many church officials are themselves emphasizing the pastoral rhetoric and even calling for further development of the moral rhetoric. The CDF also brings up one of the passages the Maida commission considered in which Nugent and Gramick talk about having to choose between defending church teaching and proclaiming Jesus' message of love. To this, the CDF boldly responds: "There is, and in fact can be, no opposition between Jesus' message of love and the teaching of the Church."[27] Perhaps Ratzinger and his cohort are selectively forgetting the history of church teaching with regard to slavery, the crusades, the Jews, usury, and religious freedom, just to name a few.

After receiving the Contestatio from their Superiors in December 1997, Gramick and Nugent were given two months to respond independently. Sister Gramick's response is dated February 5, 1998, and Father Nugent's is dated February 6, 1998. Both are lengthy and deal with more of the same; the difference is each of them is much more conciliatory by this point. They concede the need to clarify the moral rhetoric in many ways more strongly in the future. I suspect they were advised to do so by their canon lawyers given the high level of the proceedings. The only thing they really contest is the language used to communicate the moral rhetoric. They are both careful to reiterate the condemnation of homogenital acts, but in language they feel is pastorally palatable and still theologically accurate.[28] Despite this and the positive assessment of their obedience by their Superiors General, the CDF was still not satisfied because neither of them unequivocally expressed *personal* agreement with the church's moral condemnation of homosexual behavior and relationships. It seems the debate over the orthodoxy of their ministry had reached an impasse and the crux of the investigation now hinged on Nugent and Gramick's private feelings. They each were asked to formulate a declaration of personal assent, using the formula "I firmly accept and hold that . . . ," and to ask for pardon for the errors contained in their publications. On July 29, 1998, Gramick submitted her declaration, stating she would not reveal her personal beliefs regarding the moral rhetoric of church teaching: "The approach I have taken in my pastoral ministry requires this reticence."[29] Nugent submitted his declaration on August 6, 1998, stating, in effect, he had never publicly denied church teaching regarding homosexual acts. In turn, the CDF drafted its own "Profession of Faith" for Nugent to sign, which he promptly modified and returned on January 25, 1999.[30] The CDF found both of their responses unacceptable and on July 10, 1999, informed their religious superiors of the order to cease all ministry to homosexuals.[31] Both of them accepted this order in the spirit of religious obedience, but by narrowly interpreting the edict, they continued to speak and write about the subject. Within a year, the order was expanded, forbidding them to speak or write about the case or anything having to do with lesbian and gay concerns.[32] The end result (for now, anyway) of the long investigation is thus an internal power struggle, while the bifurcation problem, which caused the whole unhappy situation in the first place, remains.

Notes

Preface

1. John J. McNeill, *The Church and the Homosexual* (Kansas City: Andrews & McMeel, 1976; 4th ed., Boston: Beacon, 1993); also *Taking a Chance on God: Liberating Theology for Gays, Lesbians, and Their Lovers, Families, and Friends* (Boston: Beacon, 1988); and *Freedom, Glorious Freedom: The Spiritual Journey to the Fullness of Life for Gays, Lesbians, and Everybody Else* (Boston: Beacon, 1995).

2. For example, Gareth Moore, *The Body in Context: Sex and Catholicism* (London: SCM, 1992); also *A Question of Truth: Christianity and Homosexuality* (London: Continuum, 2003). Also see Mark D. Jordan, *The Ethics of Sex* (Oxford: Blackwell, 2002); Other moral theologians of relevance include Charles Curran, Margaret Farley, Lisa Sowle Cahill, Daniel Maguire, Joan Timmerman, Rosemary Radford Ruether, and James P. Hanigan. A useful anthology is Robert Nugent, ed., *A Challenge to Love: Gay and Lesbian Catholics in the Church* (New York: Crossroad, 1983).

3. Some of the most significant of these include: Rebecca Alpert, *Like Bread on the Seder Plate: Jewish Lesbians and the Transformation of Tradition* (New York: Columbia University Press, 1997); Marilyn Bennett Alexander and James Preston, *We Were Baptized Too: Claiming God's Grace for Lesbians and Gays* (Louisville: Westminster John Knox, 1996); Christie Balka and Andy Rose, eds., *Twice Blessed: On Being Lesbian or Gay and Jewish* (Boston: Beacon, 1989); Gary David Comstock, *Gay Theology without Apology* (Cleveland: Pilgrim, 1993); Gary David Comstock and Susan E. Henking, eds., *Que(e)rying Religion: A Critical Anthology* (New York: Continuum, 1997); Comstock, *Unrepentant, Self-Affirming, Practicing: Lesbian/Bisexual/Gay People Within Organized Religion* (New York: Continuum, 1996); Marvin M. Ellison, *Erotic Justice: A Liberating Ethic of Sexuality* (Louisville: Westminster John Knox, 1996); Robert Goss, *Jesus Acted Up: A Gay and Lesbian Manifesto* (San Francisco: HarperSanFrancisco, 1993); Keith Hartman, *Congregations in Conflict: The Battle over Homosexuality* (New Brunswick, N.J.: Rutgers University Press, 1996); Carter Heyward, *Touching Our Strength: The Erotic as Power and the Love of God* (San Francisco: Harper & Row, 1989); James B. Nelson, *Embodiment: An Approach to Sexuality and Christian Theology* (Minneapolis: Augsburg, 1978); Jeffrey S. Siker, ed., *Homosexuality in the Church: Both Sides of the Debate* (Louisville: Westminster John Knox, 1994); Leanne McCall Tigert, *Coming Out While Staying In* (Cleveland: Pilgrim, 1997).

4. Needless to say, they reach a variety of conclusions. Some of the most notable are John Boswell *Christianity, Social Tolerance, and Homosexuality: Gay People in Western Europe from the Beginning of the Christian Era to the Fourteenth Century* (Chicago: University of Chicago Press, 1980); Bernadette J. Brooten, *Love Between Women: Early Christian Responses to Female Homoeroticism* (Chicago: University of Chicago Press, 1996). Robert L. Brawley, *Biblical Ethics and*

Homosexuality: Listening to Scripture (Louisville: Westminster John Knox, 1996); L. William Countryman, *Dirt, Greed and Sex: Sexual Ethics in the New Testament and Their Implications for Today* (Philadelphia: Fortress, 1988); Daniel A. Helminiak, *What the Bible Really Says about Homosexuality* (San Francisco: Alamo Square, 1994); Marti Nissinen, *Homoeroticism in the Biblical World: A Historical Perspective*, trans. Kirsi Stjerna (Minneapolis: Fortress Press, 1998); Saul M. Olyan, "'And with a Male You Shall Not Lie the Lying Down of a Woman': On the Meaning and Significance of Leviticus 18:22 and 20:13," *Journal of the History of Sexuality* 5 (October 1994): 179–206; Robin Scroggs, *Homosexuality in the New Testament: Contextual Background for Contemporary Debate* (Philadelphia: Fortress, 1983); Mark Smith, "Ancient Bisexuality and the Interpretation of Romans 1:26–27," *Journal of the American Academy of Religion* 64, no. 2 (Summer 1996): 223–56. For an interesting peek into the kinds of debates over homosexuality going on among biblical scholars, see Robert Gagnon, *The Bible and Homosexual Practice: Texts and Hermeneutics* (Nashville: Abingdon, 2001), and the subsequent review of and dialogue about it: Walter Wink, "To Hell with Gays?" *Christian Century* 119 (June 5–12, 2002): 32–34; Gagnon, "Gays and the Bible" and Wink, "A Reply by Walter Wink," *Christian Century* 119 (August 14–27, 2002): 40–44.

5. For example: Mary Hunt, *Fierce Tenderness: A Feminist Theology of Friendship* (New York: Crossroad, 1991); Lisa Sowle Cahill, *Sex, Gender and Christian Ethics* (Cambridge: Cambridge University Press, 1996); Kelly Brown Douglas, *Sexuality and the Black Church: A Womanist Perspective* (Maryknoll, N.Y.: Orbis, 1999); Christine E. Gudorf, *Body, Sex, and Pleasure: Reconstructing Christian Sexual Ethics* (Cleveland: Pilgrim, 1994); Anne Bathurst Gilson, *Eros Breaking Free: Interpreting Sexual Theo-Ethics* (Cleveland: Pilgrim, 1995); Rosemary Radford Ruether, *Sexism and God-Talk: Toward a Feminist Theology* (Boston: Beacon, 1983); and contributors to anthologies such as: Ruether, ed., *Religion and Sexism: Images of Woman in the Jewish and Christian Traditions* (New York: Simon & Schuster, 1974); Catherine Mowry LaCugna, ed., *Freeing Theology: The Essentials of Theology in Feminist Perspective* (San Francisco: HarperSanFrancisco, 1993); Lois K. Daly, ed., *Feminist Theological Ethics: A Reader* (Louisville: Westminster John Knox, 1994); Charles E. Curran, Margaret A. Farley and Richard A. McCormick, eds., *Feminist Ethics and the Catholic Moral Tradition* (New York: Paulist, 1996); Rebecca S. Chopp and Sheila Greeve Davaney, eds., *Horizons in Feminist Theology: Identity, Tradition, and Norms* (Minneapolis: Fortress, 1997).

6. I will discuss autobiography theory at some length in chapter 1. I should note the turn to literary theory in religious studies has become more and more "fashionable" as part of the postmodern movement. It offers a useful way of gleaning new insights about religious identity and expression. In Catholic studies, a good example is found in many of the contributions to Thomas J. Ferraro, ed., *Catholic Lives, Contemporary America* (Durham: Duke University Press, 1997). Also see Marian Ronan, "Tracing the Sign of the Cross" (Ph.D. diss., Temple University, 2000).

7. Adrienne Rich, "Compulsory Heterosexuality and Lesbian Existence," in *The Lesbian and Gay Studies Reader* ed. Henry Abelove, Michele Aina Barale, and David M. Halperin (New York: Routledge, 1993), 239. The gay civil rights movement still struggles to strike an appropriate balance between gender differences. Some theorists also note masculine assumptions in the way autobiographical selves are configured, e.g., Susan Henking, "The Personal Is the Theological: Autobiographical Acts in Contemporary Feminist Theology," *Journal of the American Academy of Religion* 59, no. 3 (Fall 1991): 511–26; and Biddy Martin, "Lesbian

Identity and Autobiographical Difference[s]," in *Lesbian and Gay Studies Reader,* 274–93.

8. Michel Foucault, *The History of Sexuality, Volume 1: An Introduction,* trans. Robert Hurley (New York: Vintage, 1990; trans., 1978; Fr., 1976), 43.

9. Though the term "homosexual" was not coined until 1870, some scholars disagree with Foucault's marking of this as the birth of same-sex desire as an identity category. The histories by Boswell and Brooten, for example, which I mentioned earlier, describe a different reality. See also, Amy Richlin, "Not Before Homosexuality: The Materiality of the *Cinaedus* and the Roman Law against Love Between Men," *Journal of the History of Sexuality* 3, no. 4 (1993): 523–73.

10. Sadly, "gay" has also been reappropriated as negative slang by most kids in high school today.

11. Erving Goffman expounds on the difference between the terms in relation to the concept of deviance. See Erving Goffman, *Stigma: Notes on the Management of Spoiled Identity* (New York: Simon & Schuster, 1963), 143–44. John Cameron Mitchell's father recently declared his son is homosexual rather than gay because he "doesn't march in parades or festivals, . . . and he dresses very conservatively." This is despite the fact his son plays a flamboyant transsexual in a movie he also wrote and directed. A very revealing usage of the terms. Warren Epstein, "Parents Proud of 'Hedwig' Star . . . Sort Of," *Philadelphia Inquirer,* August 19, 2001, H6.

12. In mapping out these theoretical issues, I have drawn heavily on Annamarie Jagose, *Queer Theory: An Introduction* (New York: New York University Press, 1996). I strongly recommend this book to anyone seeking a concise articulation of the theoretical issues at stake in the study of sexual identity. As for sexual identity being essential or constructed, I think it is most useful to theorize it as both, rather than either/or.

13. Ibid., 3.

14. Ibid., 115. Civil unions and gay marriage, for example, rely on normative ideas of coupling and monogamy, rather than overturning such traditional ethical assumptions.

15. "Homosexuals engaged in religious communities are warring over a place at the table and so cannot devote much energy to anything beyond the polarizations and solidifications of identity that come in times of war." Laurel Schneider, "Homosexuality, Queer Theory, and Christian Theology," *Religious Studies Review* 26, no. 1 (January 2000): 11.

16. Interestingly, the use of "queer" predates the use of "gay" for homosexual men in this century. George Chauncey notes "queer" was a term of self-identification for homosexual men in the second and third decades of the twentieth century. George Chauncey, *Gay New York: Gender, Urban Culture, and the Making of the Gay Male World, 1890–1940* (New York: Basic Books, 1994), 101.

17. Even the editors of *The Lesbian and Gay Studies Reader,* queer theorists themselves, opted not to use the term "queer studies" in their title, as a way of acknowledging "the force of current usage" (Abelove et al., xvii). In my opinion, the institutionalization of "queer studies" as an academic discipline works against the ideals of the "queer agenda." Max Kirsch suggests queer theory paradoxically mirrors capitalist production rather than building resistance to it. See Max Kirsch, *Queer Theory and Social Change* (London: Routledge, 2000), 17–18.

18. I will explicate these categories more fully in chapter 2.

19. An important exclusion from my study I should mention is Henri Nouwen, whose spiritual journals have been so popular and influential in America. Although

his homosexuality was known by those close to him, he never publicly claimed a homosexual identity. By all accounts, he lived a celibate life; yet, he still experienced love and wrote eloquently of the devastation of a broken relationship. See Michael Ford, *Wounded Prophet: A Portrait of Henri J. M. Nouwen* (New York: Doubleday, 1999).

20. As the saying goes, "Once a Catholic, always a Catholic." Although this phrase is not literally precise, it suggests an important factor about religion. Religious identity is transmitted primarily through the context of everyday domestic life and when an adult "leaves" the religion, he/she is still likely to be influenced by that interpretive scheme. This is illustrated by the contributors to Peter Occhiogrosso, ed., *Once a Catholic: Prominent Catholics and Ex-Catholics Discuss the Influence of the Church on Their Lives and Work* (Boston: Houghton Mifflin, 1987). Peter Mullan, whose film *The Magdalene Sisters* is a scathing indictment of the now-closed Magdalene Asylums for "fallen" Catholic girls, still admires the material culture of Catholicism and says his religion is "in the bloodstream." See Steven Rea, "Mullan Proud of 'Prison Film' with Twist," *Philadelphia Inquirer,* August 17, 2003, H9.

21. By including ex-Catholics, but excluding "ex-gays" from my study, it may seem that I do not accept the former as a legitimate self-identification label. This is not my intention. In fact, I find the latter label to be much more questionable, hence my consistent usage of quotation marks to frame it. What I am doing is mapping out which identifications are pertinent for this particular study, which inevitably reflects my own biases and the way I formulate the issues involved. Because the problem I address in this book concerns religious teachings, I decided to cast a wider net in terms of religious identity, in order to account for a range of personal responses to the problem.

22. Ken Plummer, *Telling Sexual Stories: Power, Change and Social Worlds* (London: Routledge, 1995), 82.

Introduction: Whispers from the Housetop

1. For example, after coverage of a couple going to Canada to have their union blessed, the *Philadelphia Inquirer* received several letters criticizing the paper for running such a story and picture (in addition to several letters in support). One letter writer said the image of two men kissing was "the most revolting picture that I ever saw depicted in any newspaper." While this is incredible to me, it demonstrates the level of emotional response this issue engenders. *Philadelphia Inquirer,* August 21, 2003, A14.

2. In late June 1969, police raided the Stonewall Inn, a gay bar in New York's Greenwich Village. Although raids and arrests at gay establishments had been somewhat routine up to then, this time the patrons fought back and refused to back down for three days. Despite the fact that gay rights work was going on before this with groups like the Mattachine Society and the Daughters of Bilitis, especially in places like Los Angeles, New York, and Philadelphia, this event has taken on a mythic significance for the gay community—becoming a symbolic marker of a shift in gay visibility, definition, empowerment, and activism. A headline in the popular press a week after the event indicates how much things have changed: "Homo Nest Raided, Queen Bees Are Stinging Mad," story by Jerry Lisker, *New York Daily News,* July 6, 1969.

3. Hanna Rosin and Richard Morin, "As Tolerance Grows, Acceptance Remains Elusive," *Washington Post,* December 26, 1998, A1. The article suggests

gay rights would become the same kind of ideological litmus test for electoral candidates as abortion. I think this bore itself out in the 2000 presidential election when the candidates were repeatedly asked their views on gay marriage. Even more telling is the news that Randall Terry, former leader of Operation Rescue and a visible antiabortion activist, is now shifting his focus to the gay marriage issue. See Russ Bynum, "Activist Targets Gay Marriage," *Philadelphia Inquirer*, August 22, 2003, A2.

4. This is according to a Gallup Poll cited in Alfred Lubrano, "Supporting Gays, but Not Gay Marriage," *Philadelphia Inquirer*, October 12, 2003, A6. Unfortunately, the number finding it acceptable has dropped to 46 percent since the Supreme Court's overturning of state anti-sodomy laws in June 2003 — a reflection of the ever-changing context surrounding gay rights issues. These numbers should rebound and shift again with time.

5. Alan Wolfe, *One Nation, After All: What Middle-Class Americans Really Think about God, Country, Family, Racism, Welfare, Immigration, Homosexuality, Work, The Right, The Left, and Each Other* (New York: Viking, 1998), 77.

6. Ibid., 79.

7. As quoted in *Respect*, the news magazine of the Gay, Lesbian and Straight Education Network (GLSEN), Issue 12 (Summer 2003), 18.

8. Ibid., 18.

9. Quoted in Dick Polman, "Gays' Wins Met by Line in the Sand," *Philadelphia Inquirer*, August 10, 2003, A1, A14.

10. Quoted in ibid., A14.

11. Echoing Wolfe's findings, Richard Rodriguez observes that he is welcome to speak to religious groups about race and ethnicity, but he faces objections if he discusses same-sex love. These audiences have problems with his particular diversity. Richard Rodriguez, *Brown: The Last Discovery of America* (New York: Viking, 2002), 208.

12. Richard Morin and Alan Cooperman, "Poll: Many Americans Oppose Gay Unions," *Philadelphia Inquirer*, August 14, 2003, A4. Actually, the numbers immediately after the Supreme Court ruling were closer to four out of ten supporting the blessing of same-sex unions, but the numbers were almost 50–50 three months earlier before the Court's action. I suspect the numbers will shift back as people observe the world not coming to an end as a result of the removal of barriers to gay equality.

13. Quoted in ibid., A4.

14. From the *Lexicon on Ambiguous and Colloquial Terms about Family Life and Ethical Questions*, quoted in David O'Reilly, "New Church Glossary Angers Gay Community," *Philadelphia Inquirer*, April 2, 2003, C1.

15. Quoted in John L. Allen Jr., "Vatican Calls on All Catholics to Oppose Same-Sex Unions," *National Catholic Reporter*, August 15, 2003, 3. In a stunning bit of symbolism underscoring the document's defensive tone, it was signed on June 3, 2003, commemorating St. Charles Lwanga and his companions, who were martyred in Uganda in the nineteenth century for refusing a king's homosexual advances.

16. Quoted in *America* 189, no. 4 (August 18–25, 2003): 4.

17. The history of Christianity demonstrates dramatic shifts in attitudes toward marriage. Our modern glorification of marriage and family is a far cry from early Christianity and its apocalyptic call to sever all earthly ties. See Rosemary Radford Ruether, *Christianity and the Making of the Modern Family: Ruling Ideologies, Diverse Realities* (Boston: Beacon, 2000). Even in America's short history,

marriage has mirrored changes in society. See Nancy Cott, *Public Vows: A History of Marriage and the Nation* (Cambridge, Mass.: Harvard University Press, 2000).

18. Quoted in *America* 189, no. 4 (August 18–25, 2003): 4. Marianne Duddy, Executive Director of Dignity USA at the time, quickly condemned the document as "an absolute perversion of the Catholic social justice tradition." Media Release, July 29, 2003.

19. "Develop," in this case, is a euphemism for "change." Church leadership has always been reluctant to admit doctrine can change, opting instead to say doctrine develops over time as a result of historical circumstances and the concurrent maturation of human understanding. Nonetheless, church teaching has changed and will continue to change over time. See John T. Noonan Jr., "On the Development of Doctrine," *America* 180, no. 11 (April 3, 1999): 6–8; also, Maureen Fiedler and Linda Rabben, eds., *Rome Has Spoken: A Guide to Forgotten Papal Statements and How They Have Changed Through the Centuries* (New York: Crossroad, 1998).

20. For example, "Deep within his conscience, man discovers a law which he has not laid upon himself but which he must obey. . . . For man has in his heart a law inscribed by God. His dignity lies in observing this law, and by it he will be judged. His conscience is man's most secret core, and his sanctuary. There he is alone with God whose voice echoes in his depths." "Pastoral Constitution on the Church in the Modern World" (*Gaudium et Spes*), no. 16, from Austin P. Flannery, O.P., ed., *The Documents of Vatican II* (New York: Pillar Books, 1975), 916.

21. The 1960s were a time of volcanic changes for American Catholics in particular. With the election of John F. Kennedy in 1960, Catholics were symbolically seen as coming into their own as full-fledged Americans. This, combined with the Vatican II mandate to dialogue with the modern world and the new liturgy in the vernacular, caused a significant shift in consciousness and self-understanding among American Catholics. See Jay P. Dolan, *The American Catholic Experience: A History from Colonial Times to the Present* (Notre Dame, Ind.: University of Notre Dame Press, 1992), 421–54; and Robert S. Ellwood, *The Sixties Spiritual Awakening* (New Brunswick, N.J.: Rutgers University Press, 1994), 61–69, 210–19, 296–303.

22. This has been the primary teaching underlying the legacy of Christian sexual ethics. Our struggle today is to appropriately integrate contemporary understandings of sexuality into the tradition, so that we do not perpetuate faulty assumptions.

23. While some contemporary Catholic theologians have suggested alternative interpretations of the term "procreative," Pope Paul VI's encyclical *Humanae Vitae* (1968) was notoriously firm about all sexual acts being open to the possibility of pregnancy. It prohibited all so-called artificial means of birth control. Poll after poll reveals a solid majority of Catholics do not agree with or follow this particular teaching.

24. Andrew Sullivan, "Virtually Normal," in *Catholic Lives, Contemporary America*, ed. Thomas J. Ferraro (Durham: Duke University Press, 1997), 180.

25. CDF, "Letter to the Bishops of the Catholic Church on the Pastoral Care of Homosexual Persons," October 31, 1986: no. 3, in Jeannine Gramick and Pat Furey, eds., *The Vatican and Homosexuality* (New York: Crossroad, 1988), 2. The 1986 "Halloween" Letter was issued in response to what the CDF perceived was an "overly benign interpretation" being given to the homosexual condition itself since the 1975 document.

26. *Catechism of the Catholic Church,* nos. 2357, 2358 (Ligouri, Mo.: Ligouri Publications, 1994), 566. This phrase was echoed verbatim in the recent document against the recognition of gay unions, discussed above.

27. Robert Westerfelhaus, "A Significant Shift: A Pentadic Analysis of the Two Rhetorics of the Post–Vatican II Roman Catholic Church Regarding Homosexuality," *Journal of Gay, Lesbian, and Bisexual Identity* 3, no. 4 (October 1998): 269–94.

28. Ibid., 287.

29. Quoted in Michael Maher, *Being Gay and Lesbian in a Catholic High School: Beyond the Uniform* (New York: Harrington Park Press, 2001), 53.

30. From the 1991 USCC statement, "Human Sexuality: A Catholic Perspective for Education and Lifelong Learning," quoted in ibid., 119.

31. *Catechism,* no. 2358, p. 566.

32. CDF, "Some Considerations Concerning the Response to Legislative Proposals on the Non-Discrimination of Homosexual Persons," July 23, 1992 (personal copy).

33. From "Considerations Regarding Proposals to Give Legal Recognition to Unions Between Homosexual Persons," quoted in *America* 189, no. 4 (August 18–25, 2003): 4–5.

34. There are no exact numbers, but a report by the Urban Institute, based on the 2000 census, found more than 67,000 male couples and 167,000 female couples with children. This makes up about 32 percent of same-sex couples as reported in the census, so it does not even count gay single parents or those who did not report the relevant data. See Eils Lotozo, "Gay and Lesbian Parents Fueling a 'Gayby Boom'," *Philadelphia Inquirer,* June 29, 2003, A22; also, Lisa Leff, "Parents Change Face of Gay Pride," *Denver Post,* June 29, 2003, 11A.

35. This, of course, collides with the church's ban on artificial birth control in addition to the ban on homosexual acts. See Richard L. Smith, *AIDS, Gays, and the American Catholic Church* (Cleveland: Pilgrim, 1994). A growing number of moral theologians and bishops are calling for change in the doctrinal prohibition of condom usage in light of the global increase in HIV-infection. Bishop Kevin Dowling of South Africa notes that in sub-Saharan Africa, the infection rate in some countries is as high as 40 percent. One might justify condom usage as the lesser of two evils (protected sex or spreading a deadly virtus), but Bishop Dowling argues that condom usage need not be defined as an evil at all. Promoting good health and preventing death is a moral imperative. See Kevin Dowling, "Let's Not Condemn Condoms in the Fight against AIDS," *US Catholic* 68, no. 11 (November 2003): 20–22. Also see Catholics for a Free Choice, *Sex in the HIV/AIDS Era: A Guide for Catholics* (Washington, D.C.: Catholics for a Free Choice, 2003). Finally, for the most comprehensive treatment of numerous ethical issues related to AIDS, see *Catholic Ethicists on HIV/AIDS Prevention,* ed. James F. Keenan, with Jon D. Fuller, Lisa Sowle Cahill, and Kevin Kelly (New York: Continuum, 2000). This "landmark contribution to worldwide efforts to respond to HIV/AIDS," in Margaret Farley's words, includes presentations by thirty-six Roman Catholic moral theologians and AIDS workers from all over the world.

36. National Conference of Catholic Bishops, October 1, 1997.

37. In other words, people with same-sex desires do not simply "decide" to have such feelings, even when this orientation seemingly shifts over time. What one does with these desires and how one defines them is another matter.

38. This statement borrows directly from the *Catechism*. Teresa Malcolm, "Vatican Approves Changes to Message for Parents of Gays," *National Catholic Reporter*, July 17, 1998, 12.

39. Released on the Dignity listserv, July 1998.

40. Bishop William Newman, "Baltimore Bishop Asks Forgiveness of Gays/Lesbians," *Bondings: A Publication of New Ways Ministry* (Spring 2001), 1.

41. Raymond P. Kempisty, "Reaffirming Teaching," *National Catholic Reporter*, May 4, 2001, 20.

42. Courage was founded in 1980 by Father John Harvey, and is based on the twelve-step model to encourage homosexuals to live chaste lives and ultimately reverse their orientation if possible.

43. Various bishops have attempted to "rein in" Dignity over the years by banning its members from meeting on church property or by forbidding priests to preside at Dignity liturgies. While such actions have been disheartening, they have also inspired Dignity to refine its mission and reassert its recognition of same-sex relationships.

44. Released by the National Conference of Catholic Bishops, November 11, 1976, "To Live in Christ Jesus" notes that homosexuals "have a right to respect, friendship and justice. They should have an active role in the Christian community." This "pastoral letter on moral values" reconfirms the separation between homosexual acts and persons. Jeannine Gramick and Robert Nugent, eds., *Voices of Hope: A Collection of Positive Writings on Gay and Lesbian Issues* (New York: Center for Homophobia Education, 1995), 10.

45. In 1971, Gramick met a young gay Catholic man who issued the challenge that the church was not doing enough for gay people. She began meeting with lesbian and gay Catholics and was soon joined by Nugent. Thus began their informal ministry.

46. This statement from the original order was quoted in a later letter (May 9, 1988) from Pio Laghi, the Apostolic Pro-Nuncio, to then-bishop of Green Bay, Wisconsin, Adam J. Maida, requesting that he chair the commission to investigate the orthodoxy of Gramick and Nugent's ministry. All documents related to the investigation and cited in this study, unless otherwise noted, were made publicly available in a nonpaginated format by Gramick and Nugent through the website of the *National Catholic Reporter*, www.natcath.com/NCR_Online/documents; accessed October 6, 1999.

47. Deeply related to this underlying issue is the matter of power and the fear that heterodoxy will undermine that power. I do not want to minimize this. In these kinds of controversies, church officials are often most concerned with maintaining the status quo and are reluctant to change moral teachings because it might upset the power structure which grants them their privileged position. For an excellent treatment of the way church proscriptions against homosexual acts reinforce the gendered hierarchy of power, see Kathy Rudy, *Sex and the Church: Gender, Homosexuality, and the Transformation of Christian Ethics* (Boston: Beacon, 1997). My concern in this book, however, is to focus specifically on the inadequacy of current moral doctrine and subsequent pastoral practice.

48. Dignity/USA, "Gay Catholics Dismayed and Angry at Vatican Authorities," July 13, 1999 (personal copy).

49. It would seem Gramick, after defying the order of complete silence, had one of her busiest years of speaking engagements ever. Her talks in the year following the last notification were about conscience and the use of silencing as a discipline

in the church. Nugent has addressed some groups on the topic of obedience in church history.

50. In fact, a year 2000 poll conducted by Belden, Russonello and Stewart, for Catholics for a Free Choice, revealed only 44 percent of "highly committed" Catholics look to church leaders for authoritative guidance on the issue of homosexuality. Patricia Miller, "Chasing Conservative Catholics," *Conscience* 22, no. 2 (Summer 2001): 14.

51. From an April 14, 2000, editorial in the *Southern Nebraska Register*, quoted in Tom Roberts, "Gramick on Conscience in Lincoln," *National Catholic Reporter*, May 5, 2000, 6. Bruskewitz is also the only American bishop to make the unprecedented move of excommunicating all Call to Action members in his diocese.

52. Thomas J. Billitteri, "Gay and Lesbian Catholics Beg to Differ," *U.S. Catholic* 62, no. 11 (November 1997), 11–12. Gumbleton has acknowledged his views have been shaped by the fact that he has a gay brother. He is the only bishop thus far to have spoken at a national Dignity convention (Denver, 1999).

53. Dignity was not permitted to be an official exhibitor and the president was disinvited from participating in a workshop because of Dignity's opposition to the moral rhetoric condemning homosexual expression.

54. Chuck Colbert, "Rifts, Questions Emerge at Meeting on Gays," *National Catholic Reporter*, October 2, 1998, 9.

55. The removal was in response to a letter from Cardinal Ratzinger of the CDF. It is widely believed the letter was instigated by Michael Macaluso, a member of the Rochester diocese who had complained for years about Bishop Clark's pastoral approach to gays and lesbians. See the A.P. news story of August 20, 1998. Also, Chris Schenk, "We Are the Body of Christ," *Focus on FutureChurch* 6 (Fall 1998), 1–2.

56. News brief in *National Catholic Reporter*, December 25, 1998, 7.

57. News brief in *National Catholic Reporter*, December 18, 1998, 8.

58. Ed Griffin-Nolan, "The Body of Christ Torn Asunder on 'Gray Day'" in Rochester," *National Catholic Reporter*, March 12, 1999, 5.

59. Both ordinations were presided over by a bishop of the Old Catholic Church. The Old Catholic Churches are a group of national churches that broke away from Rome for reasons unrelated to the sixteenth-century Protestant reformation. Most were formed to protest the decree of papal infallibility during the First Vatican Council in 1870.

60. Quoted in Teresa Malcolm, "Letter Ends Parishioners' Two Decades of Service," *National Catholic Reporter*, November 5, 1999, 3.

61. Quoted in ibid.

62. Quoted in ibid.

63. See Gill Donovan, "Santorum's Remarks Draw Both Affirmation, Criticism from Catholics," *National Catholic Reporter*, May 9, 2003, 12.

64. Ibid., 12. Also see Lara Jakes Jordan, "Santorum Says Gays OK but Acts Aren't," *Philadelphia Inquirer*, April 23, 2003, A2.

65. "Response to the Report of the Findings of the Commission Studying the Writings and Ministry of Sister Jeannine Gramick, SSND, and Father Robert Nugent, SDS," January 12, 1995.

66. There are, of course, homosexual Catholics who experience their sexuality as a pathological condition, who would seek out ministries such as Courage to help them with their illness. They would eschew gayness as an identity category. My concern in this book is with those Catholics who self-identify as gay.

67. Another, more technical but helpful definition: "Subjectivity is the product of learning to think and handle the self in terms of the social practices and conceptualities of the culture in which a person lives." Ronald E. Long, "The Sacrality of Male Beauty and Homosex: A Neglected Factor in the Understanding of Contemporary Gay Reality," in *Que(e)rying Religion: A Critical Anthology*, ed. Gary David Comstock and Susan E. Henking (New York: Continuum, 1997), 268. When I speak of subjectivity, I am not here speaking of the concept of "agency," as in being the author of one's destiny. Postmodern theory has called the notion of an autonomous "subject" into question. I will take up the question of gay subjective moral agency in chapter 4.

68. James Nelson discusses a widely accepted quadrilateral combination of sources for moral reflection which includes scripture, tradition, reason, and experience. Most Catholic moral theologians since Vatican II have embraced this formula, though magisterial leaders are consistently leery of including experience, especially with regard to sexual ethics. James B. Nelson, "Sources for Body Theology," in *Sexuality and the Sacred: Sources for Theological Reflection*, ed. James B. Nelson and Sandra P. Longfellow (Louisville: Westminster John Knox: 1994), 374–86.

69. In a study of gay, lesbian, and bisexual Catholics in England, the vast majority of respondents ranked "personal experience" as the most important reference for their faith and sexual ethics. They then looked to "the Bible" and "human reason" as sources for theological inquiry. "Church authority" was consistently ranked the least important, which demonstrates the decreasing relevance church teaching holds for gay and lesbian Christians. See Andrew Yip, "The Persistence of Faith Among Nonheterosexual Christians: Evidence for the Neosecularization Thesis of Religious Transformation," *Journal for the Scientific Study of Religion* 41, no. 2 (2002), 199–212.

70. Robert Nugent and Jeannine Gramick, *Building Bridges: Gay and Lesbian Reality and the Catholic Church* (Mystic, Conn.: Twenty-Third Publications, 1992), 189.

71. At present, the magisterium is composed entirely of men due to the church's ban on women's ordination, so all church teaching is always already gendered.

72. Mark D. Jordan, *The Silence of Sodom: Homosexuality in Modern Catholicism* (Chicago: University of Chicago Press, 2000).

73. "Nugent Urges Homosexuals to Speak for Themselves," *National Catholic Reporter*, February 11, 2000, 9.

74. Pamela Schaeffer, "Seeking a 'Quantum Leap' on Homosexuality," *National Catholic Reporter*, June 30, 2000, 4.

75. It is not my goal to reify any one picture of gay Catholic identity or reality. The diversity of lives in these texts will speak for itself.

76. "Preliminary Draft of Responses to Questions Posed by the Commission," Submitted to Maida Commission, July 26, 1994.

77. From the Jerusalem Bible. My interpretation is part of a strategy in lesbian and gay studies to "queer" the reading of traditional texts. In this case, I am "queering" scripture.

78. James Olney, *Metaphors of Self: The Meaning of Autobiography* (Princeton: Princeton University Press, 1972), 49.

1. Surveying Autobiographical Acts

1. For an analysis of these kinds of stories, see Lucy Bregman and Sara Thiermann, *First Person Mortal: Personal Narratives of Illness, Dying and Grief* (New York: Paragon, 1995).

2. *Religion* usually relates to an organized belief system with formal rituals, moral codes and a community structure. *Spirituality* is more focused on the individual and his/her personal way of making meaning in life, which may or may not be associated with organized religion.

3. Raymond C. Holtz, *Listen to the Stories: Gay and Lesbian Catholics Talk about Their Lives and the Church* (New York: Garland Publishing, 1991): William G. Storey, James Abdo, Toby Johnson, Joe Izzo, Tom Cunningham, Malcolm Mac-Donald, Jim Bussen, Larry Sullivan, Paul Albergo, Tom McLaughlin, Lou Tesconi, John O'Leary, Jimmy Kennedy and Derrick A. Tynan-Connolly, Bill Knox and John Brady, Tom Kaun and Kevin Calegari, Jim Revak and Michael Conley, Gerald Allen, and Joe McGuire. (Gerald Allen represents the one African American autobiographer in my study.)

4. Brian Bouldrey, ed., *Wrestling with the Angel: Faith and Religion in the Lives of Gay Men* (New York: Riverhead, 1995).

5. Catherine Lake, ed., *ReCreations: Religion and Spirituality in the Lives of Queer People* (Toronto: Queer Press, 1999).

6. Andrew Sullivan, "Alone Again, Naturally," *The New Republic* 211, no. 22 (November 28, 1994): 47, 50, 52, 54–55.

7. Jeannine Gramick, ed., *Homosexuality in the Priesthood and the Religious Life* (New York: Crossroad, 1989): William Hart McNichols, S.J.; Brother Amos; Father Paul; Matthew Kelty, OCSO; Richard John Cardarelli, OFM Cap.; Brother Jonathan; and Father Aelred.

8. James Wolf, ed., *Gay Priests* (San Francisco: Harper & Row, 1989): Rev. T. Thompson; Rev. R. Roberts.

9. See my discussion of Mark Jordan's work above and in chapter 3.

10. I will give the full citation for each of these when they are specifically addressed in subsequent chapters.

11. Again, these will be fully acknowledged when they are cited in later chapters.

12. John J. McNeill, *Both Feet Firmly Planted in Midair: My Spiritual Journey* (Louisville: Westminster John Knox, 1998).

13. Fenton Johnson, *Keeping Faith: A Skeptic's Journey* (Boston: Houghton Mifflin, 2003).

14. Brian McNaught, *A Disturbed Peace: Selected Writings of an Irish Catholic Homosexual* (Washington, D.C.: Dignity, 1981); and *On Being Gay: Thoughts on Family, Faith, and Love* (New York: St. Martin's, 1988).

15. Andrew Sullivan, *Love Undetectable: Notes on Friendship, Sex, and Survival* (New York: Alfred A. Knopf, 1998).

16. James Morrison, *Broken Fever: Reflections of Gay Boyhood* (New York: St. Martin's, 2001).

17. Patrick E. Horrigan, *Widescreen Dreams: Growing Up Gay at the Movies* (Madison: University of Wisconsin Press, 1999).

18. Frank DeCaro, *A Boy Named Phyllis: A Suburban Memoir* (New York: Viking, 1996).

19. Will Fellows, *Farm Boys: Lives of Gay Men from the Rural Midwest* (Madison: University of Wisconsin Press, 1996, 1998): James Heckman, Larry Ebmeier, Rick Noss, Lon Mickelsen.

20. Richard Rodriguez, *Hunger of Memory: The Education of Richard Rodriguez* (New York: Bantam, 1982); and *Days of Obligation: An Argument with My Mexican Father* (New York: Penguin, 1992).

21. Richard Rodriguez, "Irish Catholic," in *Political Passages: Journeys of Change through Two Decades 1968–1988*, ed. John H. Bunzel (New York: Free Press, 1988).

22. Richard Rodriguez, *Brown: The Last Discovery of America* (New York: Viking, 2002). Rodriguez says *Brown* is "the most dynamically gay book that I've written." Quoted in Michael Depp, "An Angry Young Man Grows Older," *Chronicle of Higher Education* (August 2, 2002), accessed September 10, 2002, at www.chronicle.com.

23. Tommi Avicolli Mecca, Giovanna (Janet) Capone, and Denise Nico Leto, eds., *Hey Paesan! Writings by Lesbians and Gay Men of Italian Descent* (Oakland, Calif.: Three Guineas Press, 1999); Anthony Julian Tamburri, ed., *Fuori: Essays by Italian/American Lesbians and Gays* (West Lafayette, Ind.: Bordighera, 1996).

24. Rafael Campo, *The Desire to Heal: A Doctor's Education in Empathy, Identity, and Poetry* (New York: W. W. Norton, 1997); *The Other Man Was Me: A Voyage to the New World* (Houston: Arte Publico Press, 1994); *What the Body Told* (Durham, N.C.: Duke University Press, 1996); and *Diva* (Durham, N.C.: Duke University Press, 1999).

25. José Zuniga, *Soldier of the Year: The Story of a Gay American Patriot* (New York: Pocket Books, 1994).

26. David Kopay and Perry Dean Young, *The David Kopay Story: An Extraordinary Self-revelation* (New York: Donald I. Fine, 1988).

27. Dave Pallone with Alan Steinberg, *Behind the Mask: My Double Life in Baseball* (New York: Viking, 1990).

28. Fr. Robert L. Arpin, *Wonderfully, Fearfully Made: Letters on Living with Hope, Teaching Understanding, and Ministering with Love, from a Gay Catholic Priest with AIDS* (San Francisco: HarperSanFrancisco, 1993).

29. Fenton Johnson, *Geography of the Heart: A Memoir* (New York: Scribner, 1996).

30. Patrick Merla, ed., *Boys Like Us: Gay Writers Tell Their Coming Out Stories* (New York: Avon Books, 1996).

31. Andrew Holleran, *Nights in Aruba* (New York: William Morrow, 1983); and *The Beauty of Men* (New York: Plume, 1997); David Plante, *The Catholic* (New York: Atheneum, 1986); Daniel Curzon, *The World Can Break Your Heart* (Stamford, Conn.: Knight's Press, 1984).

32. Bregman and Thiermann suggest four different voices within the text separate from the human being who writes the text and stands outside of it: the author, the narrator, the protagonist, and the intended reader (18–19).

33. Olney, *Metaphors of Self*, 34.

34. James Olney, "Autobiography and the Cultural Moment," in *Autobiography: Essays Theoretical and Critical*, ed. James Olney (Princeton: Princeton University Press, 1980), 21.

35. Ibid., 22.

36. Some theorists contend the self in autobiography is never "discovered," but entirely created. Autobiographical discourse encourages an illusion of self-discovery that puts the self before language, even as it suggests the power of

language to reveal and sustain the self. Autobiographical acts would be disabled without this illusion. See Paul John Eakin, *Fictions in Autobiography: Studies in the Art of Self-Invention* (Princeton: Princeton University Press, 1985), 190–91.

37. "Indeed autobiography is fiction and fiction is autobiography: both are narrative arrangements of reality." Robert Elbaz, *The Changing Nature of the Self: A Critical Study of the Autobiographic discourse* (London: Croom Helm, 1988), 1. Paul de Man and Michael Sprinker also advocate this position.

38. Sidonie Smith, for example, borrows from Judith Butler's theory of gender performativity to insist that the unified self of an autobiography is strictly a performance, a repetition of convention. Sidonie Smith, "Performativity, Autobiographical Practice, Resistance," *a/b: Auto/Biography Studies* 10 (Spring 1995): 17–33.

39. Louis A Renza, "The Veto of the Imagination: A Theory of Autobiography," in Olney, ed., (1980), 268–95. For a similar position and an excellent overview of the range of theories and concerns, see Barry N. Olshen, "Subject, Persona, and Self in the Theory of Autobiography," *a/b: Auto/Biography Studies* 10 (Spring 1995): 5–16.

40. Plummer, 168. In Olney's most recent work, he borrows the term "peri-autography," from Vico, to express a similar idea: "writing about or around the self." James Olney, *Memory and Narrative: The Weave of Life-Writing* (Chicago: University of Chicago Press, 1998), xv.

41. Georges Gusdorf, "Conditions and Limits of Autobiography," trans. James Olney, in Olney, ed. (1980), 45.

42. Philip Lejeune calls this the autobiographical pact. See Philip E. Baruth, "Consensual Autobiography: Narrating 'Personal Sexual History' from Boswell's *London Journal* to AIDS Pamphlet Literature," in *Getting a Life: Everyday Uses of Autobiography*, ed. Sidonie Smith and Julia Watson (Minneapolis: University of Minnesota Press), 181–82.

43. More sophisticated contemporary authors may disrupt this understanding through rhetorical manipulations. See Albert Stone, "Modern American Autobiography: Texts and Transactions," in *American Autobiography: Retrospect and Prospect*, ed. Paul John Eakin (Madison: University of Wisconsin Press, 1991), 100.

44. Olney, *Memory and Narrative*, 343.

45. Ibid., 371. Diaries or journal entries may come closer to first perceptions of experience, but even these memories undergo a certain amount of editing and rethinking in the process of narrating them.

46. Gusdorf, 38.

47. Bregman and Thiermann, 53.

48. Plummer, 172.

49. See Goffman, 105.

50. Paul Ricoeur, "Narrative Identity," trans. Mark S. Muldoon, *Philosophy Today* 35 (Spring 1991): 73, 79.

51. Mark I. Wallace, ed., "Introduction" in Paul Ricoeur, *Figuring the Sacred: Religion, Narrative, and Imagination*, trans. David Pellauer (Minneapolis: Fortress, 1995), 13.

52. "The nature of the identity conflict often depends on the latent panic or, indeed, the intrinsic promise pervading a historical period." Erik Erikson, *Life History and the Historical Moment* (New York: W. W. Norton, 1966), 21.

53. Goffman, 100. Goffman describes this as moving from the position of being "discreditable," which requires vigilant secrecy to avoid stigma, to that of "discredited," which is managed without the ever-present fear of disclosure.

54. I have extended this argument in an unpublished paper, "The Coming Out Narrative in Gay and Lesbian Autobiographies," May 1996.

55. Goffman, 102.

56. Robert McRuer, "Boys' Own Stories and New Spellings of My Name: Coming Out and Other Myths of Queer Positionality," in *Genders 20: Eroticism and Containment*, ed. Carol Siegel and Ann Kibbey (New York: New York University Press, 1994), 263.

57. Karl J. Weintraub, "Autobiography and Historical Consciousness," *Critical Inquiry* (June 1975): 837.

58. Paul Robinson, *Gay Lives: Homosexual Autobiography from John Addington Symonds to Paul Monette* (Chicago: University of Chicago Press, 1999), xxii. The three contemporary autobiographers he profiles are Andrew Tobias, Martin Duberman, and Paul Monette, in a chapter entitled, "The Closet and Its Discontents."

59. Morrison, *Broken Fever*, 101 (emphasis mine).

60. See Goffman, 37.

61. Plummer, 87.

62. Olney, "Autobiography and the Cultural Moment," 13.

63. Ibid., 41.

64. This is Mark Wallace describing Ricoeur's theology of the narrative self. Wallace, in Ricoeur, *Figuring the Sacred*, 14.

65. Bregman and Thiermann, 56.

66. Wallace, in Ricoeur, 13.

2. Narrating Gay Identification

1. Holleran, *Beauty*, 69.

2. Ritch C. Savin-Williams, *"... And Then I Became Gay": Young Men's Stories* (New York: Routledge, 1998), 3. One could, of course, act sexually against one's sexual orientation, but this usually is distressing for the individual. This is the reason conversion therapists attempt to change not only the behavior but also the orientation of gay people. Some Catholic theologians like McNeill and Curran even suggest that acting against one's orientation is unnatural and thus morally problematic.

3. Ibid., 3.

4. C. Warren, *Identity and Community in the Gay World* (New York: Wiley, 1974), quoted in Barry D. Adam, "Love and Sex in Constructing Identity Among Men Who Have Sex with Men," *International Journal of Sexuality and Gender Studies* 5 (October 2000): 337.

5. Some studies of sexual orientation begin with an exploration of the "causes" of homosexuality, both psychological and physiological, and whether or not people are born this way. While the autobiographers I study may have their own ideas about such causes, it is not the focus of my project. My concern with self-identification and discourse renders debates about the biological origins of homosexuality irrelevant. For an interesting look at biology-based projects, see Simon LeVay and Dean H. Hamer, "Evidence for a Biological Influence in Male Homosexuality," and William Byne, "The Biological Evidence Challenged," in *Scientific American* 270 (May 1994), 44–55. Also, Bruce Bagemihl, *Biological Exuberance: Animal Homosexuality and Natural Diversity* (New York: St. Martin's Press, 1999).

6. Adam, 337.

7. See Foucault, *History of Sexuality*. The usefulness of identity as a tool for personal and political liberation is hotly debated among some gay/queer academics and activists. I have already highlighted some of these concerns in my prior discussion of gay communal identity and metanarratives. Bearing these in mind, I still find the concept useful in terms of self-definition and to overcome reductive notions of sexuality as desire and behavior completely isolated from personhood.

8. Michel Foucault, *Ethics: Subjectivity and Truth*, ed. P. Rabinow (New York: New Press, 1997), quoted in Jonathan Alexander, "Beyond Identity: Queer Values and Community," *Journal of Gay. Lesbian, and Bisexual Identity* 4 (October 1999): 306.

9. Schneider, 8.

10. From Tess Tessier, *Dancing after the Whirlwind: Feminist Reflections on Sex, Denial, and Spiritual Transformation* (Boston: Beacon, 1997), 10.

11. Alexander, 295.

12. Brian Utter, "Bisexuality and the Spiritual Continuum," in Lake, ed., 146.

13. A useful essay drawing on social scientific findings in order to critique the simplistic way sexuality is currently understood by both church and society is David T. Ozar, "Harming by Exclusion: On the Standard Concepts of Sexual Orientation, Sex, and Gender," in *Sexual Diversity and Catholicism: Toward the Development of Moral Theology*, ed. Patricia Beattie Jung, with Joseph Andrew Coray (Collegeville, Minn.: Liturgical Press, 2001), 252–66.

14. Brother Dave Berceli, M.M., quoted in Dan Grippo, "Why Lesbian and Gay Catholics Stay Catholic," *U.S. Catholic* 55 (September 1990), 23. It seems even the American bishops recognize a certain depth to the concept of sexuality: "Sexuality refers to a fundamental component of personality in and through which we, as male or female, experience our relatedness to self, others, the world, and even God." Quoted in Maher, 92.

15. See Patricia Beattie Jung and Ralph F. Smith, *Heterosexism: An Ethical Challenge* (Albany: SUNY, 1993). Jung and Smith offer an excellent analysis of the pervasiveness of heterosexism and shift the "problem" of homosexuality to straight people, whom they call to overcome bias and ignorance.

16. Rob Nixon, "Avondale: A Memoir of Identity," in Mecca et al., eds., 42.

17. As Lucy Bregman points out, this feeling of difference in childhood is common in autobiographies and may be the "spur toward cultivating the kind of interiority which makes autobiography possible." Part of the autobiographical project is fitting this sense of difference into a discernable category or pattern (private communication, January 31, 2002).

18. Philip Gambone, "Learning and Unlearning and Learning Again the Language of *Signori*," in Tamburri, ed., 63.

19. Tommi Avicolli Mecca, "Memoirs of a South Philly Sissy," in Tamburri, ed., 18.

20. Toby Johnson, in Holtz, ed., 38.

21. DeCaro, 15.

22. Horrigan, 60.

23. "Mark: A Spiritual Ancestry," interview in David Shallenberger, *Reclaiming the Spirit: Gay Men and Lesbians Come to Terms with Religion* (New Brunswick, N.J.: Rutgers University Press, 1998), 158.

24. I will discuss this more in the following chapter.

25. Johnson, *Keeping Faith*, 22.

26. Morrison, *Broken Fever*, 7.

27. DeCaro, 4.

Notes to Pages 53–60

28. Ibid., 109.
29. Campo, *Desire to Heal*, 109.
30. McNeill, *Both Feet*, 19.
31. Pallone, 12.
32. William Hart McNichols, "A Priest Forever," in Gramick, ed. (1989), 118.
33. Brother Jonathan, "You Are My People," in Gramick, ed. (1989), 160.
34. Rodriguez, *Brown*, 203.
35. Ibid., 206.
36. Ibid., 202, 205.
37. Ibid., 209–10.
38. Johnson, *Geography*, 55. This statement, with its blatant Catholic imagery, is an example of how intertwined sexual and religious identity can be. A nonreligious gay child would not have shared this feeling of being tested by God.
39. Ibid., 55–56.
40. Ibid., 56.
41. Fenton Johnson, "God, Gays, and the Geography of Desire," in Bouldrey, ed., 244.
42. Lon Mickelsen, in Fellows, 257.
43. Andrew Sullivan, "Virtually Normal," 172.
44. Allen Barnett, in Philip Gambone, ed., *Something Inside: Conversations with Gay Fiction Writers* (Madison: University of Wisconsin Press, 1999), 79.
45. In urban areas, there were gay bookstores for those gay boys with the self-confidence to enter them, and there was probably a richer collection of texts available in some public libraries by the late 1980s, though access could still be an issue. In any case, none of the autobiographers in my study are young enough to have come of age solidly in the "information age." For better or worse, the Internet has now become one of the primary sources for children and teens to learn about sex.
46. DeCaro, 100.
47. Ibid., 101–2.
48. Morrison, *Broken Fever*, 209.
49. Philip Gambone, "Searching for Real Words," in Bouldrey, ed., 229.
50. Campo, *Desire to Heal*, 86.
51. Ibid., 87.
52. Pallone, 17.
53. Matthew Bartosik, "A Winter Break," in *Equal Times* 7, no. 1 (Spring 2000), 7.
54. Morrison, *Broken Fever*, 213.
55. Kopay, 121.
56. Ibid., 129.
57. Campo, *Desire*, 68–69.
58. Sullivan, *Love Undetectable*, 141.
59. Zuniga, 48, 51.
60. Ibid., 108.
61. Ibid., 135.
62. Mickelsen, in Fellows, 254.
63. DeCaro, 136.
64. Johnson, *Geography*, 73.
65. Ibid., 79.
66. Johnson, *Keeping Faith*, 197.
67. Andrew Holleran, "Memories of Heidelberg," in Merla, ed., 93.

68. Ibid., 97.

69. Holleran, *Beauty*, 73.

70. Or something else. Some people are born with what doctors call "ambiguous genitalia," something other than the set of organs, chromosomes, and/or hormones considered to be standard for either male or female. The numbers are not insignificant, with over 2,000 such children born in the United States each year. It has become standard practice for doctors to assign a sex to these children and alter them accordingly. Over 90 percent are transformed into girls because it's "easier." This practice is being challenged by the visibility of intersexed people who are speaking out against such methods. Their existence and recognition should serve to further shake up the rigid binary economy of normative sex and gender expectations. We are obviously more than just male and female. See Cheryl Chase (Executive Director Intersex Society of North America), "What is Intersexuality?" in *PFLAGpole* (Fall 2001), 8–9; Also, Emily Nussbaum, "A Question of Gender," *Discover* 21, no. 1 (January 2000), 92–99. For thorough academic study and analysis, see Anne Fausto-Sterling, "The Five Sexes," *The Sciences* (March–April 1993): 20–25; "The Five Sexes, Revisited," *The Sciences* (July–August 2000): 18–23; and *Sexing the Body: Gender Politics and the Construction of Sexuality* (New York: Basic Books, 2000); Alice Dreger, *Hermaphrodites and the Medical Intervention of Sex* (Cambridge, Mass.: Harvard University Press, 1998); Bernice Hausman, *Changing Sex: Transexualism, Technology, and the Idea of Gender* (Durham: Duke University Press, 1998); and Suzanne Kessler, *Lessons from the Intersexed* (New Brunswick, N.J.: Rutgers University Press, 1998). For an excellent discussion of the religious ramifications of this knowledge, see Christine E. Gudorf, "The Erosion of Sexual Dimorphism: Challenges to Religion and Religious Ethics," in *Journal of the American Academy of Religion* 69, no. 4 (December 2001), 874–80.

71. In saying this, I want to emphasize the social relativity of gender roles and expectations over and against gender as something natural and inborn. This is not to dismiss the fact that many people experience gender factors as integral to their identity and selfhood, as transgendered people assert. I would liken this to my theoretical understanding of sexual identity, which I have already discussed. Here again, postmodern theorists following Foucault resist using identity language with gender because they want to destabilize subject categories like *man* and *woman*. Judith Butler sees these categories as "repetitions" rather than ontological truths, and uses the idea of gender "performance" as a way of subverting oppressive compulsory gender categories. See Judith Butler, *Gender Trouble: Feminism and the Subversion of Identity* (New York: Routledge, 1991). For a very insightful and articulate theological application of Butler's theory, see Mary McClintock Fulkerson, "Gender — Being It or Doing It? The Church, Homosexuality, and the Politics of Identity," in *Que(e)rying Religion: A Critical Anthology*, ed. Gary David Comstock and Susan E. Henking (New York: Continuum, 1997), 188–201.

72. Obviously, masculinity is more complicated than this explanation implies. It is not necessary for all men to fully live up to the ideal of hegemonic masculinity for it to be enforced, nor is it true that the bearers of the hegemonic ideal are the most powerful. Some correlation between the actual and the ideal is necessary, however, even if the imagery has to be forced by those in power. Most men do not in fact display all the qualities of hegemonic masculinity, but they may still benefit from its production and are thus complicit in sustaining it. See R. W. Connell, *Masculinities* (Berkeley: University of California Press, 1995); Stephen B. Boyd, W. Merle Longwood, and Mark W. Muesse, *Redeeming Men: Religion and Masculinities* (Louisville: Westminster John Knox, 1996); Krondorfer, Bjorn, ed.,

Men's Bodies, Men's Gods: Male Identities in a (Post-) Christian Culture (New York: New York University Press, 1996); Harry Brod and Michael Kaufman, eds., *Theorizing Masculinities* (Thousand Oaks, Calif.: SAGE, 1994); Michael Kimmel, *Manhood in America: A Cultural History* (New York: Free Press, 1996). For an interesting look at masculinities and the bible, see Howard Eilberg-Schwartz, *God's Phallus and Other Problems for Men and Monotheism* (Boston: Beacon, 1994). For a feminist analysis of the constrictions of current constructions of masculinity, see Susan Faludi, *Stiffed: The Betrayal of the American Man* (New York: William Morrow, 1999).

73. This too is not uncomplicated. Many gay men enjoy performing masculine gender identities, and attraction to masculinity is usually a primary component of gay sexual identity; so although gay men are victimized by hegemonic masculinity, they too can be complicit in its production. At the same time, the fact that these men engage in same-sex erotic behavior makes gay male gender identity a site where the scripts of normative masculinity are not exactly reproduced but rather interrogated and potentially rewritten. I like R. W. Connell's analysis of this, "A Very Straight Gay," in his book *Masculinities*, 143–63.

74. Horrigan, 80.

75. Ibid., 109–10.

76. In adulthood, these categories become somewhat less simplistic as masculinity becomes more associated with things like power and control (being figuratively on top). Still, the memory of these childhood and teenage categories remains as a point of reference in adult masculinity. The impressions are lasting, as the memories of these autobiographers attest.

77. Horrigan, 32.

78. Morrison, *Broken Fever*, 41.

79. Ibid., 164.

80. DeCaro, 97, also 106.

81. Arpin, 6.

82. McNaught, *On Being Gay*, 45.

83. Zuniga, 19–20, 35.

84. Rick Noss, in Fellows, 235–36.

85. Kopay, 50–51.

86. Ibid., 53–54.

87. Rodriguez, *Hunger*, 126.

88. McNeill, *Both Feet*, 14.

89. DeCaro, 158–65.

90. Ibid., 124.

91. Horrigan, 83.

92. Morrison, *Broken Fever*, 99–100.

93. Rodriguez, *Days*, 37, 32–33.

94. In his most recent book, Rodriguez deals openly with the fact that he never actually says he is gay in his memoirs. He uses the voice of a student interviewer to both raise the issue and speak the words: "He said it was cool with him that I was gay but he wanted to know how I measured the influence of homosexuality...*on your writing, since you never say.*" (Ellipsis and italics in original). See Rodriguez, *Brown*, 223.

95. Rodriguez differentiates American macho from Mexican machismo. He says in English, "the macho is publicly playful, boorish, counter-domestic. American macho is drag — the false type for the male — as Mae West is the false type

for the female." See Rodriguez, *Days,* 56–57. While his portrait of American macho is insightful, his usage of it to exalt Mexican machismo as something more
about chivalry than power is perhaps a bit oversimplified. A number of studies of
machismo have been published recently. See, for example, Matthew C. Guttman,
The Meanings of Macho: Being a Man in Mexico City (Berkeley: University of
California Press, 1996); also, Michael Hardin, "Altering Masculinities: The Spanish Conquest and the Evolution of the Latin American Machismo," *International
Journal of Sexuality and Gender Studies* 7, no. 1 (January 2002), 1–22. For an insightful study of Chicano sexual identities, see Tomas Almaguer, "Chicano Men:
A Cartography of Homosexual Identity and Behavior," in Abelove et al., eds.,
255–73.

96. Rodriguez, *Hunger,* 128–30.

97. Rodriguez, *Days,* 46.

98. Ibid., 47.

99. James Heckman, in Fellows, 98.

100. Horrigan, 39; McNaught, *On Being Gay,* 45.

101. In addition to its relationship to masculine expectations, the drive to over-
achieve and appear "perfect" could also be interpreted as a response to internalized
homophobia. This points out even more clearly the connection between gender
expectations and sexual identity. The feared implication of falling short in terms
of masculinity is that one is also a homosexual. It is no surprise then that reac-
tions to falling short of the masculine ideal are also wrapped up in homophobia.
Thanks to Rebecca Alpert for this insight.

102. Sullivan, *Love Undetectable,*138. Ironically, this ambition and scholarship
while growing up has its own rewards later in life and can pay off in terms of career
and intellectual success. Thanks to Lucy Bregman for this insight.

103. Gerald Allen, in Holtz, ed., 220.

104. "Dan: HIV Doubled My Spirituality," in Shallenberger, 41.

105. "Mark: A Gay Spiritual Ancestry," in Shallenberger, 142.

106. Campo, *Desire,* 105.

107. Philip Gambone, "Searching for Real Words," in Bouldrey, ed., 224.

108. James Abdo, in Holtz, ed., 22.

109. Toby Johnson, in ibid., 38; Tom Cunningham, in ibid., 75–76.

110. Joe Izzo, in ibid., 60.; Larry Sullivan, in ibid., 136.

111. McNaught, *On Being Gay,* 6.

112. Ibid., 29.

113. Ibid., 164.

114. Ibid.

115. Rodriguez, *Hunger,* 52.

116. Ibid., 48.

117. Joseph Kramer, "Body and Soul," in Mark Thompson, *Gay Soul: Finding
the Heart of Gay Spirit and Nature with Sixteen Writers, Healers, Teachers, and
Visionaries* (San Francisco, Harper San Francisco, 1994), 176. By the time a gay
child *is* sexual, he has so internalized the feeling of being outside his parents'
frame of reference that he is unlikely to share any concerns about his sexuality
with them. He may not feel his parents are his allies because they do not know
what it is like to grow up gay.

118. Andrew Sullivan discusses this in the context of Richard Isay's theories on
homosexuality. Sullivan uses it to critique the idea that the alienation comes first
and is a cause of homosexuality. Sullivan, *Love Undetectable,* 122–24.

119. J. D. McClatchy, "My Fountain Pen," in Merla, ed., 197.

120. Ibid., 198.
121. Stephen McCauley, "Let's Say," in Merla, ed., 189–90.
122. Brother Jonathan, "You Are My People," in Gramick, ed. (1989), 163.
123. Paul Albergo, in Holtz, ed., 146.
124. There is also no generalizable pattern of relationships to interpret as "caus-ing" homosexuality, thus refuting antiquated Freudian stereotypes about absent fathers and overwhelming mothers. The autobiographers themselves seem en-tirely uninterested in the idea that their sexuality was "caused" by anything. It simply is part of who they are.
125. Noss, in Fellows, 241.
126. Zuniga, 12.
127. Ibid., 89.
128. Ibid., 272. (Joe is the English language equivalent for José.)
129. Arpin, 32. Sadly, sometimes even a diagnosis with a serious illness is not enough to reconcile parents and children who are alienated because of sexuality. The stigma associated with AIDS is just as difficult for some people to overcome.
130. Kopay, 169.
131. Ibid., 256.
132. Mecca, "Memoirs," 23.
133. Ibid., 28.
134. DeCaro, 207–12.
135. Ibid., 199.
136. Ibid., 203–4.
137. These would include Provincetown, Fire Island, and Key West. Like New York and San Francisco, they are at land's end, close to borders — metaphorically on the margins. This is the imagery Richard Rodriguez uses when he calls San Francisco the "farthest-flung possibility." Rodriguez, *Days,* 28. For another explicit use of this imagery, see Mark Doty, *Heaven's Coast* (New York: Harper Perennial, 1997).
138. DeCaro, 184.
139. Ibid., 88, 91.
140. Campo, *Desire,* 73.
141. Holleran, in Philip Gambone, ed., *Something Inside: Conversations with Gay Fiction Writers* (Madison: University of Wisconsin Press, 1999), 174.
142. DeCaro, 157.
143. Tom Cunningham, in Holtz, ed., 78.
144. Kramer, in Thompson, 177.
145. Nixon, "Avondale," 37.
146. Ibid., 37.
147. Johnson, *Geography,* 81, 83.
148. Heckman, in Fellows, 100–101.
149. Rodriguez, *Hunger,* 57.
150. Ibid., 189–90.
151. McNaught, *On Being Gay,* 20.
152. Ibid., 142.
153. Johnson, *Geography,* 83.
154. Campo, *Desire,* 177–78.
155. Philip Gambone, "Searching," 223.
156. Pallone, 88–89.
157. Peter M. Krask, "The Way the Stars Come Home," in Bouldrey, ed., 147.
158. Campo, *Desire,* 129–30.

159. Ibid., 119.
160. Ibid., 120.
161. Gambone, "Learning," 64.
162. Rev. R. Roberts, "The Fears of a Gay Priest," in Wolf, ed., 147.
163. Ebmeier, in Fellows, 158.
164. James Abdo, in Holtz, ed., 28.
165. Nixon, "Avondale," 32–33.
166. Gambone, "Learning," 79.
167. See Jonathan Ned Katz, *The Invention of Heterosexuality* (New York: Dutton Books, 1995). Also see his *Sex Between Men Before Homosexuality* (Chicago: University of Chicago Press, 2001), for a study of same-sex desire before gay identity was available.
168. William D. Glenn, "As God Intended: Reflections on Being a Gay Student at a Jesuit High School," *America* 184, no. 17 (May 21, 2001), 29.
169. As of 2002, legal protection from discrimination based on sexual orientation remains elusive in the majority of states. Where inclusion in protection ordinances is won, the victory is usually close. Many such protections face regular legal challenges.
170. Andrew Holleran, in *American Contradictions: Interviews with Nine American Writers*, ed. Wolfgang Binder and Helmbrecht Breinig (Hanover: Wesleyan University Press, 1995), 39.

3. Orbiting the Catholic Axis

1. Two volumes that use and explore these terms of identification are Mary Jo Weaver and R. Scott Appleby, eds., *Being Right: Conservative Catholics in America* (Indianapolis: Indiana University Press, 1995); and Mary Jo Weaver, ed., *What's Left? Liberal American Catholics* (Indianapolis: Indiana University Press, 1999). An approach that tries to steer the middle ground is Peter Steinfels, *A People Adrift: The Crisis of the Roman Catholic Church in America* (New York: Simon & Schuster, 2003). At the heart of the liberal/conservative dynamic is the question of authority as related to ideology. For an analysis of this issue with regard to the church hierarchy, see Gene Burns, *The Frontiers of Catholicism: The Politics of Ideology in a Liberal World* (Berkeley: University of California Press, 1992).
2. How political parties are positioned with respect to various issues also changes over time and in turn affects what is defined as liberal and conservative. In the late 1960s and 1970s, for example, positions on abortion were not easily linked with a particular party as they are today. Many democrats favored abortion restrictions and five of the seven Supreme Court justices joining in the Roe v. Wade opinion were Republican appointees. See Joe Feuerherd, "Politics and the Pro-Life Movement," *National Catholic Reporter*, January 17, 2003, 5.
3. Michele Dillon, *Catholic Identity: Balancing Reason, Faith, and Power* (Cambridge: Cambridge University Press, 1999).
4. (Lat., "from the chair"). This requirement must be met for a specific teaching to be considered infallible. The standard is so high that it is rarely met. It has only been employed with regard to the Immaculate Conception and the Assumption, both Marian dogmatic pronouncements. Scalia also emphasized the need for Catholic judges to follow American law on the death penalty. Interestingly, Scalia made his remarks about the same time the Pope urged American Catholic lawyers not to handle divorce cases because of the inherent conflict with church teachings. See David O'Reilly, "Pope's Words Unsettle Catholic Lawyers," *Philadelphia Inquirer*, February 3, 2002, B5.

5. Dillon, 4.

6. This is true for most religions practiced in the United States. While the American value of "separation of church and state" (however unevenly this ideal is actually realized) allows for the free practice of religion, it also insists upon a separation of sacred and secular that does not always make sense in the historical development of religions. This has a special resonance in American Catholic history, which demonstrates a tension between Catholic communal solidarity and American notions of individual autonomy. See John T. McGreevy, *Catholicism and American Freedom: A History* (New York: W. W. Norton, 2003).

7. See R. Laurence Moore, *Religious Outsiders and the Making of Americans* (New York: Oxford University Press, 1986). In addition to the texts discussed in the following paragraphs, other useful studies of American Catholicism include: James T. Fisher, *Communion of Immigrants: A History of Catholics in America* (New York: Oxford University Press, 2000); Bryan T. Froehle and Mary L. Gautier, *Catholicism USA: A Portrait of the Catholic Church in the United States* (Maryknoll, N.Y.: Orbis, 2000); Mark S. Massa, *Catholics and American Culture: Fulton Sheen, Dorothy Day, and the Notre Dame Football Team* (New York: Crossroad, 1999); Claire E. Wolfteich, *American Catholics Through the Twentieth Century: Spirituality, Lay Experience and Public Life* (New York: Crossroad, 2001). For excellent collections of original source documents, see Steven M. Avella and Elizabeth McKeown, eds., *Public Voices: Catholics in the American Context* (Maryknoll, N.Y.; Orbis, 1999); and Anne M. Butler, Michael E. Engh, and Thomas W. Spalding, eds., *The Frontiers and Catholic Identities* (Maryknoll, N.Y.: Orbis, 1999).

8. Jay P. Dolan, *The American Catholic Experience,* see especially his chapter on "The Catholic Ethos," 221–40.

9. Ann Taves, *The Household of Faith: Roman Catholic Devotions in Mid-Nineteenth-Century America* (Notre Dame: University of Notre Dame Press, 1986); Robert Orsi, *The Madonna of 115th Street: Faith and Community in Italian Harlem, 1880–1950* (New Haven: Yale University Press, 1985).

10. This dynamic can still be observed in more recent Catholic immigrant populations, as second and third generations become more assimilated.

11. Paula M. Kane, *Separatism and Subculture: Boston Catholicism, 1900–1920* (Chapel Hill: University of North Carolina Press, 1994).

12. William M. Halsey, *The Survival of American Innocence: Catholicism in an Era of Disillusionment, 1920–1940* (Notre Dame: University of Notre Dame Press, 1980).

13. James Terence Fisher, *The Catholic Counterculture in America, 1933–1962* (Chapel Hill: University of North Carolina Press, 1989).

14. For an excellent study of the impact of race on American Catholicism, see John T. McGreevy, *Parish Boundaries: The Catholic Encounter with Race in the Twentieth-Century Urban North* (Chicago: University of Chicago Press, 1996). In addition to attention given to gender concerns in Taves and Kane, mentioned above, also see Karen Kennelly, ed, *American Catholic Women: A Historical Exploration* (New York: Macmillan Publishing, 1989). For a collection of relevant documents dealing with gender issues throughout American Catholic history, see Paula Kane, James Kenneally, and Karen Kennelly, eds., *Gender Identities in American Catholicism* (Maryknoll, N.Y.: Orbis, 2001).

15. Rodriguez, "Irish Catholic," 336.

16. Ibid., 329.

17. It is interesting that Catholics were leaving their urban ghettos just as gay urban ghettos were becoming more visible and accessible. I am not implying a causal relationship here but rather noting how this opposite movement symbolizes the dilemma of holding gay identity and Catholic identity together.

18. See Arthur Jones, "Catholic Pioneers in the Suburban Landscape," *National Catholic Reporter*, November 2, 2001, 10.

19. Rodriguez, *Hunger*, 106. It is interesting that in the current movement to "reform the reform," which seeks to rid the new liturgy of problematic "American" innovations and influences, a return to "I believe" as the opening of the creed is being suggested. If we follow Rodriguez's analysis, this attempt to solidify a more distinctly Catholic approach by returning to a Tridentine formula would only further fragment Catholic identity in the current American context.

20. Given the context of the autobiographies I examine, it is worth noting that sexual identities, though increasingly multiple and complex, have become available and more defined at a time when Catholic identity seems especially contingent.

21. American Catholic identity is similarly implicated in Phillip Gambone's musings about the intersection of third-generation ethnicity and gay identity. See chapter 2, above.

22. Leslie Scanlon, "Here Come's Everybody's Church," *U.S. Catholic* 67 (May 2002), 28.

23. Carolyn Osiek and Laurie Brink, "Two Women, a Generation Apart, View Religious Life," *National Catholic Reporter*, February 18, 2000, 22.

24. These are also often the Catholics who want to apply an ideological litmus test for people to "prove" their Catholic identity. Unfortunately, such tests usually focus on one issue, such as abortion or homosexuality, at the expense of more central concerns.

25. Lucy Bregman aptly observes that the idealization of pre–Vatican II Catholicism — "nostalgia for a paradise now thoroughly lost" — is a response to the multileveled shifts and fragmentation that mark post–Vatican II Catholicism (personal communication, March 23, 2002).

26. Tom Beaudoin, "Our Catholic Watergate," *America* 186 (June 3–10, 2002), 19. Beaudoin believes this movement has been intensified by the clergy sexual abuse scandal made public in the first half of 2002. Andrew Sullivan also makes a generational argument in light of the scandal: "I think it's fair to say that very few people in my generation of 40-year-olds and younger can take the church's sexual teachings very seriously again." Andrew Sullivan, "Who Says the Church Can't Change?" *Time*, June 17, 2002, 63.

27. Dillon, 119.

28. Ibid., 203–16.

29. Published in detail in a series of articles and summaries in the *National Catholic Reporter*, October 29, 1999, 11–20.

30. Discussed in Dean R. Hoge, "What Is Most Central to Being a Catholic?" in *National Catholic Reporter*, October 29, 1999, 13.

31. "U.S. Catholics: Who Do We Think We Are? The Editors Interview James Davidson," *U.S. Catholic* 65, no. 2 (February 2000), 13.

32. I should note here a few important and useful texts that deal with negotiating an integrated Catholic identity that includes a conscious faith commitment: Daniel Donovan, *Distinctively Catholic: An Exploration of Catholic Identity* (New York: Paulist Press, 1997); Penelope Ryan, *Practicing Catholic: The Search for a*

Livable Catholicism (New York: Henry Holt, 1998); and Paul Wilkes, *The Seven Secrets of Successful Catholics* (New York: Paulist Press, 1998).

33. Lawrence S. Cunningham, *The Catholic Experience* (New York: Crossroad, 1985).

34. Andrew Greeley, *The Catholic Imagination* (Berkeley: University of California Press, 2000), 1. Also see Richard Blake, *Afterimage: The Indelible Catholic Imagination of Six American Filmmakers* (Chicago: Loyola Press, 2000).

35. Greeley, 1.

36. Ibid., 6. Here, Greeley draws on David Tracy's concept of "analogical" imagination in his discussion of metaphor.

37. Rosemary Haughton, *The Catholic Thing* (Springfield, Ill.: Templegate, 1979).

38. For many of these men, part of their Catholic identity was communicated to them in Catholic schools. Not surprisingly, it was not only from the educational content that these men learned about Catholicism but also through the whole atmosphere of the school system and from the brothers, nuns, and priests who ran it. I initially expected to find more stories resembling the darkly humorous stereotype of Catholic schools, in which cruel nuns exact unjust punishments on innocent students. There simply were not enough to warrant a special discussion. And for every mean nun mentioned in these autobiographies, there is another story of an encouraging teacher or positive experience.

39. McNaught, *Disturbed*, 94.

40. Kopay, 33–36.

41. Zuniga. 14.

42. Johnson, "God, Gays," 249.

43. Ibid., 249.

44. Johnson, *Geography*, 103.

45. Ibid., 139, 176.

46. Bouldrey, *Wrestling*, ix–x.

47. McNeill, *Both Feet*, 28.

48. Tony Laveccia, in Holtz, ed., 156.

49. Scott Trepania, "Prayer Life Provides a Focus as I cope with Dropping T-Cell Counts," *National Catholic Reporter*, September 2, 1994, 7.

50. Pallone, 176.

51. Ibid., 178.

52. Campo, *Desire*, 44, 45.

53. Ibid., 44–45.

54. Horrigan, 25, 28.

55. Ibid., 100.

56. Ibid., 85.

57. Rodriguez, *Hunger*, 77.

58. Ibid., 80.

59. Ibid., 78.

60. Sullivan, *Love Undetectable*, 58.

61. Rodriguez, *Hunger*, 84.

62. Johnson, *Keeping Faith*, 33. In another passage, he is even more descriptive: "Like all great theater, the mass transports the audience to a time outside of time, to the place where time is open to eternity, to the authentic experience of God. . . ." Ibid., 283.

63. Horrigan, 162.

64. Nixon, "Avondale," 34.

65. Rodriguez, *Hunger*, 105.

66. I should mention here that the liturgical reform was instituted in varying degrees and with varying levels of expertise in different parts of the country (and the world, for that matter). By the mid-1980s, the pendulum of liturgical innovation was beginning to swing back so that some of the qualities of the old liturgy would be recovered. Some of this is due to Vatican interventions and their tightening grip of control, but some of it is also due to a greater attention to aesthetic detail and nostalgia for the Latin Mass.

67. Morrison, "Saved," in Bouldrey, ed., 64.

68. Johnson, *Geography*, 163.

69. Toby Johnson, in Holtz, ed., 39.

70. Rodriguez, *Days*, 29.

71. Ibid., 180.

72. Jim Bussen, in Holtz., ed., 132–33.

73. Tom Kaun and Kevin Calegari, in Holtz, ed., 208.

74. See Joe McGuire, in Holtz., ed., 232; and Father Paul, "We Shall Not Cease from Exploration," in Gramick, ed. (1989), 143.

75. Heckman, in Fellows, 98.

76. It would be interesting to do an analysis like this of heterosexual Catholic men's life writings. If "feeling different" is indeed part of what drives autobiographical writing in the first place, their life narratives may evidence more of them feeling drawn to the priesthood than I would initially expect.

77. Horrigan, 147.

78. Ibid., 15.

79. Zuniga, 15.

80. McNaught, *A Disturbed Peace*, 75.

81. Thanks to Lucy Bregman for this insight.

82. Donald B. Cozzens, *The Changing Face of the Priesthood: A Reflection on the Priest's Crisis of Soul* (Collegeville, Minn.: Liturgical Press, 2000).

83. See Garry Wills, *Papal Sin: Structures of Deceit* (New York: Doubleday, 2000), 194.

84. In a recent survey of 1,200 priests, 55 percent said a gay subculture exists in their dioceses or religious orders. "Survey: Half of Priests Detect Gay Subculture," *National Catholic Reporter*, September 6, 2002, 20.

85. James Martin, "The Church and the Homosexual Priest: Facing the Challenges and Accepting the Gifts Offered by Homosexual Priests in the Catholic Church," *America* 183, no. 14 (November 4, 2000), 14–15. Now, if only church leaders would recognize God is also calling women and married men as priests, then we could also acknowledge the special gifts these sets of people would bring to the priesthood.

86. Kevin Killian, "Chain of Fools," in Bouldrey, ed., 126.

87. Ibid., 128.

88. I will deal with the sexual abuse crisis more deeply in chapter 5.

89. Jordan, *Silence*, 107.

90. Johnson, *Geography*, 45.

91. Jordan, *Silence*, 159.

92. McNeill, *Both Feet*, 34.

93. Ibid., 42.

94. Ibid., 67.

95. McNichols, "A Priest Forever," 120.

96. Matthew Kelty, "The Land I Love In," in Gramick, ed., 145.

97. Richard John Cardarelli, "Lord, Make Me an Instrument of Your Peace," in Gramick, ed., 153, 155–56.

98. Brother Jonathan, "You Are My People," 166.

99. Rev. T. Thompson, "A Christian Spirituality," in Wolf, ed., 139.

100. Father Aelred, "Without Shame," in Gramick, ed., 177.

101. Arpin, 7.

102. Ibid., 153.

103. Ibid., 48.

104. Ibid., 150.

105. The legalities of the laicization process can be cumbersome and discouraging. Monetary compensation is also an issue, especially for priests who lived in community and have no savings of their own. Additionally, priests who have resigned are technically forbidden to be lay ministers or teachers of religious education.

106. This reflects the idea of the Catholic imagination as theorized by Greeley.

107. David Plante, "Images of the Body from My Religion," in Bouldrey, ed., 172.

108. Ibid., 172–73. This theme also appears in Plante's novel *The Catholic*, when the protagonist Dan imagines his night of love-making with Henry as a reenactment of Christ's love for the Mystical Body of the church. Dan concludes by saying, "In my Church, to deny your body was to deny your soul." Plante, *The Catholic*, 72.

109. Morrison, "Saved," 70.

110. Ibid., 80.

111. Ibid. Morrison echoes the traditional Catholic formula of "faith and works," over and against the "faith alone" or "grace alone" formula of the Protestant Reformation. Of course, Evangelical converts are expected to demonstrate the practical "fruits" of their conversion, which sometimes amounts to an even more severe moralism than that which is typically associated with Catholicism.

112. Kopay, 38.

113. Ibid., 39.

114. Johnson, *Keeping Faith*, 35.

115. Ibid.

116. Ebmeier, in Fellows, 157.

117. Zuniga, xii.

118. Ibid., 156.

119. Ibid., 28.

120. Mecca, "Memoirs," 18.

121. Gambone, "Beyond Words," in Merla, ed., 110.

122. Joseph Kramer, in Thompson, 171.

123. Richard John Cardarelli, "Lord, Make Me," 154.

124. Andrew Holleran, "The Sense of Sin," in Bouldrey, ed., 84.

125. Ibid., 85.

126. Ibid., 88.

127. Ibid., 92.

128. Ibid., 86–87. This story also shows up in his quasi-autobiographical novel *Nights in Aruba*, when the protagonist, Paul, says, "As I put my towel away I concluded that the Catholic Church was right: The body was the temple of the Holy Ghost — nothing more, nothing less." Holleran, *Nights*, 87–88.

129. Holleran, "Sense of Sin," 88. It is interesting that a remarkable number of these authors quote St. Augustine, whose autobiography is so influential and

whose views on sexuality are largely responsible for the sexual ethics we have inherited in the West.

130. Ibid., 95. Also see Holleran, *Nights*, 42–43.

131. David Plante, in Gambone, ed., *Something Inside*, 223.

132. Ibid., 224, 226.

133. Plante, *The Catholic*, 75.

134. In particular, he looks at autobiographies by Kathleen Norris, Terry Tempest Williams, China Galland, Patricia Hampl, and Mary Daly.

135. John D. Barbour, *Versions of Deconversion: Autobiography and the Loss of Faith* (The University Press of Virginia, 1994), 187.

136. Ibid., 200.

137. Campo, *Desire*, 40.

138. Ibid., 42.

139. Ibid., 47.

140. Ibid., 50.

141. Ibid., 40.

142. Gambone, "Searching," 227.

143. Ibid., 232.

144. Ibid., 239. (Ellipsis and format in original.)

145. Ibid., 238.

146. Johnson, *Keeping Faith*, 37.

147. Ibid., 31.

148. Ibid., 14.

149. See Ibid., 34–35.

150. Ibid., 92.

151. Ibid., 245.

152. Ibid., 198.

153. Ibid., 138 (italics in original).

154. Rodriguez, *Brown*, 224.

155. Ibid., 225.

156. Ibid., 230.

157. Ibid.

158. Krask, "The Way the Stars Come Home," 162.

159. Ibid., 164.

160. Kopay, 43–44.

161. Ibid., 244.

162. Killian is the only one of the autobiographers in my study who mentions being sexually abused by clergy. I will say more on this subject in chapter 5.

163. Kevin Killian, "Chain of Fools," 128.

164. Ibid., 128.

165. McNaught, *On Being Gay*, 32.

166. McNaught, *A Disturbed Peace*, 101.

167. McNaught, *On Being Gay*, 147.

168. Ibid., 126.

169. Johnson, *Keeping Faith*, 298.

170. Tony Laveccia, in Holtz, ed., 157.

171. Gerald Allen, in Holtz, ed., 223.

172. William G. Storey, in Holtz, ed., 11.

173. Rodriguez, *Brown*, 226.

174. Ibid., 226–27.

175. Jim Revak, in Holtz, ed., 211.

176. Tony Laveccia, in Holtz, ed., 156.

177. Tom McLaughlin, in Holtz, ed., 154.

178. This is supported in Dillon's study on Catholic identity. See Dillon, 119, 125.

179. Jon Soucy, "Speaking the Unspeakable," *The Hoya* (March 4, 2003), www.thehoya.com.

4. *"Homosexual Acts"*

1. Donna McKenzie calls this "the ethical importance of context," and notes, along with Charles Curran, how the church has refused to take this approach to sexual ethics. Donna M. McKenzie, "Is There a Moral Theologian in the House?" *Religion in the News* 5, no. 2 (Summer 2002): 19. It is disturbing that the church is usually more amenable to a range of opinion on war and killing than it is on sexual matters. This was abundantly clear with the 2003 U.S. military invasion of Iraq. Even though the pope said the action was not morally justified, many American Catholics voiced their dissent without fear of reprisal. The U.S. ambassador to the Vatican even invited a conservative American Catholic theologian to Rome to make a case for the war. Indeed, some conservative Catholics who insist there is no room for dissent on the church's sexual teachings found themselves on the other side of the "church teachings vs. sense of the faithful" debate. Why is this grayness and range of legitimate opinion not allowed when it comes to matters of gender and sexuality? It makes one wonder if the church's main problem with abortion is not so much about the sanctity of life but rather its aversion to sex.

2. Again, one of the best examples is the insistence that every sexual act must be so open to procreation that "artificial" contraception is forbidden. Yet a whopping 96 percent of all Catholic women who have ever had sex have used modern contraceptive methods at some point in their lives, and 73.5 percent of sexually active Catholic women who attend church once a week or more use a contraceptive method forbidden by the church. See the 1995 National Survey of Family Growth, quoted in "The Facts Tell the Story: Catholics and Contraception," brochure produced by Catholics for Contraception (undated).

3. Christine Gudorf, *Body, Sex, and Pleasure*, 29–32.

4. Kathy Rudy, *Sex and the Church*, 115.

5. Fulkerson, "Gender," 198–99. Fulkerson would advocate abandoning any reliance on the sexual identities which inform the heterosexual grid. I want to acknowledge the role these identities play in modern self-definition but also complicate how these identities are perceived and defined.

6. Sullivan, *Love Undetectable*, 45.

7. Margaret Farley, "A Feminist Version of Respect for Persons," in Curran, Farley, and McCormick, eds., 177.

8. Ibid., 178.

9. Andre Guindon, "Homosexual Acts or Gay Speech?" in Gramick and Furey, eds., 211.

10. Ibid.

11. Sullivan, *Love Undetectable*, 50.

12. From her remarks at "The Personal and the Political" panel, Second Sex Conference, New York, September 29, 1979. Reprinted in *Sister Outsider: Essays and Speeches by Audre Lorde* (Freedom, Calif.: Crossing Press, 1984), 110–13.

13. Lucy Bregman has pointed out how the majority of AIDS autobiographies reflect a pre-infection ethic of absolute sexual freedom that could almost be characterized as an absence of sexual ethics altogether. The focus is on sex acts, minus

any substantive attention to relationships. This might be a peculiarity of the genre, a reflection of persons whose identities are partially organized around a disease. The autobiographers in my study who are HIV-positive, like Andrew Sullivan and Robert Arpin, do not match that model. When they do allude to sexual "promiscuity," they do so with some regret, not primarily for themselves but for the stigma and marginalization that makes gay intimacy so hard to find and, in turn, exacerbates the need for casual or furtive encounters.

14. In general terms, one finds Eric Rofes, Michael Bronski, Urvashi Vaid, and Sarah Schulman on the left, rebutting Andrew Sullivan, Bruce Bawer, Gabriel Rotello, Larry Kramer, and Michelangelo Signorile, who have critiqued various aspects of gay activism as it has developed. Of course, the categories of right and left, or liberal and conservative, in no way capture their varied positions. Some relevant works include: Eric Rofes, *Dry Bones Breathe: Gay Men Creating Post-AIDS Identities and Cultures* (New York: Harrington Park Press, 1998); Michael Bronski: *The Pleasure Principle: Sex, Backlash, and the Struggle for Gay Freedom* (New York: St. Martin's Press, 1998); Andrew Sullivan, *Virtually Normal: An Argument about Homosexuality* (New York: Alfred A. Knopf, 1995); Bruce Bawer, *A Place at the Table: The Gay Individual in American Society* (New York: Poseidon Press, 1993). For an interesting treatment of sexual freedom by scholars of religion who are also queer activists, see Janet Jakobsen and Ann Pellegrini, *Love the Sin: Sexual Regulation and the Limits of Religious Tolerance* (New York: New York University Press, 2003).

15. James Morrison is the only one who calls explicitly for the abandonment of conventional norms in gay relationships. Others certainly problematize traditional norms and expectations, and they experiment with a variety of possibilities for their lives and relationships, but they are generally most concerned with how best to configure their desires and relationships within the ethical possibilities currently available to them. Even when they engage in casual or anonymous sex, they are conflicted in some way about it.

16. Remember that none of these life writers are explicitly engaged in an ethical project or writing especially to effect a change in church teachings. They are doing autobiography and I am interpreting their stories with these issues in mind. When I cite examples from their texts, I am lifting up the aspects most relevant to this project. That does not mean these are the most relevant issues for each of their projects.

17. Marilyn Gottschall, "The Ethical Implications of the Deconstruction of Gender," *Journal of the American Academy of Religion* 70, no. 2 (June 2002), 291–92.

18. Ibid., 296.

19. Diane Bjorklund, *Interpreting the Self: Two Hundred Years of American Autobiography* (Chicago: University of Chicago Press, 1998), 159.

20. Ibid.

21. Ibid., 160. Remember, it is always reality as the autobiographer sees it, not necessarily as the reader would. This is why Bjorklund says autobiographers "justify" their actions and choices. This is also the factor that makes these autobiographies so usable as examples of gay subjectivity.

22. See John Gettys, "Daniel Curzon (1938–)," in *Contemporary Gay American Novelists: A Bio-Bibliographical Critical Sourcebook*, ed. Emmanuel S. Nelson (Westport, Conn.: Greenwood Press, 1993), 93.

23. Daniel Curzon, *The World Can Break Your Heart*, 177.

24. As Gottschall says, quoting Judith Butler, "The ethico-political task that matters is neither revolution or critique — both of which inevitably take place 'immanent to the regime of power/discourse whose claims it seeks to adjudicate' — but, rather, subversion." Gottschall, 295.

25. Rev. R. Roberts, "Fears," 146.

26. Ibid., 146.

27. Campo, *Desire*, 93.

28. Ibid., 23.

29. Ibid., 23–24.

30. McNaught, *On Being Gay*, 65.

31. Ibid., 56–57.

32. Rodriguez, *Hunger*, 6.

33. Zuniga, 303.

34. See McNeill's book which takes this phrase as its title.

35. Johnson, *Keeping Faith*, 275.

36. Ibid., 204. This sentiment lies in stark contrast with what Johnson observes in church leaders. He says the church encourages men to become priests "who have so successfully repressed their experience of desire that they're able to speak with conviction about its evils." Ibid., 190.

37. Johnson, "God, Gays," 248.

38. Holleran, *Nights*, 156.

39. The hope at the time was for then-President Clinton to lift the ban. Instead, the ensuing debate resulted in the compromise that is the "don't ask, don't tell" policy, which has ironically resulted in more discharges of gay and lesbian soldiers each year. Gay activists have repeatedly denounced this policy for its simplistic assumptions about gay identity. Much like the bifurcation problem in church teaching, it assumes an easy separation between gay identity and its expression. It is a policy founded upon the use of facades masquerading as discretion. Consequently, it requires the same lack of personal integrity that is promoted by problematic church teaching. In Zuniga's words, "There is no on-off switch when dealing with human identity. This proposed policy affected gays at the core of who we are as a people. In essence, it forced us on an ongoing basis not to accept ourselves, to constantly live a lie." Zuniga, 254.

40. Zuniga, 44–45.

41. Ibid., 44.

42. Horrigan, 206.

43. Ibid., 205–6.

44. Pallone, 143.

45. Ibid., 266.

46. Ibid., 168.

47. Spousal health insurance is typically available for employees, even if they have only been married a short time. Gay and lesbian employees are typically not eligible for such benefits even if they have been with the same partner for a long time. While this unfairness seems fairly obvious, the majority of employers have yet to correct it. Only about 130 of the Fortune 500 firms offer domestic partner benefits (see Dianna Marder, "Gay, Lesbian Wedding Market Embraced," *Philadelphia Inquirer*, April 3, 2002, E1, E4). The reasons these companies offer such benefits are usually driven by the need to attract qualified employees. This makes these benefits vulnerable to the whims of the market. A more helpful and farsighted approach would be to disassociate benefits from marriage and find other foundations on which to provide fairly for basic human rights.

48. Mark Blasius, *Gay and Lesbian Politics: Sexuality and the Emergence of a New Ethic* (Philadelphia: Temple University Press, 1994), 134, 136–37. Other useful texts which explore the public/private issue and gay political strategies include: Timothy Murphy, ed., *Gay Ethics: Controversies in Outing, Civil Rights, and Sexual Science* (New York: Harrington Park Press, 1994); Steven Seidman, *Embattled Eros: Sexual Politics and Ethics in Contemporary America* (New York and London: Routledge, 1992); Ann Snitow, Christine Stansell, and Sharon Thompson, eds., *Powers of Desire: The Politics of Sexuality* (New York: Monthly Review Press, 1983). Another useful text, not specifically focused on gay and lesbian issues, is Iris Marion Young, *Justice and the Politics of Difference* (Princeton: Princeton University Press, 1990).

49. Sullivan, "Virtually Normal," 173.

50. Ibid., 185.

51. Sullivan, *Love Undetectable*, 43.

52. Derrick A. Tynan-Connolly, in Holtz, ed., 180.

53. Rodriguez, *Days*, 43.

54. Morrison, *Broken Fever*, 240.

55. Campo, *Desire*, 191.

56. Ibid., 192.

57. Ibid., 267.

58. Ibid., 192.

59. Ibid., 193.

60. Zuniga, 184. The report is called "Gay Male and Lesbian Youth Suicide, Report of the Secretary's Task Force on Youth Suicide." The document was never given full administrative support and it was not formally released, reputedly because of these "controversial" statistics and their implications.

61. Heckman, in Fellows, 99–100.

62. Cardarelli, "Lord, Make Me an Instrument," 156.

63. McNaught, *On Being Gay*, 12.

64. Ibid., 150–51.

65. Kopay, 279.

66. Fr. Raymond Calabrese, "One Gay Priest's Story," *U.S. Catholic* 68 (February 2003), 50.

67. McCauley, 192.

68. Rodriguez, *Brown*, 207.

69. Ibid., 208.

70. See, for example, *Catechism of the Catholic Church* no. 1644, which quotes *Familiaris consortio* about the love of spouses, who "are called to grow continually in their communion through day-to-day fidelity to their marriage promise of total mutual self-giving." *Catechism*, 410.

71. Johnson, *Geography*, 34.

72. Ibid., 70.

73. Ibid., 31.

74. Ibid., 92–93.

75. McNeill, *Both Feet*, 68.

76. Heckman, in Fellows, 100.

77. Kopay, 145.

78. Ibid., 179.

79. Ibid., 180.

80. Pallone, 76–77.

81. Ibid., 80–81.

82. Larry Sullivan, in Holtz, ed., 136.
83. William G. Storey, in Holtz, ed., 10.
84. James Abdo, in Holtz, ed., 26.
85. Ibid., 27.
86. Gerald Allen, in Holtz, ed., 223. Allen still identifies as gay rather than bisexual.
87. Morrison, *Broken Fever*, 148–49.
88. Zuniga, 171–72. Zuniga also identifies as gay rather than bisexual.
89. McNaught, *On Being Gay*, 118.
90. Ibid., 118.
91. Johnson, *Geography*, 129.
92. Ibid.
93. Morrison, *Broken Fever*, 214–15.
94. Ibid., 190.
95. Gambone, "Beyond Words," 112.
96. William G. Storey, in Holtz, ed., 10.
97. Campo, *Desire*, 155.
98. Eugene Kennedy, "Ministry, Homosexuality, and Psychological Wholeness" (plenary address made to the New Ways Ministry Symposium, "Out of Silence God Has Called Us: Lesbian/Gay Issues and the Vatican II Church," Louisville, Ky., March 8–10, 2002), Audio Recording #02094-0020, Chesapeake Audio/Video Communications, Inc., Elkridge, Md. Also see Kennedy's *The Unhealed Wound: The Church and Human Sexuality* (New York: St. Martin's Griffin, 2001), for an analysis of the way the church's teachings on sexuality uphold the institution at the cost of personal wholeness.
99. Johnson, "God, Gays," 255.
100. Johnson, *Geography*, 76–77.
101. Johnson, "God, Gays," 251.
102. This theme of authority over sexual lives by those who live them is further developed in Evelyn E. and James D. Whitehead, *Wisdom of the Body: Making Sense of our Sexuality* (New York: Crossroad, 2001).
103. A recent study indicates that as nonheterosexual Christians develop their sexual ethics based on lived experience, they do not wish this to mean one is simply free to do whatever one wants. Rather, they seek to locate sexual morality within a Christian framework. See Yip, 208.
104. Schneider, 4.
105. Ibid., 11.
106. Holleran, "Sense of Sin," 96.

5. Reconciliation

1. See, for example, *Catechism*, nos. 1749–61, in which we are told the morality of human acts depends on object, intention, and circumstances. It is interesting this formula in itself reflects the necessity of contextualizing human acts, yet church leaders avoid applying this formula to gay acts by branding all such acts *intrinsically* disordered.
2. Jordan, *Silence*, 4.
3. This principle "constitutes one of the central theological characteristics of Catholicism." Richard McBrien, ed., *The HarperCollins Encyclopedia of Catholicism* (San Francisco: Harper San Francisco, 1995), s.v. "Sacramentality," 1148.
4. Susan A. Ross, "God's Embodiment and Women: Sacraments," in Catherine Mowry LaCugna, ed., *Freeing Theology: The Essentials of Theology in*

Feminist Perspective (San Francisco: Harper San Francisco, 1993), 187. Eventually, the Latin *Sacramenta,* from the root *sacer* (sacred) was used as a translation for these moments of God's grace. Also see Mark Francis, "Sacrament," in McBrien, ed., 1146.

5. Doris Donnelly, "Reconciliation: The Continuing Challenge," in *Reconciliation: The Continuing Agenda,* ed. Robert J. Kennedy (Collegeville, Minn.: Liturgical Press, 1987), 284.

6. Bjorn Krondorfer, "The Confines of Male Confessions: On Religion, Bodies, and Mirrors," in Krondorfer, ed., 222.

7. Stephen Spender, "Confessions and Autobiography," in Olney, ed. (1980), 118.

8. Ron Hansen, "Hotly in Pursuit of the Real: The Role of the Catholic Writer," *America* 185, no. 15 (November 12, 2001): 8.

9. Johnson, *Keeping Faith,* 129.

10. Rodriguez, *Brown,* 203, 224.

11. Jordan, *Silence,* 258, 261.

12. Ibid., 258.

13. Kathleen Hughes, "Reconciliation: Cultural and Christian Perspectives," in Kennedy, ed. (1987), 119.

14. Toinette M. Eugene, "Reconciliation in the Pastoral Context of Today's Church and World: Does Reconciliation Have a Future?" in *Reconciling Embrace: Foundations for the Future of Sacramental Reconciliation,* ed. Robert J. Kennedy (Chicago: Liturgy Training Publications, 1998), 13–14.

15. Ibid., 13.

16. From the Jerusalem Bible.

17. Raymond-Jean Frontain, "A Professional Queer Remembers: Bibliography, Narrative, and the Saving Power of Memory," in *A Sea of Stories: The Shaping Power of Narrative in Gay and Lesbian Cultures,* ed. Sonya L. Jones (New York: Harrington Park Press, 2000), 227–28.

18. Walter Holland, "In the Body's Ghetto," in Jones, ed., 116.

19. Gusdorf, "Conditions and Limits," 47.

20. Jordan, *Silence,* 260.

21. Morrison, *Broken Fever,* 8.

22. Johnson, "God, Gays," 247.

23. Campo, *Desire,* 270.

24. Johnson, *Keeping Faith,* 15.

25. Warning bells about this crisis had been sounding for years from various corners of the church, and cases have been reported in previous years. See Thomas C. Fox, "What They Knew in 1985," *National Catholic Reporter,* May 17, 2002, 3, 6–7; and Thomas P. Doyle, "Reflections from the Eye of the Hurricane," *National Catholic Reporter,* June 21, 2002, 6–7. The difference this time around is the increased attention to this problem by the mainstream media and civil authorities.

26. In their defense, many bishops have noted how much more advanced our knowledge of pedophilia and ephebophilia is today than it was even two decades ago. Short-term treatment was thought to be an effective "cure." It was also normative in society as a whole to deal with such matters quietly and confidentially. Indeed, many of these cases predate our current tell-all culture. Even so, the evidence suggests the protection of priests was given a higher priority than the effective protection of children.

27. United States Conference of Catholic Bishops, "Charter for the Protection of Children and Young People," special supplement to the *Catholic Standard and Times*, June 27, 2002, not paginated. This document is far from perfect, primarily because it is a response to public pressure rather than a proactive response to the problem.

28. Kevin Clarke, "Whitewash or Renewal?" *U.S. Catholic* 68, no. 6 (June 2003): 14.

29. Gill Donovan, "Some See Big Reforms on the Horizon: Conservatives and Liberals Align in Call for Lay Involvement," *National Catholic Reporter*, July 19, 2002, 3–5.

30. See Fran Ferder and John Heagle, "Time for Bishops to Listen, Take Ordinary Catholics Seriously," *National Catholic Reporter*, July 19, 2002, 6.

31. Andrew Sullivan, "Who Says the Church Can't Change?" *Time*, June 17, 2002, 63.

32. Rachel Zoll, "Experts: Purging Gay Priests Isn't the Answer," *Philadelphia Inquirer*, March 23, 2002, A7.

33. Quoted in Jon Fuller, "On 'Straightening Out' Catholic Seminaries," *America* 187, no. 20 (December 16, 2002): 8.

34. James J. Gill, "Seminaries Await Vatican Visitation," *America* 187, no. 2 (July 15–22): 11. Fortunately, most bishops eschewed this line of thinking in addressing this crisis. Cardinal Bevilacqua even proudly announced there are no gay seminarians in Philadelphia. Apparently, he thinks he can see through closet doors.

35. A helpful article which unpacks some of these connections is Joseph J. Guido, "The Importance of Perspective: Understanding the Sexual Abuse of Children by Priests," *America* 186, no. 11 (April 1, 2002): 21–23.

36. Another dimension of this issue needing further analysis and exploration is the sexuality of teens and even children. We must always take very seriously all cases in which anyone reports being victimized, but other cases of adolescents seeking sexual "mentoring" from an adult may complicate our definitions of abuse and how we mark youth and adulthood. For a useful and challenging examination of these ideas, see Judith Levine, *Harmful to Minors: The Perils of Protecting Children from Sex* (Minneapolis: University of Minnesota Press, 2002).

37. Consider late night television ads for the phone sex line 1-800-WE-ARE-18.

38. Some abusive heterosexual priests have told therapists they believed having sex with teen boys did not technically break their vow of celibacy. As strange as this sounds to me, it reflects a societal confusion over what exactly "having sex" means, in addition to a sort of Clinton-esque tendency toward justification. See Sandra G. Boodman, "For Experts on Abuse, Priests' Orientation Isn't the Issue," *Washington Post*, June 24, 2002, B2.

39. According to Dr. Fred Berlin, associate professor of psychiatry at Johns Hopkins University: "Some of this has been about homosexual men giving in to temptation with adolescent males. At the same time, we should make it clear that homosexuals are no more risk to children than heterosexuals. In terms of the bigger picture, there are every bit as many heterosexual men giving into sexual temptation with female adolescents." Laurie Goodstein, "Homosexuality in Priesthood is Under Increasing Scrutiny," *The New York Times — on the Web*, www.nytimes.com (April 19, 2002).

40. See news brief, "Dismissing All Abusive Priests Is Ineffective Strategy, Vatican Told," *America* 188, no. 14 (April 21, 2003): 4–5.

41. In the words of A. W. Richard Sipe, an activist and writer on issues related to clergy sexual abuse, "So many of the priests are psychosexually immature, it makes them more vulnerable to taking advantage of, or falling in love with, if you will, age-inappropriate people." See Goodstein, "Homosexuality in Priesthood."

42. Linda Chavez, Michael Novak, and Richard John Neuhaus have all made assertions like this.

43. Sipe notes, "I found in my studies that homosexually oriented men are every bit as observant of their celibacy as heterosexual men." Quoted in Goodstein.

44. They were recognized as such in the early church. See Rosemary Radford Ruether, "Abuse a Consequence of Historic Wrong Turn," *National Catholic Reporter*, June 7, 2002, 19.

45. See the news brief cited earlier in *America* 188, no. 14 (April 21, 2003): 5.

46. As a result of the clergy sex abuse crisis, Bishop Wilton Gregory, current president of the U.S. Conference of Catholic Bishops, foresees "a greater collaborative approach [with the laity] to the issues that we have to face together." He says it's about "you respecting my office, my respecting your competence, realizing that together we can do an awful lot that neither of us can do apart." Amen to that! It's time for church leaders to demonstrate what "respecting our competence" can really mean. See David Van Biema, "Rebels in the Pews," *Time*, June 17, 2002, 58.

47. Maher, 15.

48. Maher, 115.

49. Hamilton College/MTV/Zogby International Gay Issues Poll, Press Release, August 27, 2001. Posted to the GLB-NEWS List, August 28, 2001.

50. Maryclaire Dale, "Cops Sued for Threat to Out Gay Teenager," *Philadelphia Daily News*, November 5, 2001, posted to the GLB-NEWS list, November 5, 2001.

51. Information based on a press release posted to the GLB-PRESS list by the Lambda Legal Defense and Education Fund, February 27, 2002.

52. This kind of problem is not peculiar to the American context. Fenton Johnson's partner Larry died in a hospital in France, and Johnson was not allowed to be at his bedside. He watched Larry die from the hall outside his door. Johnson, *Keeping Faith*, 201.

53. Quoted in Kathleen Hughes and Joseph Favazza, eds., *A Reconciliation Sourcebook* (Chicago: Liturgy Training Publications, 1997), 104.

54. Quoted in H. Kathleen Hughes, "Walking on the Edge of Two Great Abysses: Theological Perspectives on Reconciliation," in Kennedy, ed. (1998), 103.

55. Ahmar Mustikhan, "Catholic Church Fires Gay Choir Leader," a summary of an AP story, posted to the Gay.com/PlanetOut.com Network, July 1, 2003; posted to the Dignity News Service, DignityNews@yahoogroups.com, July 10, 2003.

56. Nicole Winfield, "Vatican Reaffirms Need for Penance," AP News Story, May 2, 2002, posted to GLB-NEWS list, May 3, 2002.

57. Rodriguez, quoted in Paul Crowley, S.J., "An Ancient Catholic: An Interview with Richard Rodriguez," in Ferraro, ed., 264.

58. Johnson, *Keeping Faith*, 305.

59. Quoted in Maher, 6.

Appendix: the Gramick and Nugent Investigation

1. "Cardinal Hickey's Letter to the Congregation for the Institutes of Consecrated Life and Apostolic Societies [formerly the Congregation for Religious and Secular Institutes]," October 10, 1989.

2. "Preliminary Draft of Responses to Questions Posed by the Commission," Submitted to Maida Commission, July 26, 1994.

3. Ibid.

4. Ibid.

5. Ibid.

6. Neither are these opinions *not* offered as viable alternatives, in my personal experience of their workshops. I would characterize their approach as presenting a range of Catholic opinion on the subject, all of which come across as valid because the teachings are not infallibly declared and are thus open to development. Gramick and Nugent never say church teaching should change, but they do insist that it be open to new data.

7. This highlights another difficulty for the church hierarchy: their inability to deal adequately and respectfully with dissenting voices within their own ranks. The Vatican II ideal of collegiality among all bishops seemingly has been abandoned; instead, we have a situation in which the bishops who agree with Rome are favored and others are vilified. This is especially irritating in a case such as this where the majority of American bishops are generally supportive of or at least neutral toward Nugent and Gramick's ministry.

8. "Preliminary Responses to selected passages from *Building Bridges*," Submitted to the Maida Commission, July 26, 1994 (emphasis mine). I often find all of this talk from church teachers and ministers of "confusing the faithful" annoying. I do not think we are all so easily confused; in fact, most Catholics can read between the lines of church teaching and see political biases in operation.

9. Ibid. (emphasis mine).

10. Quoted in ibid. Gramick and Nugent defend this as an example of hyperbole.

11. Quoted in ibid. In the book, they support this statement by noting two important things: (1) How thriving Dignity had been allowed to become in the United States; and (2) The fact that the 1986 (and then the 1992) letters from the CDF were both promulgated in English and likely meant for the American church. Today's situation is different. While there are still tensions between the U.S. hierarchy and Rome, many more bishops are appointees of Pope John Paul II and are more likely to agree with Rome on issues such as homosexuality. Even so, when tensions do arise between the two, it is always framed as a difference between Roman *doctrine* and American *pastoral* practice.

12. "Response to the Report of the Findings of the Commission Studying the Writings and Ministry of Sister Jeannine Gramick, SSND, and Father Robert Nugent, SDS," January 12, 1995.

13. "Report of the Findings of the Commission Studying the Writings and Ministry of Sister Jeannine Gramick, SSND, and Father Robert Nugent, SDS," October 4, 1994. Nugent and Gramick do state in their response, "We have never claimed that a moral judgment on sexual behavior is 'incidental' or that it is not 'a crucial issue,' but we believe the Commission has overemphasized this question by making it, in effect, the *only* crucial issue."

14. Ibid.

15. Ibid.

16. Quoted in "Response to Additional Questions from the Congregation for the Institutes of Consecrated Life and Societies of Apostolic Life," October 22, 1996.

17. Ibid.

18. Gramick and Nugent were not informed of the transfer until December 1997, when their Superior Generals were notified at a meeting with Cardinal Ratzinger. The two year lapse allowed time for the CDF to conduct its own internal investigation.

19. In 1995, Gramick and Nugent published *Voices of Hope: A Collection of Positive Catholic Writings on Gay and Lesbian Issues* (New York: Center for Homophobia Education). The CDF cites this book and *Building Bridges* for their evidence.

20. "Erroneous and Dangerous Propositions in the Publications *Building Bridges* and *Voices of Hope* by Sister Jeannine Gramick, SSND, and Father Robert Nugent, SDS," October 24, 1997.

21. In my project, I attempt to articulate a more realistic version of gay and lesbian reality by discussing how diverse that reality can be. Church teaching may indeed reflect some lesbian and gay reality, but it does not reflect the whole of it, as church officials might like to believe.

22. "Erroneous and Dangerous Propositions . . . "

23. See Nelson, "Sources for Body Theology." While this "quadrilateral" interpretation of authority has its roots in Protestant theology, many Catholic ethicists have embraced this formula since Vatican II. Church officials would not dispute this equation, but they would not rate these sources equally, nor would they suggest it is valid to reach different conclusions than are already in place in church teaching.

24. Quoted in "Erroneous and Dangerous Propositions . . . "

25. The same argument about critical mass could be made with regard to the church's absolute ban on "artificial" birth control. The tendency of late has been to dismiss dissenting Catholics as being caught up in modern, secular culture — what John Paul calls the "culture of death." I am struck by how this denigrates the education and moral agency of individual Catholics, not to mention how cynical this attitude is toward the world. How different this is from the optimism expressed at Vatican II!

26. Gramick and Nugent, eds., *Voices of Hope,* 67 (emphasis mine).

27. "Erroneous and Dangerous Propositions . . . "

28. For example, Nugent builds a strong distinction, rooted deeply in the history of moral theology, between objective immorality and subjective culpability, to argue that using terminology like "objective disorder" in a pastoral setting is problematic. "Response of Father Robert Nugent, SDS, to the Congregation for the Doctrine of the Faith regarding 'Erroneous and Dangerous Propositions in the Publications *Building Bridges* and *Voices of Hope* by Sister Jeannine Gramick, SSND, and Father Robert Nugent, SDS.'" February 6, 1998.

29. "Response to the Congregation for the Doctrine of the Faith," July 7, 1998. She also notes her desire that her "personal views on contentious issues remain as far as possible in the background." While much of her writing would indicate her personal advocacy for a change in the church's moral rhetoric on homosexuality, she is indeed never clear *exactly* where she herself stands on this issue, especially in her workshops. Perhaps the no-win situation with the CDF and subsequent changes she has made in terms of her congregational affiliation will allow her the freedom to more openly clarify her own views and personal motivations.

30. An example of his emendations is his changing the phrase "homosexual acts are always objectively evil" to "homosexual [genital] acts are always, objectively speaking, morally wrong." He does this, he says, to be sure his public statements embody his commitment to treat homosexuals and their families with

respect, compassion, and sensitivity. Such are the linguistic gymnastics required to try to reconcile the moral and pastoral rhetorics. "Nugent: Response to CDF Profession of Faith," January 25, 1999.

31. Lisa Sowle Cahill describes this move as an ominous shift in the Vatican's method of dealing with theologians and ministers: "Now, people are being silenced *not* for contradicting any doctrine, and not even for contradicting any 'noninfallible teaching,' but for staying within church teaching while not equally emphasizing or including other points." Lisa Sowle Cahill, "Silencing of Nugent, Gramick Sets a Novel Standard of Orthodoxy," *America* 181, no. 4 (August 14–21, 1999): 10.

32. Nugent has thus far complied with the order of silence. Gramick has defied the order and transferred to the Sisters of Loretto. She hopes to continue her full ministry to gay people with the support of this community. Mary Hunt reads the Vatican's move to "silence them further" as a tacit admission that "the Vatican has lost on the substantive issue of homosexuality and can now only 'win' some credibility through brute force . . . to compel a person's conscience, and in doing so to shore itself up." Mary E. Hunt, "Rome's Not-So-Veiled Power Play," *National Catholic Reporter,* June 30, 2000, 20.

Select Bibliography

Primary Sources (Autobiographical Acts)

Aelred, Father. "Without Shame." In *Homosexuality in the Priesthood and the Religious Life,* ed. Jeannine Gramick, 170–77. New York: Crossroad, 1989.

Amos, Brother. "Inheritance for the Disinherited." In *Homosexuality in the Priesthood and the Religious Life,* ed. Jeannine Gramick, 126–33. New York: Crossroad, 1989.

Arpin, Fr. Robert L. *Wonderfully, Fearfully Made: Letters on Living with Hope, Teaching Understanding, and Ministering with Love, from a Gay Catholic Priest with AIDS.* San Francisco: HarperSanFrancisco, 1993.

Bartosik, Matthew. "A Winter Break." *Equal Times* 7, no. 1 (Spring 2000): 7.

Binder, Wolfgang, and Helmbrecht Breinig, eds. *American Contradictions: Interviews with Nine American Writers.* Hanover, N.H.: Wesleyan University Press, 1995.

Bouldrey, Brian, ed. *Wrestling with the Angel: Faith and Religion in the Lives of Gay Men.* New York: Riverhead Books, 1995.

Calabrese, Fr. Raymond (pseud.). "One Gay Priest's Story." *U.S. Catholic* 68 (February 2003): 50.

Campo, Rafael. *The Desire to Heal: A Doctor's Education in Empathy, Identity, and Poetry.* New York: W. W. Norton, 1997.

———. *Diva.* Durham, N.C.: Duke University Press, 1999.

———. *The Other Man Was Me: A Voyage to the New World.* Houston: Arte Publico Press, 1994.

———. *What the Body Told.* Durham, N.C.: Duke University Press, 1996.

Cardarelli, Richard John. "Lord, Make Me an Instrument of Your Peace." In *Homosexuality in the Priesthood and the Religious Life,* ed. Jeannine Gramick, 151–59. New York: Crossroad, 1989.

Crowley, Paul. "An Ancient Catholic: An Interview with Richard Rodriguez." In *Catholic Lives, Contemporary America,* ed. Thomas J. Ferraro, 259–65. Durham, N.C.: Duke University Press, 1997.

Curzon, Daniel. "Why I Am an Ex-Catholic." In *ReCreations: Religion and Spirituality in the Lives of Queer People,* ed. Catherine Lake, 103–5. Toronto: Queer Press, 1999.

———. *The World Can Break Your Heart.* Stamford, Conn.: Knight's Press, 1984.

"Dan: 'HIV Doubled My Spirituality.' " Interview by David Shallenberger, *Reclaiming the Spirit: Gay Men and Lesbians Come to Terms with Religion.* New Brunswick, N.J.: Rutgers University Press, 1998.

DeCaro, Frank. *A Boy Named Phyllis: A Suburban Memoir.* New York: Viking, 1996.

Fellows, Will. *Farm Boys: Lives of Gay Men from the Rural Midwest.* Madison: University of Wisconsin Press, 1996, 1998.

Gambone, Philip. "Beyond Words." In *Boys Like Us: Gay Writers Tell Their Coming Out Stories,* ed. Patrick Merla, 98–114. New York: Avon Books, 1996.
———. "Learning and Unlearning and Learning Again the Language of *Signori.*" In *Fuori: Essays by Italian/American Lesbians and Gays,* ed. Anthony Julian Tamburri, 60–80. West Lafayette, Ind.: Bordighera, 1996.
———. "Searching for Real Words," In *Wrestling with the Angel: Faith and Religion in the Lives of Gay Men,* ed. Brian Bouldrey, 221–42. New York: Riverhead Books, 1995.
———, ed. *Something Inside: Conversations with Gay Fiction Writers.* Madison: University of Wisconsin Press, 1999.
Glenn, William D. "As God Intended: Reflections on Being a Gay Student at a Jesuit High School." *America* 184, no. 17 (May 21, 2001): 26–29.
Gramick, Jeannine, ed. *Homosexuality in the Priesthood and the Religious Life.* New York: Crossroad, 1989.
Holleran Andrew. *The Beauty of Men.* New York: Plume, 1997.
———. "Memories of Heidelberg." In *Boys Like Us: Gay Writers Tell Their Coming Out Stories,* ed. Patrick Merla, 88–97. New York: Avon Books, 1996.
———. *Nights in Aruba.* New York: William Morrow, 1983.
———. "The Sense of Sin." In *Wrestling with the Angel: Faith and Religion in the Lives of Gay Men,* ed. Brian Bouldrey, 83–96. New York: Riverhead Books, 1995.
Holtz, Raymond C. *Listen to the Stories: Gay and Lesbian Catholics Talk about Their Lives and the Church.* New York: Garland Publishing, 1991.
Horrigan, Patrick E. *Widescreen Dreams: Growing Up Gay at the Movies.* Madison: University of Wisconsin Press, 1999.
Johnson, Fenton. *Geography of the Heart: A Memoir.* New York: Scribner, 1996.
———. "God, Gays, and the Geography of Desire." In *Wrestling with the Angel: Faith and Religion in the Lives of Gay Men,* ed. Brian Bouldrey, 243–58. New York: Riverhead Books, 1995.
———. *Keeping Faith: A Skeptic's Journey.* Boston: Houghton Mifflin, 2003.
Jonathan, Brother. "You Are My People." In *Homosexuality in the Priesthood and the Religious Life,* ed. Jeannine Gramick, 160–69. New York: Crossroad, 1989.
Kelty, Matthew. "The Land I Love In." In *Homosexuality in the Priesthood and the Religious Life,* ed. Jeannine Gramick, 145–50. New York: Crossroad, 1989.
Killian, Kevin. "Chain of Fools." In *Wrestling with the Angel: Faith and Religion in the Lives of Gay Men,* ed. Brian Bouldrey, 117–29. New York: Riverhead Books, 1995.
Kopay, David, and Perry Dean Young. *The David Kopay Story: An Extraordinary Self-revelation.* New York: Donald I. Fine, 1988.
Kramer, Joseph. "Body and Soul." Interview by Mark Thompson, *Gay Soul: Finding the Heart of Gay Spirit and Nature with Sixteen Writers, Healers, Teachers, and Visionaries.* San Francisco: HarperSanFrancisco, 1994: 168–80.
Krask, Peter M. "The Way the Stars Come Home." In *Wrestling with the Angel: Faith and Religion in the Lives of Gay Men,* ed. Brian Bouldrey, 147–70. New York: Riverhead Books, 1995.
Lake, Catherine, ed. *ReCreations: Religion and Spirituality in the Lives of Queer People.* Toronto: Queer Press, 1999.
"Mark: A Gay Spiritual Ancestry." Interview by David Shallenberger, *Reclaiming the Spirit: Gay Men and Lesbians Come to Terms with Religion.* New Brunswick, N.J.: Rutgers University Press, 1998.

McCauley, Stephen. "Let's Say." In *Boys Like Us: Gay Writers Tell Their Coming Out Stories*, ed. Patrick Merla, 186–92. New York: Avon Books, 1996.

McClatchy, J. D. "My Fountain Pen." In *Boys Like Us: Gay Writers Tell Their Coming Out Stories*, ed. Patrick Merla, 193–203. New York: Avon Books, 1996.

McNaught, Brian. *A Disturbed Peace: Selected Writings of an Irish Catholic Homosexual.* Washington, D.C.: Dignity, 1981.

———. *On Being Gay: Thoughts on Family, Faith, and Love.* New York: St. Martin's, 1988.

McNeill, John J. "As My Body Grows Older, My Spirit Becomes Younger." *National Catholic Reporter,* April 14, 2000, 22–23.

———. *Both Feet Firmly Planted in Midair: My Spiritual Journey.* Louisville: Westminster John Knox, 1998.

McNichols, William Hart. "A Priest Forever." In *Homosexuality in the Priesthood and the Religious Life,* ed. Jeannine Gramick, 118–25. New York: Crossroad, 1989.

Mecca, Tommi Avicolli. "Memoirs of a South Philly Sissy." In *Fuori: Essays by Italian/American Lesbians and Gays,* ed. Anthony Julian Tamburri, 13–28. West Lafayette, Ind.: Bordighera, 1996.

Mecca, Tommi Avicolli, Giovanna (Janet) Capone, and Denise Nico Leto, eds. *Hey Paesan! Writings by Lesbians and Gay Men of Italian Descent.* Oakland, Calif.: Three Guineas Press, 1999.

Merla, Patrick, ed. *Boys Like Us: Gay Writers Tell Their Coming Out Stories.* New York: Avon Books, 1996.

Merrett, Jim. "My First Homosexual: Confessions of a Lapsed Catholic." *Advocate,* May 9, 1989, 48–49.

Minervini, Mark P. "Finding My Faith." *International Journal of Sexuality and Gender Studies* 5, no. 3 (July 2000): 279–82.

Morrison, James. *Broken Fever: Reflections of Gay Boyhood.* New York: St. Martin's, 2001.

———. "Saved." In *Wrestling with the Angel: Faith and Religion in the Lives of Gay Men,* ed. Brian Bouldrey, 59–82. New York: Riverhead Books, 1995.

Nixon, Rob. "Avondale: A Memoir of Identity." In *Hey Paesan! Writings by Lesbians and Gay Men of Italian Descent,* eds. Tommi Avicolli Mecca, Giovanna (Janet) Capone, and Denise Nico Leto. Oakland, Calif.: Three Guineas Press, 1999.

Pallone, Dave, with Alan Steinberg. *Behind the Mask: My Double Life in Baseball.* New York: Viking, 1990.

Paul, Father. "We Shall Not Cease from Exploration." In *Homosexuality in the Priesthood and the Religious Life,* ed. Jeannine Gramick, 134–44. New York: Crossroad, 1989.

Plante, David. *The Catholic.* New York: Atheneum, 1986.

———. "Images of the Body from My Religion." In *Wrestling with the Angel: Faith and Religion in the Lives of Gay Men,* ed. Brian Bouldrey, 171–74. New York: Riverhead Books, 1995.

Roberts, Rev. R. (pseud.). "The Fears of a Gay Priest." In *Gay Priests,* ed. James G. Wolf, 141–60. San Francisco: Harper & Row, 1989.

Rodriguez, Richard. *Brown: The Last Discovery of America.* New York: Viking, 2002.

———. *Days of Obligation: An Argument with My Mexican Father.* New York: Penguin, 1992.

———. *Hunger of Memory: The Education of Richard Rodriguez.* New York: Bantam, 1982.

———. "Irish Catholic." In *Political Passages: Journeys of Change through Two Decades 1968–1988,* ed. John H. Bunzel, 326–47. New York: Free Press, 1988.

Schimmel, David. "A Spiritual Self-Portrait: Using My Homosexuality to Develop an Honest Relationship with God." *National Catholic Reporter,* December 3, 1999, 34–36.

Shallenberger, David. *Reclaiming the Spirit: Gay Men and Lesbians Come to Terms with Religion.* New Brunswick, N.J.: Rutgers University Press, 1998.

Soucy, Jon. "Speaking the Unspeakable." *The Hoya,* March 4, 2003, online at www.thehoya.com.

Stahel, Thomas H. "'I'm Here': An Interview With Andrew Sullivan." *America* 168, no. 116 (May 8, 1993): 5–11.

Stoltz, Eric. "Notes From a Community — Catholic and Gay." *America* 178, no. 10 (March 28, 1998): 10–13.

Sullivan, Andrew. "Alone Again, Naturally." *The New Republic* 211, no. 22 (November 28, 1994): 47, 50, 52, 54–55.

———. *Love Undetectable: Notes on Friendship, Sex, and Survival.* New York: Alfred A. Knopf, 1998.

———. "Virtually Normal." In *Catholic Lives, Contemporary America,* ed. Thomas J. Ferraro, 171–86. Durham, N.C.: Duke University Press, 1997.

Tamburri, Anthony Julian ed. *Fuori: Essays by Italian/American Lesbians and Gays.* West Lafayette, Ind.: Bordighera, 1996.

Thompson, Mark. *Gay Soul: Finding the Heart of Gay Spirit and Nature with Sixteen Writers, Healers, Teachers, and Visionaries.* San Francisco: HarperSanFrancisco, 1994.

Thompson, Rev. T. (pseud.). "A Christian Spirituality." In *Gay Priests,* ed. James G. Wolf, 119–40. San Francisco: Harper & Row, 1989.

Trepania, Scott. "Prayer Life Provides a Focus as I cope with Dropping T-Cell Counts." *National Catholic Reporter,* September 2, 1994, 7–8.

Tucker, Scott. "Our Queer World: True Confessions." *The Humanist* 53, no. 5 (September–October, 1993): 45–46.

Utter, Brian. "Bisexuality and the Spiritual Continuum," In *ReCreations: Religion and Spirituality in the Lives of Queer People,* ed. Catherine Lake, 143–46. Toronto: Queer Press, 1999.

Wolf, James, ed. *Gay Priests.* San Francisco: Harper & Row, 1989.

Zuniga, José. *Soldier of the Year: The Story of a Gay American Patriot.* New York: Pocket Books, 1994.

Secondary Sources

Adam, Barry D. "Love and Sex in Constructing Identity Among Men Who Have Sex with Men." *International Journal of Sexuality and Gender Studies* 5, no. 4 (October 2000): 325–39.

Abelove, Henry, Michele Aina Barale, and David M. Halperin, eds. *The Lesbian and Gay Studies Reader.* New York: Routledge, 1993.

Alexander, Jonathan. "Beyond Identity: Queer Values and Community," *Journal of Gay, Lesbian, and Bisexual Identity* 4, no. 4 (October 1999): 293–314.

Alexander, Marilyn Bennett, and James Preston. *We Were Baptized Too: Claiming God's Grace for Lesbians and Gays.* Louisville: Westminster John Knox, 1996.

Almaguer, Tomas. "Chicano Men: A Cartography of Homosexual Identity and Behavior." In *The Lesbian and Gay Studies Reader,* ed. Henry Abelove, Michele Aina Barale, and David M. Halperin, 255–73. New York: Routledge, 1993.

Alpert, Rebecca. *Like Bread on the Seder Plate: Jewish Lesbians and the Transformation of Tradition.* New York: Columbia University Press, 1997.

Avella, Steven M., and Elizabeth McKeown, eds. *Public Voices: Catholics in the American Context.* Maryknoll, N.Y.: Orbis, 1999.

Bagemihl, Bruce. *Biological Exuberance: Animal Homosexuality and Natural Diversity.* New York: St. Martin's, 1999.

Balka, Christie, and Andy Rose, eds. *Twice Blessed: On Being Lesbian or Gay and Jewish.* Boston: Beacon, 1989.

Barbour, John D. *Versions of Deconversion: Autobiography and the Loss of Faith.* Charlottesville: The University Press of Virginia, 1994.

Baruth, Philip E. "Consensual Autobiography: Narrating 'Personal Sexual History' from Boswell's *London Journal* to AIDS Pamphlet Literature." In *Getting a Life: Everyday Uses of Autobiography,* ed. Sidonie Smith and Julia Watson, 177–97. Minneapolis: University of Minnesota Press, 1996.

Bawer, Bruce. *A Place at the Table: The Gay Individual in American Society.* New York: Poseidon, 1993.

Beaudoin, Tom. "Our Catholic Watergate." *America* 186, no. 19 (June 3–10, 2002): 18–20.

Billitteri, Thomas J. "Gay and Lesbian Catholics Beg to Differ." *U.S. Catholic* 62, no. 11 (November 1997): 10–15.

Bjorklund, Diane. *Interpreting the Self: Two Hundred Years of American Autobiography.* Chicago: University of Chicago Press, 1998.

Blake, Richard. *Afterimage: The Indelible Catholic Imagination of Six American Filmmakers.* Chicago: Loyola Press, 2000.

Blasius, Mark. *Gay and Lesbian Politics: Sexuality and the Emergence of a New Ethic.* Philadelphia: Temple University Press, 1994.

Boswell, John. *Christianity, Social Tolerance, and Homosexuality: Gay People in Western Europe from the Beginning of the Christian Era to the Fourteenth Century.* Chicago: University of Chicago Press, 1980.

———. *Same-Sex Unions in Premodern Europe.* New York: Villard Books, 1994.

Boyd, Stephen B., W. Merle Longwood, and Mark W. Muesse, eds. *Redeeming Men: Religion and Masculinities.* Louisville: Westminster John Knox, 1996.

Brawley, Robert L. *Biblical Ethics and Homosexuality: Listening to Scripture.* Louisville: Westminster John Knox, 1996.

Bredbeck, Gregory W. "Andrew Holleran (1943[?]–)." In *Contemporary Gay American Novelists: A Bio-Bibliographical Critical Sourcebook,* ed. Emmanuel S. Nelson, 197–204. Westport, Conn.: Greenwood Press, 1993.

Bregman, Lucy, and Sara Thiermann. *First Person Mortal: Personal Narratives of Illness, Dying and Grief.* New York: Paragon, 1995.

Brod, Harry, and Michael Kaufman, eds. *Theorizing Masculinities.* Thousand Oaks, Calif.: SAGE, 1994.

Bronski, Michael. *The Pleasure Principle: Sex, Backlash, and the Struggle for Gay Freedom.* New York: St. Martin's, 1998.

Brooten, Bernadette J. *Love Between Women: Early Christian Responses to Female Homoeroticism.* Chicago: University of Chicago Press, 1996.

Burns, Gene. *The Frontiers of Catholicism: The Politics of Ideology in a Liberal World.* Berkeley: University of California Press, 1992.

Butler, Anne M., Michael E. Engh, and Thomas W. Spalding, eds. *The Frontiers and Catholic Identities.* Maryknoll, N.Y.: Orbis, 1999.

Butler, Judith. *Gender Trouble: Feminism and the Subversion of Identity.* New York: Routledge, 1991.

Byne, William. "The Biological Evidence Challenged." *Scientific American* 270 (May 1994): 50–55.

Cahill, Lisa Sowle. *Sex, Gender and Christian Ethics.* Cambridge, Mass.: Cambridge University Press, 1996.

———. "Silencing of Nugent, Gramick Sets a Novel Standard of Orthodoxy." *America* 181, no. 4 (August 14–21, 1999): 6–10.

Catechism of the Catholic Church. Ligouri, Mo.: Ligouri Publications, 1994.

Chauncey, George. *Gay New York: Gender, Urban Culture, and the Making of the Gay Male World, 1890–1940.* New York: Basic Books, 1994.

Chopp, Rebecca S., and Sheila Greeve Davaney, eds. *Horizons in Feminist Theology: Identity, Tradition, and Norms.* Minneapolis: Fortress, 1997.

Clarke, Kevin. "Whitewash or Renewal?" *U.S. Catholic* 68, no. 6 (June 2003): 12–17.

Comstock, Gary David. *Gay Theology without Apology.* Cleveland: Pilgrim, 1993.

———. *Unrepentant, Self-Affirming, Practicing: Lesbian/Bisexual/Gay People within Organized Religion.* New York: Continuum, 1996.

Comstock, Gary David, and Susan E. Henking, eds. *Que(e)rying Religion: A Critical Anthology.* New York: Continuum, 1997.

Congregation for the Doctrine of the Faith. "Letter to the Bishops of the Catholic Church on the Pastoral Care of Homosexual Persons," October 31, 1986. In *The Vatican and Homosexuality,* ed. Jeannine Gramick and Pat Furey, 1–10. New York: Crossroad, 1988.

———. "Some Considerations Concerning the Response to Legislative Proposals on the Non-Discrimination of Homosexual Persons," July 23, 1992 (personal copy).

Connell, R. W. *Masculinities.* Berkeley: University of California Press, 1995.

Countryman, L. William. *Dirt, Greed and Sex: Sexual Ethics in the New Testament and Their Implications for Today.* Philadelphia: Fortress, 1988.

Cott, Nancy. *Public Vows: A History of Marriage and the Nation.* Cambridge, Mass.: Harvard University Press, 2000.

Cozzens, Donald B. *The Changing Face of the Priesthood: A Reflection on the Priest's Crisis of Soul.* Collegeville, Minn.: Liturgical Press, 2000.

Cunningham, Lawrence S. *The Catholic Experience.* New York: Crossroad, 1985.

Curran, Charles. "Is There Any Good News in the Recent Documents from the Vatican about Homosexuality?" In *Voices of Hope: A Collection of Positive Writings on Gay and Lesbian Issues,* ed. Jeannine Gramick and Robert Nugent, 159–72. New York: Center for Homophobia Education, 1995.

———. "Sexual Orientation and Human Rights in American Religious Discourse: A Roman Catholic Perspective," In *Sexual Orientation and Human Rights in American Religious Discourse,* ed. Saul Olyan and Martha Nussbaum. New York: Oxford University Press, 1998.

Curran, Charles E., Margaret A. Farley, and Richard A. McCormick, eds. *Feminist Ethics and the Catholic Moral Tradition.* New York: Paulist, 1996.

Daly, Lois K., ed. *Feminist Theological Ethics: A Reader.* Louisville: Westminster John Knox, 1994.

Dillon, Michele. *Catholic Identity: Balancing Reason, Faith, and Power.* Cambridge, Mass.: Cambridge University Press, 1999.

Dolan, Jay P. *The American Catholic Experience: A History from Colonial Times to the Present.* Notre Dame, Ind.: University of Notre Dame Press, 1992.

Donnelly, Doris. "Reconciliation: The Continuing Challenge." In *Reconciliation: The Continuing Agenda,* ed. Robert J. Kennedy. Collegeville, Minn.: Liturgical Press, 1987.

Donovan, Daniel. *Distinctively Catholic: An Exploration of Catholic Identity.* New York: Paulist, 1997.

Doty, Mark. *Heaven's Coast.* New York: Harper Perennial, 1997.

Douglas, Kelly Brown. *Sexuality and the Black Church: A Womanist Perspective.* Maryknoll, N.Y.: Orbis, 1999.

Dreger, Alice. *Hermaphrodites and the Medical Intervention of Sex.* Cambridge, Mass.: Harvard University Press, 1998.

Duberman, Martin B., Martha Vicinus, and George Chauncey Jr., eds. *Hidden From History: Reclaiming the Gay and Lesbian Past.* New York: New American Library, 1989.

Dukes, Thomas. "David Plante (1940–)." In *Contemporary Gay American Novelists: A Bio-Bibliographical Critical Sourcebook,* ed. Emmanuel S. Nelson, 309–15. Westport, Conn.: Greenwood Press, 1993.

Eakin, Paul John. *Fictions in Autobiography: Studies in the Art of Self-Invention.* Princeton: Princeton University Press, 1985.

———, ed. *American Autobiography: Retrospect and Prospect.* Madison: University of Wisconsin Press, 1991.

Eilberg-Schwartz, Howard. *God's Phallus and Other Problems for Men and Monotheism.* Boston: Beacon, 1994.

Elbaz, Robert. *The Changing Nature of the Self: A Critical Study of the Autobiographic Discourse.* London: Croom Helm, 1988.

Ellison, Marvin M. *Erotic Justice: A Liberating Ethic of Sexuality.* Louisville: Westminster John Knox, 1996.

Ellwood, Robert S. *The Sixties Spiritual Awakening.* New Brunswick, N.J.: Rutgers University Press, 1994.

Erikson, Erik. *Life History and the Historical Moment.* New York: W. W. Norton, 1966.

Eugene, Toinette M. "Reconciliation in the Pastoral Context of Today's Church and World: Does Reconciliation Have a Future?" In *Reconciling Embrace: Foundations for the Future of Sacramental Reconciliation,* ed. Robert J. Kennedy, 1–14. Chicago: Liturgy Training Publications, 1998.

Faludi, Susan. *Stiffed: The Betrayal of the American Man.* New York: William Morrow, 1999.

Fausto-Sterling, Anne. *Myths of Gender: Biological Theories about Men and Women* New York: Basic Books, 1985.

———. *Sexing the Body: Gender Politics and the Construction of Sexuality.* New York: Basic Books, 2000.

Farley, Margaret. "A Feminist Version of Respect for Persons." In *Feminist Ethics and the Catholic Moral Tradition,* ed. Charles E. Curran, Margaret A. Farley, and Richard A. McCormick, 164–83. New York: Paulist, 1996.

Fausto-Sterling, Anne. "The Five Sexes." *The Sciences* (March–April 1993): 20–25.

———. "The Five Sexes, Revisited." *The Sciences* (July–August 2000): 18–23.

Ferraro, Thomas J., ed. *Catholic Lives, Contemporary America.* Durham, N.C.: Duke University Press, 1997.

Fiedler, Maureen, and Linda Rabben, eds. *Rome Has Spoken: A Guide to Forgotten Papal Statements and How They Have Changed Through the Centuries.* New York: Crossroad, 1998.

Fisher, James Terence. *The Catholic Counterculture in America, 1933–1962.* Chapel Hill: University of North Carolina Press, 1989.

———. *Communion of Immigrants: A History of Catholics in America.* New York: Oxford University Press, 2000.

Flannery, Austin P., ed. *The Documents of Vatican II.* New York: Pillar Books, 1975.

Ford, Michael. *Wounded Prophet: A Portrait of Henri J. M. Nouwen.* New York: Doubleday, 1999.

Foucault, Michel. *Ethics: Subjectivity and Truth,* ed. P. Rabinow. New York: The New Press, 1997.

———. *The History of Sexuality, Volume 1: An Introduction.* Translated by Robert Hurley. New York: Vintage, 1990; trans., 1978; Fr., 1976.

Froehle, Bryan T., and Mary L. Gautier, *Catholicism USA: A Portrait of the Catholic Church in the United States.* Maryknoll, N.Y.: Orbis, 2000.

Frontain, Raymond-Jean. "A Professional Queer Remembers: Bibliography, Narrative, and the Saving Power of Memory." In *A Sea of Stories: The Shaping Power of Narrative in Gay and Lesbian Cultures,* ed. Sonya L. Jones, 217–38. New York: Harrington Park Press, 2000.

Fulkerson, Mary McClintock. "Gender — Being It or Doing It? The Church, Homosexuality, and the Politics of Identity." In *Que(e)rying Religion: A Critical Anthology,* ed. Gary David Comstock and Susan E. Henking, 188–201. New York: Continuum, 1997.

Fuller, Jon. "On 'Straightening Out' Catholic Seminaries." *America* 187, no. 20 (December 16, 2002): 7–9.

Gagnon, Robert. *The Bible and Homosexual Practice: Texts and Hermeneutics.* Nashville: Abingdon, 2001.

———. "Gays and the Bible: A Response to Walter Wink." *Christian Century* 119 (August 14–27, 2002): 40–43.

Gettys, John. "Daniel Curzon (1938–)." In *Contemporary Gay American Novelists: A Bio-Bibliographical Critical Sourcebook,* ed. Emmanuel S. Nelson, 89–95. Westport, Conn.: Greenwood Press, 1993.

Gill, James J. "Seminaries Await Vatican Visitation." *America* 187, no. 2 (July 15–22, 2002): 10–13.

Gilson, Anne Bathurst. *Eros Breaking Free: Interpreting Sexual Theo-Ethics.* Cleveland: Pilgrim, 1995.

Goffman, Erving. *Stigma: Notes on the Management of Spoiled Identity.* New York: Simon & Schuster, 1963.

Goss, Robert. *Jesus Acted Up: A Gay and Lesbian Manifesto.* San Francisco: HarperSanFrancisco, 1993.

Gottschall, Marilyn. "The Ethical Implications of the Deconstruction of Gender." *Journal of the American Academy of Religion* 70, no. 2 (June 2002): 279–99.

Gramick, Jeannine, and Pat Furey, eds. *The Vatican and Homosexuality.* New York: Crossroad, 1988.

Gramick, Jeannine, and Robert Nugent, eds. *Voices of Hope: A Collection of Positive Writings on Gay and Lesbian Issues.* New York: Center for Homophobia Education, 1995.

Greeley, Andrew. *The Catholic Imagination.* Berkeley: University of California Press, 2000.

Grippo, Dan. "Why Lesbian and Gay Catholics Stay Catholic." *U.S. Catholic* 55, no. 9 (September 1990): 18–25.

Gudorf, Christine E. *Body, Sex, and Pleasure: Reconstructing Christian Sexual Ethics.* Cleveland: Pilgrim, 1994.

———. "The Erosion of Sexual Dimorphism: Challenges to Religion and Religious Ethics." *Journal of the American Academy of Religion* 69, no. 4 (December 2001): 863–91.

Guido, Joseph J. "The Importance of Perspective: Understanding the Sexual Abuse of Children by Priests." *America* 186, no. 11 (April 1, 2002): 21–23.

Guindon, Andre. "Homosexual Acts or Gay Speech?" In *The Vatican and Homosexuality,* ed. Jeannine Gramick and Pat Furey, 208–15. New York: Crossroad, 1988.

Gusdorf, Georges. "Conditions and Limits of Autobiography." Translated by James Olney. In *Autobiography: Essays Theoretical and Critical,* ed. James Olney, 28–48. Princeton: Princeton University Press, 1980.

Guttman, Matthew C. *The Meanings of Macho: Being a Man in Mexico City.* Berkeley: University of California Press, 1996.

Halsey, William M. *The Survival of American Innocence: Catholicism in an Era of Disillusionment, 1920–1940.* Notre Dame, Ind.: University of Notre Dame Press, 1980.

Hanigan, James P. *Homosexuality: The Test Case for Christian Ethics.* New York: Paulist, 1988.

———. "Sexual Orientation and Human Rights: A Roman Catholic View." In *Sexual Orientation and Human Rights in American Religious Discourse,* ed. Saul Olyan and Martha Nussbaum. New York: Oxford University Press, 1998.

Hansen, Ron. "Hotly in Pursuit of the Real: The Role of the Catholic Writer." *America* 185, no. 15 (November 12, 2001): 6–10.

Hardin, Michael. "Altering Masculinities: The Spanish Conquest and the Evolution of the Latin American Machismo." *International Journal of Sexuality and Gender Studies* 7, no. 1 (January 2002): 1–22.

Hartman, Keith. *Congregations in Conflict: The Battle over Homosexuality.* New Brunswick, N.J.: Rutgers University Press, 1996.

Haughton, Rosemary. *The Catholic Thing.* Springfield, Ill.: Templegate, 1979.

Hausman, Bernice. *Changing Sex: Transsexualism, Technology, and the Idea of Gender.* Durham, N.C.: Duke University Press, 1998.

Helminiak, Daniel A. *What the Bible Really Says about Homosexuality.* San Francisco: Alamo Square, 1994.

Henking, Susan. "The Personal Is the Theological: Autobiographical Acts in Contemporary Feminist Theology." *Journal of the American Academy of Religion* 59, no. 3 (Fall 1991): 511–26.

Herman, Didi. *The Antigay Agenda: Orthodox Vision and the Christian Right.* Chicago: University of Chicago Press, 1997.

Heyward, Carter. *Touching Our Strength: The Erotic as Power and the Love of God.* San Francisco: Harper & Row, 1989.

Holland, Walter. "In the Body's Ghetto." In *A Sea of Stories: The Shaping Power of Narrative in Gay and Lesbian Cultures,* ed. Sonya L. Jones, 109–38. New York: Harrington Park Press, 2000.

Hughes, Kathleen. "Reconciliation: Cultural and Christian Perspectives." In *Reconciliation: The Continuing Agenda*, ed. Robert J. Kennedy. Collegeville, Minn.: Liturgical Press, 1987.

———. "Walking on the Edge of Two Great Abysses: Theological Perspectives on Reconciliation." In *Reconciling Embrace: Foundations for the Future of Sacramental Reconciliation*, ed. Robert J. Kennedy, 95–107. Chicago: Liturgy Training Publications, 1998.

Hughes, Kathleen, and Joseph Favazza, eds. *A Reconciliation Sourcebook*. Chicago: Liturgy Training Publications, 1997.

Hunt, Mary. *Fierce Tenderness: A Feminist Theology of Friendship*. New York: Crossroad, 1991.

Jakobsen, Janet R., and Ann Pellegrini. *Love the Sin: Sexual Regulation and the Limits of Religious Tolerance*. New York: New York University Press, 2003.

Jagose, Annamarie. *Queer Theory: An Introduction*. New York: New York University Press, 1996.

Jones, Sonya L., ed. *A Sea of Stories: The Shaping Power of Narrative in Gay and Lesbian Cultures*. New York: Harrington Park Press, 2000.

Jordan, Mark D. *The Ethics of Sex*. Oxford: Blackwell, 2002.

———. *The Invention of Sodomy in Christian Theology*. Chicago: University of Chicago Press, 1997.

———. *The Silence of Sodom: Homosexuality in Modern Catholicism*. Chicago: University of Chicago Press, 2000.

———. *Telling Truths in Church: Scandal, Flesh, and Christian Speech*. Boston: Beacon, 2003.

Jung, Patricia Beattie, and Ralph F. Smith. *Heterosexism: An Ethical Challenge*. Albany: SUNY, 1993.

Jung, Patricia Beattie, with Joseph Andrew Coray, eds. *Sexual Diversity and Catholicism: Toward the Development of Moral Theology*. Collegeville, Minn.: Liturgical Press, 2001.

Kane, Paula M. *Separatism and Subculture: Boston Catholicism, 1900–1920*. Chapel Hill: University of North Carolina Press, 1994.

Kane, Paula, James Kenneally, and Karen Kennelly, eds. *Gender Identities in American Catholicism*. Maryknoll, N.Y.: Orbis, 2001.

Katz, Jonathan Ned. *The Invention of Heterosexuality*. New York: Dutton Books, 1995.

———. *Sex Between Men Before Homosexuality*. Chicago: University of Chicago Press, 2001.

Kennedy, Eugene. "Ministry, Homosexuality, and Psychological Wholeness." Plenary address made to the New Ways Ministry Symposium, "Out of Silence God Has Called Us: Lesbian/Gay Issues and the Vatican II Church," Louisville, Ky., March 8–10, 2002. Audio Recording #02094-0020, Chesapeake Audio/Video Communications, Inc., Elkridge, Md.

———. *The Unhealed Wound: The Church and Human Sexuality*. New York: St. Martin's Griffin, 2001.

Kennedy, Robert J., ed. *Reconciliation: The Continuing Agenda*. Collegeville, Minn.: Liturgical Press, 1987.

———, ed. *Reconciling Embrace: Foundations for the Future of Sacramental Reconciliation*. Chicago: Liturgy Training Publications, 1998.

Kennelly, Karen, ed. *American Catholic Women: A Historical Exploration*. New York: Macmillan Publishing, 1989.

Kessler, Suzanne. *Lessons from the Intersexed.* New Brunswick, N.J.: Rutgers University Press, 1998.

Kimmel, Michael. *Manhood in America: A Cultural History.* New York: Free Press, 1996.

Kirsch, Max. *Queer Theory and Social Change.* London: Routledge, 2000.

Krondorfer, Bjorn. "The Confines of Male Confessions: On Religion, Bodies, and Mirrors." In *Men's Bodies, Men's Gods: Male Identities in a (Post-) Christian Culture,* 205–34. New York: New York University Press, 1996.

Krondorfer, Bjorn, ed. *Men's Bodies, Men's Gods: Male Identities in a (Post-) Christian Culture.* New York: New York University Press, 1996.

LaCugna, Catherine Mowry, ed. *Freeing Theology: The Essentials of Theology in Feminist Perspective.* San Francisco: HarperSanFrancisco, 1993.

Laqueur, Thomas. *Making Sex: Body and Gender from the Greeks to Freud.* Cambridge, Mass.: Harvard University Press, 1990.

LeVay, Simon, and Dean H. Hamer. "Evidence for a Biological Influence in Male Homosexuality." *Scientific American* 270 (May 1994): 44–49.

Levine, Judith. *Harmful to Minors: The Perils of Protecting Children from Sex.* Minneapolis: University of Minnesota Press, 2002.

Long, Ronald E. "The Sacrality of Male Beauty and Homosex: A Neglected Factor in the Understanding of Contemporary Gay Reality." In *Que(e)rying Religion: A Critical Anthology,* ed. Gary David Comstock and Susan E. Henking, 266–81. New York: Continuum, 1997.

Lorde, Audre. *Sister Outsider: Essays and Speeches by Audre Lorde.* Freedom, Calif.: Crossing Press, 1984.

Maher, Michael. *Being Gay and Lesbian in a Catholic High School: Beyond the Uniform.* New York: Harrington Park Press, 2001.

Martin, Biddy. "Lesbian Identity and Autobiographical Difference[s]." In *The Lesbian and Gay Studies Reader,* ed. Henry Abelove, Michele Aina Barale, and David M. Halperin, 274–93. New York: Routledge, 1993.

Martin, James. "The Church and the Homosexual Priest: Facing the Challenges and Accepting the Gifts Offered by Homosexual Priests in the Catholic Church." *America* 183, no. 14 (November 4, 2000): 11–15.

Massa, Mark S. *Catholics and American Culture: Fulton Sheen, Dorothy Day, and the Notre Dame Football Team.* New York: Crossroad, 1999.

McBrien, Richard, ed. *The HarperCollins Encyclopedia of Catholicism.* San Francisco: HarperSanFrancisco, 1995.

McGreevy, John T. *Catholicism and American Freedom: A History.* New York: W. W. Norton, 2003.

———. *Parish Boundaries: The Catholic Encounter with Race in the Twentieth-Century Urban North.* Chicago: University of Chicago Press, 1996.

McKenzie, Donna M. "Is There a Moral Theologian in the House?" *Religion in the News* 5, no. 2 (Summer 2002): 18–19.

McNeill, John. *The Church and the Homosexual.* Kansas City: Andrews & McMeel, 1976; 4th edition, Boston: Beacon, 1993.

———. *Freedom, Glorious Freedom: The Spiritual Journey to the Fullness of Life for Gays, Lesbians, and Everybody Else.* Boston: Beacon, 1995.

———. *Taking A Chance on God: Liberating Theology for Gays, Lesbians, and Their Lovers, Families, and Friends.* Boston: Beacon, 1988.

McRuer, Robert. "Boys' Own Stories and New Spellings of My Name: Coming Out and Other Myths of Queer Positionality." In *Genders 20: Eroticism and*

Containment, ed. Carol Siegel and Ann Kibbey, 260–84. New York: New York University Press, 1994.

Miller, Patricia. "Chasing Conservative Catholics." *Conscience* 22, no. 2 (Summer 2001): 11–14.

Moore, Gareth. *The Body in Context: Sex and Catholicism.* London: SCM, 1992.

———. *A Question of Truth: Christianity and Homosexuality.* London: Continuum, 2003.

Moore, R. Laurence. *Religious Outsiders and the Making of Americans.* New York: Oxford University Press, 1986.

Murphy, Timothy, ed. *Gay Ethics: Controversies in Outing, Civil Rights, and Sexual Science.* New York: Harrington Park Press, 1994.

Nelson, James B. *Embodiment: An Approach to Sexuality and Christian Theology.* Minneapolis: Augsburg, 1978.

———. "Sources for Body Theology," In *Sexuality and the Sacred: Sources for Theological Reflection*, ed. James B. Nelson and Sandra P. Longfellow, 374–86. Louisville: Westminster John Knox, 1994.

Nelson, James B., and Sandra P. Longfellow. *Sexuality and the Sacred: Sources for Theological Reflection.* Louisville: Westminster John Knox, 1994.

Newman, Bishop William. "Baltimore Bishop Asks Forgiveness of Gays/Lesbians." *Bondings: A Publication of New Ways Ministry* (Spring 2001): 1.

Nissinen, Marti. *Homoeroticism in the Biblical World: A Historical Perspective.* Translated by Kirsi Stjerna. Minneapolis: Fortress Press, 1998.

Noonan, John T., Jr. "On the Development of Doctrine." *America* 180, no. 11 (April 3, 1999): 6–8.

Nugent, Robert, ed. *A Challenge to Love: Gay and Lesbian Catholics in the Church.* New York: Crossroad, 1983.

Nugent, Robert, and Jeannine Gramick. *Building Bridges: Gay and Lesbian Reality and the Catholic Church.* Mystic, Conn.: Twenty-Third Publications, 1992.

Nussbaum, Emily. "A Question of Gender." *Discover* 21, no. 1 (January 2000): 92–99.

Occhiogrosso, Peter, ed. *Once a Catholic: Prominent Catholics and Ex-Catholics Discuss the Influence of the Church on Their Lives and Work.* Boston: Houghton Mifflin, 1987.

Olney, James. "Autobiography and the Cultural Moment." In *Autobiography: Essays Theoretical and Critical*, 3–27. Princeton: Princeton University Press, 1980.

———. *Memory and Narrative: The Weave of Life-Writing.* Chicago: University of Chicago Press, 1998.

———. *Metaphors of Self: The Meaning of Autobiography.* Princeton: Princeton University Press, 1972.

———, ed. *Autobiography: Essays Theoretical and Critical.* Princeton: Princeton University Press, 1980.

Olshen, Barry N. "Subject, Persona, and Self in the Theory of Autobiography." *a/b: Auto/Biography Studies* 10 (Spring 1995): 5–16.

Olyan, Saul. "'And with a Male You Shall Not Lie the Lying Down of a Woman': On the Meaning and Significance of Leviticus 18:22 and 20:13." *Journal of the History of Sexuality* 5 (October 1994): 179–206.

Olyan, Saul, and Martha Nussbaum, eds. *Sexual Orientation and Human Rights in American Religious Discourse.* New York: Oxford University Press, 1998.

Orsi, Robert. *The Madonna of 115th Street: Faith and Community in Italian Harlem, 1880–1950.* New Haven: Yale University Press, 1985.

Ozar, David T. "Harming by Exclusion: On the Standard Concepts of Sexual Orientation, Sex, and Gender." In *Sexual Diversity and Catholicism: Toward the Development of Moral Theology,* ed. Patricia Beattie Jung, with Joseph Andrew Coray, 252–66. Collegeville, Minn.: Liturgical Press, 2001.

Peiss, Kathy, and Christina Simmons, eds., with Robert A. Padgug. *Passion and Power: Sexuality in History.* Philadelphia: Temple University Press, 1989.

Plummer, Ken. *Telling Sexual Stories: Power, Change and Social Worlds.* London: Routledge, 1995.

Primiano, Leonard Norman. "Intrinsically Catholic: Vernacular Religion and Philadelphia's 'Dignity.'" Ph.D. diss., University of Pennsylvania, 1993.

Redmont, Jane. *Generous Lives: American Catholic Women Today.* Ligouri, Mo.: Triumph Books, 1992.

Renza, Louis A. "The Veto of the Imagination: A Theory of Autobiography." In *Autobiography: Essays Theoretical and Critical,* ed. James Olney, 268–95. Princeton: Princeton University Press, 1980.

Rich, Adrienne. "Compulsory Heterosexuality and Lesbian Existence." In *The Lesbian and Gay Studies Reader* ed. Henry Abelove, Michele Aina Barale, and David M. Halperin, 227–54. New York: Routledge, 1993.

Richlin, Amy. "Not Before Homosexuality: The Materiality of the *Cinaedus* and the Roman Law against Love Between Men." *Journal of the History of Sexuality* 3, no. 4 (1993): 523–73.

Ricoeur, Paul. *Figuring the Sacred: Religion, Narrative, and Imagination.* ed. Mark I. Wallace. Translated by David Pellauer. Minneapolis: Fortress, 1995.

———. "Narrative Identity." Translated by Mark S. Muldoon. *Philosophy Today* 35 (Spring 1991): 73–81.

Robinson, Paul. *Gay Lives: Homosexual Autobiography from John Addington Symonds to Paul Monette.* Chicago: University of Chicago Press, 1999.

Rofes, Eric. *Dry Bones Breathe: Gay Men Creating Post-AIDS Identities and Cultures.* New York: Harrington Park Press, 1998.

Ronan, Marian. "Tracing the Sign of the Cross." Ph.D. diss., Temple University, 2000.

Ross, Susan A. "God's Embodiment and Women: Sacraments." In *Freeing Theology: The Essentials of Theology in Feminist Perspective,* ed. Catherine Mowry LaCugna, 185–209. San Francisco: HarperSanFrancisco, 1993.

Rudy, Kathy. *Sex and the Church: Gender, Homosexuality, and the Transformation of Christian Ethics.* Boston: Beacon, 1997.

Ruether, Rosemary Radford. *Christianity and the Making of the Modern Family: Ruling Ideologies, Diverse Realities.* Boston: Beacon, 2000.

———. *Sexism and God-Talk: Toward a Feminist Theology.* Boston: Beacon, 1983.

———, ed. *Religion and Sexism: Images of Woman in the Jewish and Christian Traditions.* New York: Simon & Schuster, 1974.

Ryan, Penelope. *Practicing Catholic: The Search for a Livable Catholicism.* New York: Henry Holt, 1998.

Rynne, Xavier. *Vatican Council II.* With a New Introduction by the Author. Maryknoll, N.Y.: Orbis, 1999 (1968, Farrar, Straus & Giroux).

Savin-Williams, Ritch C. "... And Then I Became Gay": Young Men's Stories. New York: Routledge, 1998.

Scanlon, Leslie. "Here Come's Everybody's Church." *U.S. Catholic* 67, no. 5 (May 2002): 28–32.

Schneider, Laurel. "Homosexuality, Queer Theory, and Christian Theology." *Religious Studies Review* 26, no. 1 (January 2000): 3–12.

Scroggs, Robin. *Homosexuality in the New Testament: Contextual Background for Contemporary Debate.* Philadelphia: Fortress, 1983.

Seidman, Steven. *Embattled Eros: Sexual Politics and Ethics in Contemporary America.* New York: Routledge, 1992.

Siker, Jeffrey S., ed. *Homosexuality in the Church: Both Sides of the Debate.* Louisville: Westminster John Knox, 1994.

Smith, Richard L. *AIDS, Gays, and the American Catholic Church.* Cleveland: Pilgrim, 1994.

Smith, Mark. "Ancient Bisexuality and the Interpretation of Romans 1:26–27." *Journal of the American Academy of Religion* 64, no. 2 (Summer 1996): 223–56.

Smith, Sidonie. "Performativity, Autobiographical Practice, Resistance." *a/b: Auto/ Biography Studies* 10 (Spring 1995): 17–33.

Smith, Sidonie, and Julia Watson, eds. *Getting a Life: Everyday Uses of Autobiography.* Minneapolis: University of Minnesota Press, 1996.

Snitow, Ann, Christine Stansell, and Sharon Thompson, eds. *Powers of Desire: The Politics of Sexuality.* New York: Monthly Review Press, 1983.

Spender, Stephen. "Confessions and Autobiography." In *Autobiography: Essays Theoretical and Critical,* ed. James Olney, 115–22. Princeton: Princeton University Press, 1980.

Steinfels, Peter. *A People Adrift: The Crisis of the Roman Catholic Church in America.* New York: Simon & Schuster, 2003.

Stone, Albert. "Modern American Autobiography: Texts and Transactions." In *American Autobiography: Retrospect and Prospect,* ed. Paul John Eakin, 95–119. Madison: University of Wisconsin Press, 1991.

Sullivan, Andrew. *Virtually Normal: An Argument about Homosexuality.* New York: Alfred A. Knopf, 1995.

Swidler, Leonard. *Toward a Catholic Constitution.* New York: Crossroad, 1996.

Taves, Ann. *The Household of Faith: Roman Catholic Devotions in Mid-Nineteenth-Century America.* Notre Dame, Ind.: University of Notre Dame Press, 1986.

Tessier, L. J. *Dancing after the Whirlwind: Feminist Reflections on Sex, Denial, and Spiritual Transformation.* Boston: Beacon, 1997.

Tigert, Leanne McCall. *Coming Out While Staying In.* Cleveland: Pilgrim, 1997.

Toman, James A. "Dual Identity: Being Catholic and Being Gay." Ph.D. diss., Cleveland State University, 1997.

United States Conference of Catholic Bishops. "Charter for the Protection of Children and Young People." A special supplement to the *Catholic Standard and Times,* June 27, 2002.

"U.S. Catholics: Who Do We Think We Are? The Editors Interview James Davidson," *U.S. Catholic* 65, no. 2 (February 2000): 12–17.

Wallace, Mark I. "Introduction." In Paul Ricoeur, *Figuring the Sacred: Religion, Narrative, and Imagination.* Translated by David Pellauer, 1–32. Minneapolis: Fortress, 1995.

Warren, C. *Identity and Community in the Gay World.* New York: Wiley, 1974.

Weaver, Mary Jo, ed. *What's Left? Liberal American Catholics.* Indianapolis: Indiana University Press, 1999.

Weaver, Mary Jo, and R. Scott Appleby, eds. *Being Right: Conservative Catholics in America.* Indianapolis: Indiana University Press, 1995.

Weintraub, Karl J. "Autobiography and Historical Consciousness." *Critical Inquiry* (June 1975): 821–48.

Westerfelhaus, Robert. "A Significant Shift: A Pentadic Analysis of the Two Rhetorics of the Post–Vatican II Roman Catholic Church Regarding Homosexuality." *Journal of Gay, Lesbian, and Bisexual Identity* 3, no. 4 (October 1998): 269–94.

Whitehead, Evelyn Eaton, and James D. Whitehead. *Wisdom of the Body: Making Sense of our Sexuality.* New York: Crossroad, 2001.

Wilkes, Paul. *The Seven Secrets of Successful Catholics.* New York: Paulist, 1998.

Wink, Walter. "To Hell with Gays?" *Christian Century* 119 (June 5–12, 2002): 32–34.

———. "A Reply by Walter Wink." *Christian Century* 119 (August 14–27, 2002): 43–44.

Wills, Garry. *Papal Sin: Structures of Deceit.* New York: Doubleday, 2000.

Wolfe, Alan. *One Nation, After All: What Middle-Class Americans Really Think about God, Country, Family, Racism, Welfare, Immigration, Homosexuality, Work, The Right, The Left, and Each Other.* New York: Viking. 1998.

Wolfteich, Claire E. *American Catholics Through the Twentieth Century: Spirituality, Lay Experience and Public Life.* New York: Crossroad, 2001.

Yip, Andrew. "The Persistence of Faith Among Nonheterosexual Christians: Evidence for the Neosecularization Thesis of Religious Transformation." *Journal for the Scientific Study of Religion* 41, no. 2 (2002): 199–212.

Young, Iris Marion. *Justice and the Politics of Difference.* Princeton: Princeton University Press, 1990.

Index